INFANT–PARENT
PSYCHOTHERAPY

INFANT–PARENT PSYCHOTHERAPY

A Handbook

Stella Acquarone

KARNAC

LONDON   NEW YORK

First published in 2004 by
H. Karnac (Books) Ltd.
6 Pembroke Buildings, London NW10 6RE

British Library Cataloguing in Publication Data

A C.I.P. for this book is available from the British Library

ISBN: 18875-258-1

10 9 8 7 6 5 4 3 2 1

Edited, designed, and produced by Communication Crafts

Printed in Great Britain

www.karnacbooks.com

*Dedicated to the memory of
Ignacio and Elena, my dancing parents*

CONTENTS

ACKNOWLEDGEMENTS

I would like to thank the infants and their parents who have trusted me in their difficult times and taught me—and keep teaching me—so much about infant communication and the complex workings of the emotions and the mind.

I would like to thank my son Ignacio for suggesting that I write this book, my daughter Isabel for her positive spirit and constant encouragement to continue with my work at the Parent Infant Clinic, and my grandchildren, Camila and Zara, for their joy and cuteness, reflecting the beauty and dangers of the early years.

I am glad I can publicly thank the doctors, health visitors, community nurses, paediatric physiotherapists, and other professionals working in health clinics, paediatric and intensive-care babies wards in hospitals, the Mother-and-Baby Unit in Holloway Prison, nursery teachers, and social services who have allowed me into their institutions and interested me in the world of early difficulties in young families; their collaboration and discussions help me to attune the interventions safely, respecting the intimacy and the fragility of these situations. I would like to mention especially Dr Catherine Aitken, community paediatrician, Heather Soley, paediatric physiotherapist, Mary Lombard, Yvonne Jeremy, and Sandy Davies, health visitors, and Dr Sheila Lewis and Dr Rossiter, consultant paediatricians.

I would also like to thank innumerable colleagues at the Child Guidance Clinics in Redbridge, Enfield, Barnet, and Haringey, especially Mrs Haydene Benjamin, Principal Child Psychotherapist, who supported my wish, in the early 1980s, to do clinical research with infants. I would like to thank my colleague, Hisako Watanabe, child psychiatrist, for her collaboration, in the early 1990s at the Parent Infant Clinic, in finding clinical strategies for treating communication disorders in the first year of life. I owe very special gratitude to Esther Bick and Martha Harris, who taught me how to observe infants, and to Serge Lebovici, Bertram Cramer, and T. Berry Brazelton, with whom I discussed early psychoanalytic interventions in the early 1980s, and Colwyn Trevarthen, for enlightening discussions over the years about communication from birth and about other research in infancy; they gave their unconditional support to the Parent Infant Clinic and the School of Infant Mental Health. Furthermore, I would like to thank the many colleagues, students, and friends around the world whose enthusiasm about the prevention of mental disorders and early intervention gave me great encouragement.

I would also like to express my gratitude to Susan Grossman and my husband Don Hughston for their suggestions on the early drafts. As the drafts took shape and substance, I am indebted to Maia Raicar for the tedious and time-consuming re-ordering of the material.

This book would not have been possible without the enthusiastic support of Brett Kahr, and H. Karnac (Books), initially with Cesare Sacerdoti and later Oliver Rathbone and Leena Hakkinen.

Finally, I am indebted to the editor, Eric King, for helping me to make grammatical sense of what I wanted to say. Without his steady and experienced work, it would not have been possible for the book to be published.

FOREWORD

Brett Kahr

Senior Clinical Research Fellow in Psychotherapy and Mental Health,
Centre for Child Mental Health, London

In recent months, I have become slightly despairing each time I pick up a new book on psychotherapy or psychoanalysis. I find increasingly that our colleagues in the mental health field produce very few works of great originality or inspiration, so that the task of reading becomes a lamentable exercise in diminishing returns.

Fortunately, Dr Stella Acquarone's new book, *Infant–Parent Psychotherapy: Handbook for Professionals*, has lifted my spirits immensely. I feel privileged to be able to introduce such a bold and solid new work, one that already has huge implications for the fields of infant mental health, child psychology and child psychiatry, adult psychotherapy, marital psychotherapy, and family therapy.

Essentially, Acquarone's clearly written and carefully articulated textbook holds an important position on the bookshelf of every practising mental health clinician, whether psychoanalytically orientated or behaviourally orientated, whether systemic or pharmacological. For in this handbook, Acquarone outlines a rich tapestry exploring the unconscious mind of both the infant and his or her parents, explaining in close detail how anxieties in both infant and parents become constellated as the annoying and troubling symptoms of infancy: pathological crying, failure to thrive, refusal to eat, chronic sleeping difficulties, and so on. In an era when psychiatrists find it increasingly difficult to understand the origins of patients' symptoms without placing them under a magnetic resonance image scanner, Acquarone reveals how patently early symptomatology develops in the ordinary crucible of the daily anxieties of family life. In this way, Acquarone helps us to understand the psychological roots of infantile emotional distress, but also, most particularly, how psychotherapeutic interventions can in a relatively short period of time alleviate distress within the infant and the wider family network.

Many mental health professionals, and certainly many parents, still do not recognize that infants can suffer from mental health problems, just as children, adolescents, and adults do. By contrast, the mental health problems of infants become easily ignored or dismissed: "Oh, Mary's just teething", or, "Johnny's just cranky". Often, an infant may be teething or cranky, but if the infant displays distress continually, and if the parents do not have the immediate capacity to contain or to calm the distress, then the symptoms intensify, and one will be confronted with an infant who awakens ten or twenty times during the night, or an infant who will not stop crying, thus driving mother and father to despair and, often, to deep abuse and murderousness.

Happily, neither the baby nor the parents need suffer unduly, because, as Acquarone explains, the modern clinical practice of infant–parent psychotherapy provides a very successful means of working with families, arguably mitigating against the need for prolonged psychoanalytic or psychotherapeutic treatment in years to come. Acquarone, like all good infant mental health specialists, stresses the importance of early intervention, providing help, support, and guidance sooner rather than later, so that the early murderous impulses of parents towards screaming and fractious babies can be contained and processed and parents can be helped to become better observers of their own infants. Stella Acquarone adopts a classical public health model in her understanding of infantile mental distress. In her Introduction, she recognizes that "Early intervention is to mental suffering what jabs are to childhood diseases. But while immunization programmes have almost eradicated a number of previously widespread serious diseases, mental illness and distress are commonly left untreated, at great personal and social cost" (p. 4). Dr Acquarone understands that earlier interventions will ultimately prove to be shorter and, therefore, more cost-effective, bringing about more contentedness in family life. Furthermore, Acquarone has studied the neuropsychological and neurobiological literature with care, and she has come to appreciate that the infant brain enjoys a great deal of neuroplasticity, so that early interventions will become wired into the infant's brain with greater efficacy. As Acquarone has noted so eloquently, "the emotional trauma in the vulnerable infant brain causes an elevation of stress hormones, such as cortisol, which wash over the tender brain like acid, with the result that regions in the cortex and limbic system responsible for attachment are up to 20% smaller and have fewer synapses" (p. 24). If only parents could appreciate that screaming at an infant actually results in neuropathogenesis, we could experience a veritable revolution in infant care.

Those of us who have worked psychotherapeutically with adults in their thirties, forties, fifties, sixties, and beyond know only too well how ossified and "stuck" certain people can become. I can think of one middle-aged patient who came to see me four times a week for many years, whose therapy I often privately compared to an experience of wading through treacle. The patient did change, but at a slow, painstaking rate, in part because we had to struggle through literally decades of deeply rigidified defences. By contrast, when intervening with an infant in the context of infant–parent psychotherapy, one sees changes almost immediately. Sometimes, working with parents by themselves will even circumvent the need to see the child. As a psychoanalytic marital psychotherapist, I work with quite a number of couples who present for various reasons. Only recently, a mother and father came to see me to discuss their 8-year-old daughter, who had not had an uninterrupted night's sleep for at least the last three years. The parents could tolerate this situation no longer, and they came for a consultation. Naturally, I asked them to tell me all about their daughter and about her sleep problem, but, as one would imagine, I also took a detailed history of the marital relations between mother and father. Unsurprisingly, the daughter's sleep difficulty soon took a back seat; instead, mother and father began to enumerate a list of hurts, grievances, and injustices in the marriage, none of which they had ever articulated before. After ninety minutes of confession and tears, mother and father returned home, and they came back to see me one week later for a second consultation. To my delight, they announced that "for some strange reason", their daughter had slept through the night. And this positive result has since sustained itself. The parents entered marital psychotherapy, and they worked with me on their problems with great gusto, and with great success. Many psychotherapists will recognize this sort of situation. But, of course, if one can intervene this successfully with the parents of an 8-year-old, imagine how potent an intervention can be with the parents of an 8-week-old child.

Acquarone's case material really serves as the centrepiece of her book, and although an adept theoretician, she allows the infants and the parents to assume the central place of importance throughout her well-crafted narratives. For instance, consider Case 4, an 11-month-old boy called "Nicholas", who would cry throughout the night unless he could suckle at his mother's breast. We have all seen babies of this variety, and we have all talked to parents at their wits' end, deprived of rapid-eye-movement sleep, and in states of mental and physical collapse. In one very straightforward consultation, Acquarone established that the baby's father worked abroad, and mother "never knew when he was going to be around" (p. 45). As Acquarone has reported, "I asked this mother if perhaps the child was fulfilling the father's role, always staying in bed with her and sucking her breast as he pleased" (p. 45). After this comment, the mother started to cry, and thus she began to make some conscious links and to develop some understanding of the fact that although she consciously resented the baby's neediness, on an unconscious level she had actually fuelled this same neediness, using him as an antidepressant tablet to keep with her in bed, to mitigate against the loneliness of the absent father. Acquarone further helped the mother to recognize that her own father, the baby's grandfather, used to disappear for long periods, as he was in the navy. Thus, mother managed to choose a partner who unconsciously resembled her own father, repeating a crucial and painful aspect of her own history. By the third session, Acquarone had helped this mother to establish greater separation between herself and her son, who had become, quite understandably, a missing penis in her mind, or the missing phallic function in her life.

Grounded in all the best principles of psychoanalytic treatment, the relatively new field of infant–parent psychotherapy draws upon the work of Sigmund Freud consulting to "Little Hans", the intensive child psychoanalytic procedures of Anna Freud and Melanie Klein, and perhaps, above all, Donald Winnicott's brief psychoanalytic psychiatric consultations with the large parade of children who came to visit his "psychiatric snack-bar" at the Paddington Green Children's Hospital in London, where Winnicott endeavoured to discover how little need be done to alter the developmental trajectory of a tiny child. Drawing upon these essential psychoanalytic imagos, Acquarone has also integrated the very best of subsequent workers, such as Margaret Mahler, Serge Lebovici, Selma Fraiberg, T. Berry Brazelton, Bertrand Cramer, Daniel Stern, and Allan Schore, among others, to create her own very personal synthesis. There can be no doubt that much of her success stems not only from her incorporation and processing of a century of psychoanalytic research and treatment, but from her own passion for babies and from her respect for parents. Throughout the book,

Acquarone writes with remarkable compassion, never blaming or judging, but always trying to understand and always managing to be helpful.

Based on more than twenty years of clinical work with parents and babies, Acquarone has a unique base of experience upon which to draw, perhaps larger than that of any other infant mental health worker. Certainly she has undertaken many more psychotherapeutic consultations with infants than Donald Winnicott had done during his half-century of clinical practice. And Acquarone's unique and deep experience across a variety of settings has allowed her to theorize and to systematize with brilliance, elucidating the components of the assessment procedure and developing a rich and detailed psychoanalytic classification of the different types of problems and difficulties that the infant—parent psychotherapist may encounter, each of which requires a modification of the basic technique (cf. Acquarone, 2002).

I believe I first met Stella Acquarone in 1991, shortly after she had founded both the Parent Infant Clinic in London and its academic arm, the School of Infant Mental Health. Acquarone launched the first-ever training in infant mental health in Great Britain, long before any university began to offer a degree in this subject. In this respect, she will always be a pioneer. I found Acquarone immediately impressive, because although very experienced psychoanalytically, she also draws heavily upon her background in developmental psychology and academic psychology; this becomes a very attractive combination, allowing her not only to undertake the clinical work with compassion, but to synthesize, systematize, theorize, and engage in follow-up research, something that clinical psychotherapists have only just begun to think about. Throughout the early 1990s, I had the great privilege not only of observing many of her consultations on film—she is a most accomplished lecturer and educator—but I also attended many of her infant—parent clinics, and we shared some cases. Here, in the consulting-room, I could observe Acquarone's brilliance at first hand, watching her deploy the techniques and skills so successfully, and I became a great champion of the idea of early intervention. She talks to parents in a completely jargon-free manner but manages to convey the most complex psychoanalytic concepts about unconscious functioning in the most delicate, ambassadorial, and digestible manner. I learned a great deal about working with all age groups from working alongside Stella Acquarone.

Although infant—parent psychotherapy as a discipline is now being practised by many child psychotherapists, it must never become the exclusive province of psychoanalytic child psychotherapists—though many do it extremely well, especially those committed to working with the "under fives". The lengthy, multi-year, multi-frequency treatments that have always been the stock in trade of child psychotherapists often do not allow scope for the expression of spontaneity required by the clinician when working with infants and parents. Donald Winnicott certainly believed this to be so, much to the chagrin of Anna Freud and others. Infant–parent psychotherapy must be studied and learned and then be embraced by all members of the therapeutic community. Many adult psychotherapists already do this work and do it quite well, because of their special adeptness at talking with grown-ups.

As Acquarone has remarked, "Information leaflets talk endlessly about folic acid, proper check-ups, diet, the intake of calcium, and other physical preventative measures. However, it is rare to see guidelines that refer to the psychological state of pregnancy, conflicts within the family, new feelings aroused, explanations of why physical tests are necessary, the function of scans, or the delivery of bad news" (pp. 57–58). Obviously, the arrival of a new baby represents a period of potentially great joy for a family, but, more often than not, it is a period of great anxiety, change, and upheaval; and at this early point in the baby's life, all members of the family need psychological support. Acquarone wonders, "What is the cost, for example, of having a properly trained prenatal psychotherapist (such training is now available) as against the cost of treating the entire family at a later stage, plus the maintenance of special schools, hospital units for suicidal teenagers and drug users, psychiatric units, units for eating disorders, and so on?" (p. 58). In her writing, Stella Acquarone has echoed the wish of Melanie Klein, who wrote in 1932 that "If every child who shows disturbances that are at all severe were to be analysed in good time, a great number of these people who later end up in prisons or lunatic asylums, or who go completely to pieces, would be saved from such a fate and be able to develop a normal life" (Klein, 1932, p. 374). Klein, though a great visionary, urged children to attend five times weekly. We now know that suggesting a five-times-weekly child analysis to the young parents of an under-five would cause many parents to eschew all further mental health services or contacts. Infant–parent psychotherapy, as practised by Stella Acquarone, can be deep, it can be intensive—but when instituted early, it can also be brief, resolving knots without wrenching the child into an unusual treatment structure that can sometimes prove more disruptive to the family than the presenting problem.

We all owe a great debt of gratitude to Stella Acquarone. She has brought her intensive psychological, psychotherapeutic, and psychoanalytic training and experience to bear upon the problem of early interventions; she has developed a rigorous model of assessment and psychological treatment; and she has managed to convey both the broad sweep and the details of her work with extreme engagement and lucidity in the pages of her new book. I urge colleagues to take up the challenges posed by *Infant–Parent Psychotherapy: A Handbook*. I rank this book as one of the great classics in the child mental health and adult mental health fields, and I hope that each of you will derive as much sustenance and inspiration from its contents as I have.

PROLOGUE

This book is about a new approach within psychoanalysis: dealing with the babies in front of us—the real babies, screaming, whether thriving or troubled. We do not have to wade very deep in any psychoanalytic material before we encounter plenty of *theory* about babies. But these psychoanalytic ideas are babies "reconstructed" from the child and adult population of patients or from infants observed.

With our new approach, instead of starting with a child or adult and projecting *back* to the baby, we start with the baby and project *forward*. In view of recent infant research, empirical observation, supervision, and the emerging fields of infant psychiatry and evolutionary psychology and biology, we can no longer in good conscience treat the real babies in front of us as mere recipients of parents' projections. *Real* babies and *really* worried parents of truly troubled babies do not necessarily fit into theories made from the big-people point of view. The new approach involves a new point of view: babies have their own short story, their own frustrated expectations, and their own specific kinds of affects to mould.

This new approach is infant–parent (psychoanalytic) psychotherapy. It has roots in the major fields of psychology—psychodynamic, behavioural, cognitive, humanistic, bio-psychological, sociocultural—but the stem, the main trunk, is clinical. It is a body of knowledge emerging from the screaming—thriving or troubled—babies in front of us. Perhaps it is a branch of *applied psychoanalysis*. In time, the experts will classify it properly. But for the moment we should avoid lineage, pedigree, and classification and let the babies in front of us speak for themselves, each in their own voice and from their own point of view.

For a professional, dealing with the preverbal is counterintuitive. We are taught to ask presenting patients "What's wrong?" and from this beginning dialogue we fashion an appropriate treatment. We professionals often forget that parents, on the other hand, are pre-equipped by Nature to deal with their baby: they and their baby are caught up in a complex and magical matrix of emotions. For this reason—because parents are emotionally attached to their babies in a way professionals can never be—I ask you not to approach this book from what you know. We could spend hours fussing over what is really going on inside the head of the preverbal. But if you would suspend your judgements and opinions without theorizing—just experience and observe the nonverbal dance of infants and their parents—then the new world of infant–parent psychoanalytic psychotherapy will be revealed.

I call this new world the "parent–infant space", and to enter it as a professional—as an outsider to an intimate place—is to take on a different kind of awareness: the same kind of focused awareness, perhaps, that a surgeon adopts when entering the operating theatre.

The parent–infant space is psychodynamic. It deals with images some of which we are aware of openly but most of which are hidden, even from ourselves, in deep recesses of our minds. The images themselves are tokens of sorts, processed by the brain as it is equipped and able at the time they are delivered to it by the body and its senses. The brain sets about sorting them. The infant brain—working without words or reason or experience—coats each incoming image-token with emotion-tags so that gradually the baby responds appropriately to the outside world in the preverbal language of emotions. When development is interrupted or goes in an unexpected or undesired direction, then professionals who are psychodynamically trained are the best equipped to enter the parent–infant space and sort these tokens out.

Beginning with simple tools of experience and observation—infant observation as per Esther Bick's method, as well as ordinary observation—the psychodynamically trained can reset the parent–infant space. They are able to read and interpret the signals, signs, and markers of the preverbal dialogue, to talk nonverbally and examine the image-tokens from the earliest moments, even before words are used to structure thoughts. Allowing infants to "talk" and getting parents to recognize their own infantile aspects, psychodynamically trained parents or professionals can create a parent–infant space in which the traumatized family can interchange, negotiate, and interact from the core of their emotions without being overwhelmed with chaos and conflict or being led off-beat by the family's unique rhythms and dances, dramas or fantasies.

The emergent perspective: development in a complex world

An infant is screaming, and the worried parents present themselves to you. What questions do you ask? What do you look for? What approach and what tools do you use? And will you be able to cope without anxiety or stress?

As a clinical tool, infant–parent psychotherapy draws on its deep roots in psychoanalysis because it depends a great deal on the psychoanalytic mechanisms that Freud first developed to explore, understand, and treat worrisome behaviour springing from unconscious and preverbal areas of our minds. Unlike those trained in medicine who prescribe on the basis of symptoms, the early interventionists (we professionals who deal with the preverbal) cannot simply ask babies, "What hurts?" or "What seems to be the problem?" Instead, *we must work from the concerns and worries of parents and the distress, difficulties, and communications of infants*. While early intervention may seem straightforward, it is not altogether easy, for the simple reason that our development process is so complex and normal development can be easily derailed. As every mother knows, babies cry for many reasons.

Infant–parent psychotherapy may prove useful to clinicians, home visitors, professionals, and parents who work not only with their own babies, but with the infantile parts of themselves as well—the primitive emotions and instinctive behaviours we all carry from birth throughout life. Infant–parent psychotherapy also recognizes and deals with intergenerational transmissions, because early interventionists are aware that the present is often the past repeated, so the distress of baby and parents may well be relieved by realigning and rerouting part or the whole complex of family history and dynamics.

The clinically based methodology to deal with parents' escalating concerns, worries, and distress over real (or imagined) difficulties and disorders is relatively straightforward: simply identify, adjust, and align your questions, approaches, tools, and treatment to the emotionally based world of infant–mother–father. The secret of this approach—if there is one—is integrating what we know about an infant's individuality and development to that infant's exposure to family. It is this careful assessment of a baby's exposure to family that firmly grounds the infant–parent psychotherapy approach.

While we must have respect for all theories of emotional development, we should not be blinded or blinkered by them; rather, we should keep them on one side and try to go further, to describe what we see in front of us: the individual infant and the parents. The essence of their relationship is what forms the core of emotions that is contained within the bond between an infant and his or her parents, seemingly magic or tragic, depending on the circumstances.

Integrating what we know about babies' brains, the parent–infant space, and the eternal triangle, we are preconfigured, it seems, to deal with our family, to communicate and sense emotions, and to cope with the circumstances of our situation and environment. Infant–parent psychotherapy—early intervention—is an emerging framework centred around our growing awareness of the different forces and influences that sometimes derail development.

The imperative for mastering the "art" of early intervention is paramount. More and more, mothers are "trusting their instincts" and demanding specialist attention at the first signs of concern. No parent wants to live with the thought that, had they not listened to their paediatrician or doctor saying "everything will be all right", "there's nothing to worry about", "it's normal", or their baby will "grow out of it", their baby's disorder could have been avoided. Because today's parents are better informed, today's professionals must be better trained.

Mastering this art of early intervention has five prerequisites:

- *understanding* the dynamics of the baby and the family (chapters one and two)
- *using* the psychodynamic approach (chapter three)
- *building an expertise* with the troubled baby—the assessment, diagnosis, and treatment (chapters four, five, and six) of infants, parents, and families at risk
- *handling* the special-needs baby (chapter seven)
- *working* with the troubled mother (chapter eight)

Part I of this volume—chapters one, two, and three—investigates the theoretical foundations upon which infant–parent psychotherapy is

built. There are two explanations underlying the effectiveness of infant–parent psychotherapy: one neurobiological, the other psychodynamic. The neurobiological, discussed in chapter one, relates to how
hundreds of thousands of genes, billions of neurons, and trillions of
connections settle down into coherent, orderly development, with maternal and paternal genes each separately influencing different parts of
the brain. The chapter also looks at the neurobiological effects of the
emotional and physical environment—how the brain adjusts in response to outside influences and is therefore still open at this stage to
correction if things do go wrong.

The psychodynamic, discussed in chapter two, relates to a better
understanding of the mother–baby–father relationship. I have developed the concepts of the *parent–infant space* and the *eternal triangle* as
means to encapsulate the complexity and density of the baby–parent
relationship in a way that allows us to talk coherently about the psychodynamic concepts involved. So often overlooked, the role of the
second adult—usually the father—in the family dynamics is shown to
be crucial, whether this adult is present or not. This new triangle of
father–mother–this-particular-baby (presenting distress) is explored,
bringing to light aspects to understand and help development. Case
studies—which are used throughout this volume to put flesh on the
topics discussed—are presented here to illustrate the different forms
that this eternal triangle can take.

In chapter three, we move on to the psychoanalytic basis of infant–
parent psychotherapy. If we are serious about helping babies, if we
sincerely want to lower the volume of crying and distress in the infant
world, parents and professionals alike must somehow adopt *their baby's* points of view, use *the baby's* systems and methods of communication, and move *with the baby* into a space to thrive. Approaching the
parent–infant space psychodynamically with psychoanalytic tools allows the early interventionist to first form a picture of the internal
world and then work within it. The parent–infant space itself is the
blueprint of all the actions of the people who occupy it—infant/
mother/father, the parents' relationship with their parents, and the
internalized model of infant/mother/father that the parents carry in
their own minds.

To be effective, the professional must approach troubled infants or
parents already familiar with the *theoretical background* of the early
intervention and already practised in the use of the psychodynamic
tools needed to hold, contain, and map the primary drivers in the
infant–parent relationship. This theory has emerged from develop-

mental psychology, research in infancy, and psychoanalysis of early life. And although infant observations, infant interaction time, and home visits are not treatments proper, these are included in chapter three because it is important that we acquire a proper *experiential background* to the early intervention by examining and acquiring a proficiency in these foundation activities, methodologies, and skills.

Part II puts into practice the theoretical foundations laid down in Part I. While the paediatrician sees "normal" and troubled babies alike, we infant–parent professionals just see the *troubled* babies, and usually we are invited in only when parents are concerned, worried, or distressed. Any good outcome consistently achieved will then be the result of accurate assessment (chapter four), skilful diagnosis (chapter five), and proper treatment (chapter six). But however accurate and skilful the practitioner, and however proper the intervention is intended to be, good outcomes are best achieved by starting with a proper assessment.

Part III is an extension of chapter six, and it takes into account special-needs infants (chapter seven) and troubled mothers (chapter eight). When I speak of my experience of working with severely disturbed mothers (chapter eight), I do it with more wonder than I usually feel, mainly because it is another area that almost belonged solely to the psychiatric field; my venture into this area had to be in conjunction with psychiatrists, working with them with outpatients or inpatients, or being involved for consultations. However, the chapter talks about work other than the psychiatric care-keeping/treatment of the mother. It talks about the observation, monitoring, reflection, and help that a mother (who might develop puerperal psychosis, suffer from severe endogenous depression, develop severe postnatal depression, have a schizophrenic breakdown, manic-depressive episodes, compulsive thoughts, etc.) can or is able to receive, since her mental state is so fragile and could be dangerous for the infant's physical and mental welfare. Strategies are presented to assess and help a mother and her baby in this situation at such a vulnerable and important moment in the baby's life.

We start, though, by looking, in the Introduction, at what infant–parent psychotherapy is and what it takes to be an infant–parent psychotherapist. When parents bring in *screaming babies*, what the professional hears in the consultation may seem like a fairy tale, replete with monsters, good and evil characters, treacheries, and trickeries. To the untrained, it may even appear that the successful early intervention is a magic wand waved over a batch of stress-producing anxieties and that we infant–parent psychotherapists are wizard practitioners of a mysterious art. But the atmosphere of the fairy tale shares many features of the landscape of primitive emotions where new parents sometimes act like characters stuck in relationships and stages of development with a limited understanding of what is happening around them. And if magic is the heart of the fairy tale, then psychodynamics is the heart of the early intervention, for it is difficult to quiet screaming babies unless you can quickly change from verbal to nonverbal communication and exercise a professional intuition. Fortunately, infant–parent psychotherapy is a kind of applied art and a scientific skill that can be learned and used, whatever the reasons for a baby crying.

INFANT–PARENT PSYCHOTHERAPY

Introduction

WHAT IS INFANT–PARENT PSYCHOTHERAPY?

This book concerns the field of early emotions in all of us, making an analysis across emotions reactivated, beyond behaviour in the present, delving into the past and coming out with precious understanding that allows us better to help the baby and parents in distress.

The aim of infant–parent psychotherapy is to understand and facilitate normal communication and the development of emotions and relationships. In exploring the internal world of the infant, the therapist focuses on the mental representation each parent has of themselves, of each other, and of their baby, each in relation to the other.

In general the work is brief. It is brief because the infant–parent relationship itself is so new and thus difficulties are thought to be short-lived and can usually be quickly rectified. It is this *early* intervention that gives the therapy its impact and effectiveness.

As an adult and child psychoanalytic psychotherapist, it naturally follows that I use psychoanalytic ideas and instruments. That means I have to differentiate between long-term psychoanalytic psychotherapy and early short-term interventions (including infant–parent and particularly infant–*mother* psychotherapy).

The two types of treatment can take place simultaneously. The relationship between mother and baby cannot wait for the resolution of past conflicts in the mother or the father. In cases where there is a need for both kinds of therapy, two different psychotherapists could be involved in the work. A contract, agreement, or schedule of work is made according to need. Individual long-term psychotherapy may be offered to either of the parents where it is felt that the mother or father is overwhelmed by past experiences. Or, after an assessment, the recommendation may be that just the infant and mother meet regularly with the therapist.

The analysis and understanding of the observations and interventions that come from the work are based on certain premises or axioms, the main one being that every baby has a mental apparatus capable of registering needs and feelings and is also able to function in active interaction with the mother's feelings. In time, as Mahler pointed out in a study in 1975, "the infant learns to use his mother as a beacon or orientation and internalise this experience as an inner mother. The psychotic child has been unable to make effective use of the inner mother and carries fragments of her that are unreliable and, therefore, is terrified of moving towards selfhood and separateness" (Mahler, 1975, p. 434).

Psychoanalytic theories of the mind and the psychoanalytic tools of using the transference and the countertransference to know about deep layers of the mind, together with infant research, provides the basis for an understanding of the complex positive or negative interaction and the way to help effectively and in a timely way.

Understanding the baby in front of us

To construct a psychodynamic context is to use ideas and technical instruments of psychoanalysis integrated with other theories of infant emotional development, evolution, behaviour, cognition, music, art, psychology, and neuropsychological research. This is *psychotherapy*. It is a technique of going through in a systematic and creative way not only the mother's narrative (and the father's, if he is present at the consultation), but the baby's as well. This is why the *early intervention*—understanding, shared with those in the consulting-room, from professionals who can position the story unfolding in front of them in a proper psychodynamic context—is both an art form and a science. It is a performance achieved by personality and applied knowledge shaped and tempered by an emerging body of thought, evidence, and experience we call infant–parent psychotherapy or infant psychoanalysis.

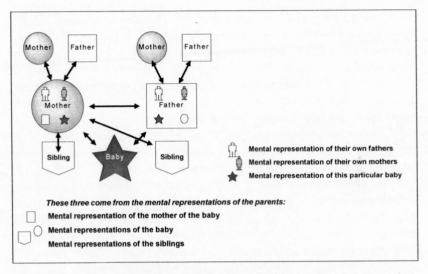

These three come from the mental representations of the parents:

Mental representation of their own fathers

Mental representation of their own mothers

Mental representation of this particular baby

Mental representation of the mother of the baby

Mental representations of the baby

Mental representations of the siblings

FIGURE I.1.   The basic model of relationships [mother–father–baby] used in infant–parent psychotherapy.

In addition to parenthood, many types of work position a professional in front of under-5s: nurse, paediatrician, nursery staff, ante- and postnatal clinician, developmental and educational psychologist, counsellor, doctor, social worker, midwife, adoption agency staff, pre- and primary-school teacher, and volunteer. Infant–parent psychotherapy added to any one of these roles and careers allows practitioners to intervene *early*, confident that best outcomes will appear very quickly and last longer.

The effective early intervention—if an intervention is needed at all—is difficult to achieve. Knowing what to do requires an understanding of the baby in front of you, of the capacities it is born with and without and the forces push and pull it through development.

EARLY INTERVENTION

Often when faced with early signs of alarm, those in the medical profession will counsel mothers to "wait and see if the child grows out of it". This worrying practice of deflecting a mother's concerns ignores her real instinct for danger. It compromises the child's potential for healthy development by stifling an early and more effective response.

I started as a child psychotherapist. This book is based on my observations and treatment of over 3,500 parents and their infants over a period of twenty years. With each new baby I see, I grow more convinced of the extraordinary effectiveness of early intervention. Not only is it possible to thus detect the first signs of emotional problems, but inherently pathological processes that could otherwise lead to permanent organic damage (retardation, autism, early psychosis, and other serious disorders of childhood, adolescence, and even adulthood) can be corrected. Early diagnosis can also help to treat or even prevent many "psychosomatic" illnesses.

I continue to see a steady stream of mothers, fathers, and infants referred to me by GPs, health visitors, and paediatricians. Parents are commonly concerned about their baby's sleeping habits, excessive crying, feeding difficulties, extreme quietness, or inability to separate from the mother. Within a few sessions many parents can be helped to understand both their baby's messages and their own reactions and feelings to their baby's behaviours. Sometimes I ask the siblings and grandparents to join us. Babies will often react in simple ways to complex family dynamics, and parents can be encouraged to observe and correct interactions that affect their new baby adversely.

To better understand screaming babies and children—both thriving and troubled—we have to be able to act decisively when our intuition tells us something is wrong. But in order to intervene early, we need to know how to do so effectively.

Early intervention is to mental suffering what jabs are to childhood diseases. But while immunization programmes have almost eradicated a number of previously widespread serious diseases, mental illness and distress are commonly left untreated, at great personal and social cost. If we ignore the early signs, then not only will vulnerable children prove to be a continual drain on medical, social, and educational resources, but their parents will be destined to a lifetime of constant care and worry.

Let's face it: a new child generates turmoil—some necessary and some not. Just as new content alters its context, a baby's arrival alters its family's dynamics. And these dynamics—the baby's behaviour and the family's response—are tied not only to elements we can see, but to genetic codes and recessive tendencies we cannot see, not to mention the intergenerational, social, and cultural factors at work as well. Whatever turmoil the baby causes and for whatever reason, the family usually wishes (consciously or not) to resolve baby's distress and find some sort of harmony and rhythm, coming to terms with what is expected and what is possible.

This wish to resolve creates a developmental dialectic in the "parent–infant space" into which professionals can enter, measure, assess, and intervene (or not). The space itself is a bit of a mystery. Over a lifetime it can be said to spiral—babies gradually become parents of their own babies—and for all the reasons discussed in this book, the parent–infant space may wobble or warp, even break. The usual intent of the intervening professional is to help baby and parents find a balance, a unique space to develop mature patterns of behaviour and emotion.

There are several reasons why intervening early is so effective:

1. *Childbirth is a crucial time for parents*, since it reactivates unresolved issues, which, left untreated, can flare into more complex chronic conditions or even pathology.

2. *First emotions are being imprinted.*

3. *The brain is being wired.*

4. *Earlier interventions are much shorter*—corrections made early on lead to better outcomes than years of treatment later in life.

5. *It is cost-effective*—there can generally be a few interviews by a well-trained professional intervening early, instead of a team of professionals treating difficulties and disorders later in life.

6. *The quality of family life is improved*—effective early intervention can help a family avoid years of unnecessary misery.

My goal is to help parents to understand their baby better. Professionals need to be alert and sensitive to early warning signs of problems. All of us must do what is best for babies. In helping them, we enrich society and ourselves by removing obstacles to healthy development through simple cost-effective early intervention.

The need for early intervention

Recognizing a baby as a person

When does a baby begin to be a "person"? Does it begin from conception or birth, or does it evolve from upbringing and environment? There are many theories about this. Perhaps the question is better put by asking when a baby has a personality. Any mother can tell you that, almost from conception, her baby has a personality. However, my work has shown me that most adults do not fully recognize that a baby has a complex personality. And if the behaviour of the little person is a problem, there seems to be a tiresome tendency to blame the mother.

The answer to this question is important because from the time that babies show their personality, they are also demonstrating behaviour. And when babies behave inappropriately—when, for example, they do not respond to sound—the problem must be addressed at once. Such an early intervention needs to be both sensitive and skilful to be effective. Intervention has the power to change behaviour; early intervention has the power to change outcomes, because it recognizes that outcomes and development are self-organizing, adaptive, and emergent:

- *Self-organizing*, because a baby will spontaneously organize a whole series of complex structures into a way of life—development will "get organized" and reinforce itself. The human brain constantly organizes and reorganizes its billions of neural connections so as to learn from experience. If an early intervention can change conditions on the outside, babies stand a better chance of developing the inner resources needed to survive and thrive.

- *Adaptive*, because babies try to turn whatever happens to their advantage.

- *Emergent*, because our lives are the natural expression of our beginnings. When we understand the tremendous dynamics at work in early life, then we may find certain points where intervention is possible and our children's lives can be transformed for the better.

Thus, for optimal results, professionals should intervene early. Parents sense that their babies are born with predisposed personal characteristics. Depending on upbringing and environment, these characteristics define the relationship that babies share with their parents. It can be stressful or happy or somewhere in between. I have worked with babies so vital and strong that they seem to pull entire families, and everyone around them, into their orbit. Other babies simply fail to thrive. Each of them, however, carries personal and unique responses, reactions, feelings, tendencies, and temperament. Newborns know and recognize what they want, how to get it, and at what cost to themselves. Parents, too, know what kind of help they need, but often they do not know how to get it.

One aim of this book is to bring into sharper focus the subtle ways in which babies and parents interact and change each other. If our babies are, in any case, going to change us, it is as well to take the opportunity to change for the better. Parenting then becomes easier and more enjoyable; babies thrive. And perhaps old cycles of inter-generational problems can be broken at last and replaced by healthy parent–child and family relationships.

To facilitate such a radical shift in perspective, we must first of all be aware of the potential for change, taking the following into account:

- *The baby's individuality*—a unique make-up, including temperament, tendencies, needs, and ways of dealing with time, frustration, annoyance, pain, gratitude, adaptability, and intensity of reactions.

- *The quality of the baby's interactions* and its importance in assessing the state of the infant's relationship with parents and what part intergenerational dynamics will play in the baby's family life.

- *The integration of the baby into a family structure*, especially how the individual make-up and personality of the child affects the parents' ability to fit the child into their lives—what happens to each parent when the baby comes along, and to the relationship between the mother and father.

In subsequent chapters we assess whether the baby's development is within the wide range of normality and illustrate how behaviour, reactions, and various activities demonstrate the baby's progress. Clinical examples are presented to illustrate how some mothers, who have had damaged relationships with their own mothers, struggle to rectify their own mother–child conflicts, and how they instinctively seek professional help in order to try to change the way they feel about their own babies. It is gratifying, however, to observe how mothers who are securely attached—who have secure relationships with *their* mothers or mother-substitutes—behave in a similar way with their own babies.

By recognizing familiar problem behavioural patterns between the parents and their babies, it is possible to see how all kinds of difficulties can be resolved. It is especially worth considering how parents deal with their own expectations for their baby in order to compensate for their own adverse childhood experiences—for example, if they themselves were abused or neglected.

Not everything, however, is within an individual's control. Inside and outside forces push and pull individuals in such ways that each

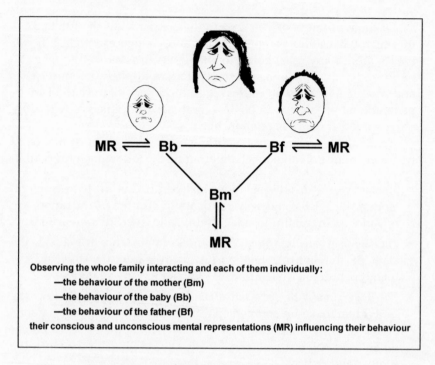

Observing the whole family interacting and each of them individually:
—the behaviour of the mother (Bm)
—the behaviour of the baby (Bb)
—the behaviour of the father (Bf)
their conscious and unconscious mental representations (MR) influencing their behaviour

FIGURE I.2.   Troubled faces in the consulting-room

life is unique. Unexpected events, traumas, and changes can be seen as either dreadful or challenging. Even child rearing itself can stifle creativity, and both parents may need help to move forward.

The task is to widen perspectives and open doors to allow for a different kind of thinking that will enable each member of a fused mother–father–baby unit to move forward. This is not fairy-tale thinking, although the results can make it seem so.

How early?

Our main strategy is to help babies before the age of 12 months, and even as early as birth or pregnancy, to get the best start. This presents an opportunity for the parents to be referred as well, to provide services to help them to sort out deep-seated conflicts that have been reactivated by the parenting experience. It is important, though, to remember that extreme vulnerability goes along with the openness that is characteristic of this early stage. Whoever engages in working with adults becoming parents has to do so carefully and sensitively, because making unconscious communications more available as they are reactivated by the care of a baby brings more awareness of past and present conflicts. With fragile mothers, the possibility of being helped runs parallel to a greater risk of breaking down and having to be hospitalized and separated from their baby. Sometimes awareness of this vulnerability may prevent us from intervening at an early stage. We need to look precisely at each situation and patient to consider when, where, and how to go about the intervention.

Why do we intervene?

Parents and professionals often ask me to help in situations that they find uncomfortable, painful, annoying, strange, confusing, or worrying. Their wish for change may or may not be conscious. They may be in a state of mind in which they actively resist change, distancing themselves from anxiety and mental pain. Psychoanalytic work in such situations can be long and hazardous, and patients can become stuck in their treatments and restricted in their lives. However, our task when a baby reactivates the more infantile parts of the parent is to find an opening. We intervene because we wish to facilitate the change, and the new and refreshing perspective that the real infant brings to the consultation often surprises us. With expressions and behaviour so closely tied to their emotional sensitivities, babies often help emotionally paralysed parents to make links and to understand better their own experiences.

Pregnancy and birth promote physical changes, so visible in a woman, but even thinking of having a child can push both parents into parental reverie. This reverie opens up unconscious pathways within the parents to make them more available to the infant's primitive communications. Through this physical and emotional internal stimulation, old conflicts, enmeshed with fantasies and new constructions, create an imaginary child based on the experience of the foetus and their own projections of wishes about the child.

We thus have an excellent avenue for helping babies and their parents to change in a painless way.

Altering the shape of a family's future is not an exercise in magic, although the early intervention may seem so, given the immediate relief and long-term benefits it can bring. Because of its inherent structural and dynamic complexities, effective early intervention is an expertise that must be mastered more than memorized, practised more than contemplated. But, mastered or not, if intervening does nothing more than unlock a future less bleak than one awaiting a distressed family, then everybody—baby included—will profit at least to some extent from your expertise.

Parents in psychoanalysis, psychotherapy, or counselling

Given such opportunities for promoting a family's health, psychoanalysts and adult psychotherapists need to review their way of in-depth work with adults who have had a baby, bearing in mind the fields of infant research, infant observation, and infant psychotherapy. If parents are already in a traditional psychoanalysis, it is recommended that infant–parent psychotherapy should only be undertaken at this time if they seem to have insight into their baby also being in conflict. In this case, different skills are needed.

If the pregnancy occurs while in treatment, the impetus given by the foetus and familyhood extends psychoanalytic understanding through the formation of new ideas and the *baby's reality*. In this context, the past can be reviewed, and the pull from the foetus and motherhood or fatherhood can serve as a new link into the unconscious, which is now steadily and forcefully led by the parental "reverie". Understanding this as a healthy development *or the wish for it* should underlie the whole process, so as not to push it into a primitive area that cannot be managed by either therapist or parent.

Counsellors and psychiatric nurses work with depressed mothers, confused mothers, and deeply disturbed mothers, and they do this for a period that is longer than early short interventions, although not long enough for a well-resolved psychoanalytic treatment. The outcome is not as comprehensive as it could be, but the fact that these professionals are not trained to work deeply with primitive anxieties can protect the full integrity of the parents during this sensitive period and keep them out of going into hospital with a mental breakdown.

A major aim of this book, however, is to provide tools for the use of adult and child psychoanalysts and psychotherapists and counsellors. Having supervised and worked with all types of professionals in health-related fields, I find that it is important to value the range of contributions available if we really want to be effective in helping infants and parents.

THE MAIN ELEMENTS THAT PROFESSIONALS REQUIRE FOR INFANT–PARENT PSYCHOTHERAPY

Personal qualities

Why do we choose to engage in early intervention? Is it a mission? Is it where the money is? Is it a new slant on an old job? Many organizations have slightly altered their remit, causing therapists to change their focus—for example, to drug addiction, alcohol abuse, abortion clinics, or refugee or family centres. But are we prepared for such mentally and emotionally challenging work?

We look within to review the events that have led us in this direction, in our personal life, work experience, or psychoanalytic treatment. Insight into our vulnerabilities may lead us to seek appropriate help. Do we acknowledge contributions from our personal make-up, sensitivities, and visceral and body responses to others' behaviour? How aware are we of the contributions of our cultural and family origins, our likes and dislikes, our special interests, our skills and hobbies? It is important to be honest in this exercise.

How ready are we to get into identifications with others and find a solution from within? Can we tolerate being dragged into collusive attitudes or being invaded by projective identifications that feel disturbing and difficult to understand, to learn from it all, and yet to be prepared for a different set of behaviours to move us deeply and with compassion?

In accepting involvement in this extremely delicate area of work, it is important to review our knowledge of it aside from that gained through our children or through our specific training in child development or in child psychotherapy. This means becoming acquainted with the literature on infant research, developmental psychoanalysis, neurobiology, infant observations, and observation of babies and toddlers.

Life experiences

Professionals can contemplate standards of health and its variations in different ways, depending on their background, culture, and personal experiences. Those who have lived in extreme poverty or on drugs (or had relatives in these circumstances) or have survived wars will have very basic standards of the minimum requirement for healthy development. The opposite also applies. Those who have always lived in the confines of a protective or overprotective family, where everything was the same, without any curiosity about other people in the world, may find it difficult to identify or sympathize with others and their unfamiliar ways of living. A tendency to judge, rather than try to understand, other people's reality may arise.

On the other hand, life experience can make for greater sensitivity. For example, a professional might be motivated by the experience of having a disabled baby brother who did not live long or an insane parent, spouse, or sibling who taught them more about psychiatry than did their training or their patients. Others may have survived a natural catastrophe, a major accident, or a fire in a high-rise building. These disasters do not just happen in films: they can and do happen in everyday life. It is useful to recall traumatic experiences that extend our understanding of human nature and the behaviours that can be triggered in extreme circumstances.

Others may have travelled to places where they do not know the language, yet they managed for two weeks, or a year. Travelling alone, camping, surviving with little or no money, learning a new language, and recalling their expectations and difficulties or the humiliation of being treated like a moron because their accent is strange or because they got words or syntax mixed up—all these experiences broaden the range of empathy. It is useful to review such experiences to help us empathize with infants, especially children with disabilities. Their accommodation to the new experiences that suddenly occur after birth, without any previous knowledge with which to understand what is happening, might have some resemblance to adult ways of reacting in a new or traumatic situation. Similarly, difficulty in understanding what is going on around us in a strange place, or understanding a new language or adjusting to a new cultural setting, may be similar to the efforts of disabled or fragile babies who go through life with no one to identify with or to understand their daily trauma.

Somehow, as adults, we have learned to communicate at visual, verbal, and intellectual levels, putting meaning to events and the world around us. We learn to feel secure in the world of familiar people and actions, avoiding too much anxiety. It is important to enlarge our experience and consciousness, not only by understanding our own unconscious conflicts and what we experience as traumatic, but also by keeping them alive in a way that is reparatory towards ourselves and others. This does not mean that we should keep alive the trauma in a compulsively repetitive way. Working through difficulties will provide an imprint of matters so resolved, enabling us to sympathize and empathize with others. Our reflection on their experience will then be grounded in real thinking about feelings, rather than simply thinking about thinking.

It is also important to actively exercise our senses with experiences that will enrich our awareness of other dimensions or possibilities of being—for example, by blindfolding ourselves and trying to cope for a whole weekend; by making ourselves unable to hear and see, or restraining our movements, and finding out how it is possible to manage for a period of time; or by trying an unknown language or unknown experiences. In the training for infant–parent psychotherapy, it is enlightening to lead trainees into this extension of their awareness in order to help them to be more open to all types of communications in the infant–parent encounter.

It is useful to emphasize the importance of living every day with courage and pride. There is a lot to learn and use from within us, and our attitude has to include a continuous self-examination and valuing of our impressions, sensations, memories. By this means we are contributing to our personal psychotherapy and training, with the maximum possibility of healthy integration and creativity.

Formal training

When we talk about what it is in a training programme that makes it special, it is helpful to remember that psychoanalytic techniques for working with adults are different from those for treating children. In the same way, new techniques and training needs are developing in the field of infant psychotherapy.

The formal training programme that we have developed includes reading and discussion of infant research, diagnostic classification from 0 to 3 years (called infant psychiatry), different visions of infancy and infant observation, and different psychoanalytic theories of the development of the self and emotions. The training also includes discussion of the trainees' own work in seminar groups on a three-monthly rotation of observations of different clinical settings for babies and their parents, ranging from paediatric wards, to home visits, to families at risk.

Our programme lasts two to three years. Clinical work with parents and babies is closely supervised when the student is considered to be mature enough to undertake it.

The experience of working in different settings is a requirement. Apart from the one they are already working in, trainees are required to experience four other settings for at least four months in each placement. It is considered important that they observe, note, discuss, and reflect on behaviours between infant, toddlers, and their parents in order to become aware of the wide range of normal, everyday conflicts and their resolutions. In this way, a quick attunement is acquired to enable the trainee to know when an interaction feels, and can be explained, as pervasive or entrenched.

Infant observation is a discipline that consists of weekly observation of the same mother–baby pair, along with the father and siblings if possible, from birth to 2 years of age. This lasts for one hour at the same time each week, with detailed notes being taken immediately afterwards and then discussed with a seminar leader in a group of four to six trainees. The aim is to be able to witness and to bear the emotional intensity of the growth of a special kind of relationship: the first and most important imprinting of emotions at play. The two years enable the trainee to observe the growth of the baby's relationships from the raw expressions of the neonate and its new mother to those of the verbal, toilet-trained, independent toddler and its parents. The experience will include close observation of the visceral reactions, body language, images, fantasies, and memories awakened in the observer, but without their being communicated to the parents. The observer has to be careful not to fulfil roles expected or needed in the baby's household, but sensitively to stay as neutral, humane, and passive as possible in order not to interfere in the natural development of the infant–parent relationship by having either a too-distancing or a too-helpful attitude. (This discipline provides the basis for the attitude needed eventually by qualified infant–parent psychotherapists in the consultation, prior to intervention.) Social observations of infant–parent interaction outside the home—in friends' houses, parks, and swimming-pools or in supermarkets—are also required. Detailed observations of the dyad are discussed to extend the group's learning about the extreme behaviours that are part of normal interaction and development.

Personal psychoanalytic work is of great help, and skilled supervision is provided in infant-observations seminars and clinical work discussion. This is necessary because the primitive nature of the experiences reactivated in the professional makes it almost impossible for the work to be done at a level where there is no collusion with internal resistance from the family.

THEORETICAL FOUNDATIONS

CHAPTER ONE

The dynamics of the infant space

The process of development in infancy seems magical. Everything happens very fast, following patterns that develop through the interaction of genetics and the environment, the positive stimulus of good relationships, or the damning effects of bad ones. Traumatic or pleasant experiences are imprinted on the brains of tiny infants, working hand in hand with unpredictable physiological changes, for the better or for the worse.

When the effects of this process are harmful, are they permanent, or can we alleviate them? If so, how can we change the inevitable, what kind of help is available, and where can we find it?

Answers to such questions are offered throughout this volume, and the when, where, and what of the kind of help babies and parents need is described. There are many possibilities, but common to them all is the understanding that infants carry within them their own story, each a particular vision of the world put together in response to the difficulties confronting them and their parents. It may well be that much of their story is a response to the expectations and reactions of parents, in whom the infant may have awakened unresolved conflicts, but it is still the infant who comes first to the consultation. Whatever the cause of the problem, the answer is to be found, first and foremost, in the baby.

"ONCE UPON A TIME, there lived a happy couple in a far-away land. When their child was born, they vowed to give it everything and threw a wonderful party to celebrate. Good fairies were invited to the party, but bad fairies also turned up. And then the trouble started.

"The mother died and the father brought home a new mother. This wicked stepmother treated the baby badly, and everything began to fall apart. Monsters appeared and followed the growing child everywhere. Life became frightening.

"But dreams, hopes, wishes, and the memory of a loving mother comforted the child, keeping evil away during the long journey to becoming a tall, strong adult in the big, bad world."

Fairy-tales have always enchanted us, adults and children alike. By their very structure, fairy-tales move us through terrors, to hope, to happiness when everything works out in the end. As we turn the final pages and put the story down, it seems as if the glow of good triumphing over evil will last forever—though no follow-up studies of the central characters can exist to confirm this!

In fairy-tales, the heroine tends to be born into good-enough conditions, but, shortly afterwards, everything changes. Babies born to good mothers may be placed at the mercy of bad, wicked [step-]mothers. Or wonderful fathers become gruesome and abusive. There is often a fear of incest and nasty collusion, but the hope that good will triumph over evil is always there. The fairies symbolize this deeply held hope, showering the central characters with love and care and the promise of a future that is wealthy and trouble-free.

This magical potential for transformation can teach us how to change the troubled circumstances of real lives. Perhaps the biggest secret that therapists can learn from fairy-tales is the value of carefully examining the beginnings. In our work with adults, adolescents, and children, we hear stories that can best be understood by going right back to the beginning. Patients often come with stories of horror not dissimilar to those in fairy-tales. Children with sleeping problems talk of "monsters in the bedroom", or adults may come with feelings of being "trapped" at home, of being unable to go out and have any pleasure in life because of some "tyrant in the house". The sessions can be filled with talk of constant trials and of endless advice from others, as in rites of initiation.

In therapy sessions, as patients recover the memory of traumatic events that they had forgotten, these stories come to life again in rapid succession. Monsters suddenly revisit them in the consulting-room in the form of screaming babies and helpless mothers trying to escape from blaming fathers, despair, and tears. Horrifying masks are seen on the angelic faces of newborn babies, and mistrust, paranoia, and rage are projected upon these innocent souls. As their stories unfold in the consulting-room, the parents marvel at the magic wands of therapist– fairies when links are made and peace, calm, and understanding trans- form their monstrous landscapes. In five sessions or so, skilled psychotherapists with years of experience and understanding can rec- ognize familiar scenarios and perform their magic, so that goodness and healing lift a seemingly doomed child into a happy future with a newly aware family.

How can we analyse a nonverbal complaint made by a baby? All kinds of people spend their lives understanding inanimate objects (e.g. by getting the remains of early civilizations to speak). But though babies may be nonverbal, they are *very* animated, and parents know all too well that babies will not be dismissed because they cannot speak. They *will* be heard.

What do they need us to hear? By going back to the beginning and understanding these infants, it is possible to alter the outcome for the children, adolescents, and parents that they will become. It is a magical process that can end well, as in fairy-tales, because the key to an ending in which they live happily ever after is held by the infant at the very beginning.

The magic of the brain

When we first began our work with infants and parents three decades ago, we were working from clinical intuition. Today, neurobiological research seems to be validating our early findings that healthy bonds and healthy brains depend on quality relationships with the primary caregivers (usually parents) and on the connections of neurons in the brain.

The number of cells (neurons) in the brain—about 100 billion— remains the same throughout our lives as at birth. In the first year of life, each neuron forms about 15,000 synapses (connections). By the end of the second year, the brain will have formed 1,000 trillion connections (see Fig. 1.1). It is all these connections that make the brain of a 2-year-old so much heavier than the newborn's—four times as much. At this time some serious pruning must begin in order for the brain to be "wired up" efficiently. Each neuron may prune up to 10,000 of these connections if they are not needed or have not been used. Early events determine which circuits in the brain will be reinforced and retained. New synapses can in fact be formed at any time during life, whenever completely new situations demand it, but never with the same ease as in the early years.

As the number of connections decreases, the density of this complex and powerful wiring system is reinforced in the baby's brain by the quality and content of the emotional surroundings. Neurobiologists show us that the wiring is related directly to the quality of the parent–infant relationship, the kind of care the baby receives, and the quality of the baby's attachments with its parents and others.

The capacity of the developing brain to modify itself is an adaptive mechanism that has emerged out of the process of natural selection. It meets the need to develop a mechanism that could enable a highly complex neurological structure to become efficiently wired up without demanding vastly more chromosomal information. This is a crucial point. Since most knowledge cannot be anticipated, development depends upon a way to incorporate experiences into the developing

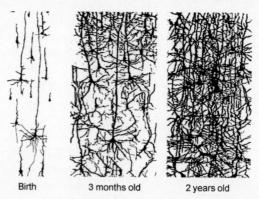

Birth   3 months old   2 years old

FIGURE 1.1.   Scans of the brain at birth, 3 months, and 2 years reveal the increasing density and complexity of connections among the neurons.

(Reprinted by permission of the publisher from *The Postnatal Development of the Human Cerebral Cortex, Vols. I-VIII* by Jesse LeRoy Conel, Cambridge, Mass.: Harvard University Press, Copyright ©1939, 1975 by the President and Fellows of Harvard College.)

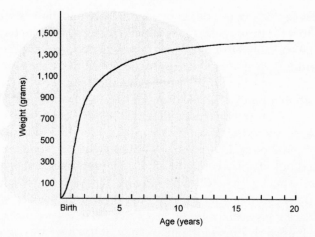

FIGURE 1.2.   Rate of growth in brain weight due to increasing complexity, from birth to age 20 years: the rate is greatest during the first three years (after Schore, 1994).

brain. By initially overproducing connections that have been spread to a variety of targets and then selecting from among these on the basis of their different functional characteristics, highly predictable and functionally adaptive patterns of connectivity can be generated with minimal pre-specification of the details (Deacon, 1997).

The brain's ability to change its own structure in response to the environment is known as neuroplasticity: "The single most significant distinguishing feature of all nervous tissue—of neurons—is that they are designed to change in response to external signals. Those molecular changes permit the storage of information by neurons and neural systems" (Perry et al., 1995)

The prime task of brain development in the first few years of life is the forming, and then reinforcing into permanence, of necessary connections. It is during these early years that the brain is most open to being influenced (see Fig. 1.2), which points to the benefits of early intervention.

Emotions and the basic emotional system

So the complexity of the mind seems to increase because the infant not only has to regulate its innate needs for intersubjectivity in actually relating to the mother but, in parallel, has to start the process of recognizing its own reactions, likings, and how to satisfy them, all in a brain firing to be connected and to develop without getting overexcited/

hyperaroused or fearing death or rage. However, the brain contains feelings that for three reasons—to satisfy, to regulate, or to have fun—need to be contained or modulated by somebody, making the vulnerable infant then feel at one with a mature brain that can protect, has a cortex attuned to its own, and can induce pleasure.

Christopher Badcock (2000) has pointed to a further complexity in brain integration, and this has to do with the different origin of parts of the brain in any individual. He talks about Freud's fundamental discovery of psychological dynamics based on a mental topography that developed out of early conflict with the parents and remained latent thereafter. There is, according to Badcock, a neurophysiological basis for this theory in that conflicting parental genes have been shown to build different parts of the brain, programmed in ways consistent with Freud's characterization of the id and ego. It has been discovered that some genes are expressed when they are inherited from one parent, but not when they come from the other. Such genes are said to be "imprinted". Imprinted genes are reset each generation. A gene that is maternally imprinted in a male will be paternally imprinted when passed on to the man's children, and similarly for a female gene.

Keverne, Martel, and Nevison (1996b) found that maternal cells were present in large numbers in the neocortex and forebrain but that very few were found in the limbic brain—especially the hypothalamus. They were particularly clustered in the frontal lobes of the cortex. Paternal cells, by contrast, were the exact opposite: these were found in the hypothalamus and limbic brain, but not in the neocortex. Allen and colleagues (1995) reported that cells in the brainstem appear to be the work equally of maternal and paternal genes. The maternal brain, or neocortex, would be a neural buffer for instinctual drives and demands arising in the limbic, paternal brain. Mother's genes may have control of the breast and the milk it produces; Haig (1999) suggests that paternal genes within the infant may command its mouth and how it is used.

Interaction

Babies are born into this world with their brain ready to relate to others and to learn, but they cannot do this by themselves. Colwyn Trevarthen mentions how even a premature baby can, if approached with sufficient gentleness, interact in rhythmic "proto-conversational" patterns in time with the adult's vocalizations, touches, and expressions of face or hands, turn-taking within the evenly spaced emotionally enhanced movements that are characteristically displayed by an attentive and affectionate adult (Trevarthen, 1999, 2001; Trevarthen, Kokkinaki, & Fiamenghi, 1999; Van Rees & de Leeuw, 1987).

Millions of years of evolution have provided the human neonate with the ability to elicit sympathetic action by caregivers who know more and have greater power for protection. So in part the infant is building its own purpose and awareness, and for that it will adapt to the parents, provided that they are good at reading the infant's cues and motives and have shared emotions and cognitions. The process of mutual discovery enriches the adult too and certainly helps the development of the brain, by encouraging neurons to get connected, thereby leading to increased complexity and psychological power. The infant has to detect the interest of adults, interpret their intentions, and evaluate their emotions and link them with its own experience. The world of shared experience becomes extended by trusting the behaviours and emotions of the adult and being able to predict future pleasurable reality, such as the satisfaction of needs required for well-being. Memory gets engaged in storing experiences, classifying and extending them over longer periods according to personal experiences. It is essentially subjective, as the infant learns to live with the consequences of doing things and has to think its way around to get what it wants and needs, from that couple of parents or environment. The infant learns to live creating a sense of identity.

The human competence of the neonate is further indicated by its recognition, acquired in utero, of the voice of its mother, as can be demonstrated by the infant orientating itself towards her and by its attentiveness, and then recognizing her smell and touch. The newborn enters the parent–infant space fully equipped physically and emotionally to handle the early burst of neural wiring and configuration needed to build mental processes and procedures to handle incoming images, sounds, and bodily sensations and to enter into joyful dialogic companionship over and above its need for physical support, affectionate care, and protection. Infants communicate with attentive relatives and siblings too, influencing their attempts to gain playful reactions, until by the end of the first year the infant is expected to be an alert partner in recognized games and collaborative activities.

Early relationships

It is now accepted that a baby's emotional environment will influence the neurobiology that is the basis of mind. From the infant's point of view the most vital part of the surrounding world is the emotional connection with its caregiver. It is this that the newborn is genetically pre-programmed to immediately seek out, register, and exuberantly respond to:

> The ecological niche to which the baby has evolved the ability to adapt is the relationship with the mother. Research suggests that emotion operates as a central organising process within the brain. In this way, an individual's abilities to organise emotions—a product in part of earlier attachment relationships—directly shapes the ability of the mind to integrate experience and to adapt to future stressors. [Seigal, 1999, p. 4]

There are four main types of care and resulting forms of attachment (see Figure 1.3):

1. *Caregiving:*
   Normal development—secure attachment

   In most families the baby is loved by its parent(s) on arrival, and this translates into appropriate care, interaction, and stimulation. Expected infant-brain development in relation to caregivers produces emotional and cognitive growth. However, even in caregiving relationships, some children do feel insecurely attached.

2. *Scare-giving:*
   Hypervigilant development—anxious/avoidant attachment

   Unfortunately the parents are not always caregivers, and instead they may be "scare-givers" as a result of difficult circumstances: drugs, domestic violence, abuse or neglect in their own infancy, or psychiatric disorders. Research has shown that, under such circumstances, the emotional trauma in the vulnerable infant brain causes an elevation of stress hormones, such as cortisol, which wash over the tender brain like acid, with the result that regions in the cortex and limbic system responsible for attachment are up to 20% smaller and have fewer synapses. This may lead to great interference in the cognitive and emotional development of the brain and in the capacity of the infant for using its intelligence creatively, and it may also lead to repetition of the trauma later in life.

   Scare-givers produce trauma and dissociation. However, in some families, often where the parents themselves had received inadequate care as children, there are inner and outer stresses that adversely influence the caregiving relationship. The baby has no alternative but to fit in to what it finds and adapt its responses, and the neurobiology behind them, to the only world it knows.

RELATIONSHIP	CONSEQUENCES	HELP

1. *CAREGIVING*

Secure attachment	**Normal development**	
Main feeling: security, joy	Promotes brain growth of positive connections	None needed
Some babies may feel insecurely attached	Upsets promote negative connections	Could benefit from infant–parent psychotherapy: *Brief insightful type*

2. *SCARE-GIVING*

Anxious/avoidant attachment	**Hypervigilant development**	
Main feelings: anger or panic and stress in the relationship. More resilient babies learn to dissociate	Inhibits brain growth of positive connections; promotes negative connections, hyperarousal, constriction, and addiction. In babies who learn to dissociate, violent behaviour is usual	Regulatory functions needed, to be developed through a new attachment. Could benefit from infant–parent psychotherapy: *Paediatric supportive type & Infant-focused therapy*

3. *LITTLE OR NO CAREGIVING*

Poor attachment	**Delayed development**	
Little or no relationship	Inhibits much brain growth (unless very resilient)	Could benefit from infant–parent psychotherapy:
Ambivalent relationship	Emotional/cognitive impairment ("hospitalism" or the like). Helpless violence towards others	*Paediatric supportive type & Infant-focused therapy to the mother and infant*

4. *CAREGIVING, BUT VULNERABLE INFANT*

No attachment	**Delayed/deficient development**	
Distraught relationship with parents and siblings, lack of empathy	Inhibits brain growth of positive experiences; promotes brain growth of self-comforting and stereotypic behaviour. Some apparent developmental delay, becoming deficient. May become violent against self and others	Exploration needed of hidden sensibilities in the child. Early and skilful intervention essential: *Immediate infant-focused therapy with parents and siblings from 6 months*

FIGURE 1.3. Summary of relationships between parents and infants, consequences for attachment and development, and help needed.

3. *Little or no caregiving:*
   Delayed development—poor attachment

   There is another unfortunate experience possible in development: that instead of caregivers the infant has "no caregiver", because the place is too full of babies demanding attention or because the mother suffers from, say, postnatal depression and, even though present physically, is not in a meaningful relationship with her baby nor encountering its needs.

4. *Caregiving, but vulnerable infant:*
   Delayed or deficient development (autistic, etc.)—
   no attachment possible

   Some babies, because of unfathomable sensibilities or particular needs, do not feel their needs met, no matter how good-enough their parenting space has been. It is then necessary to explore the infant space as unique and more subtle to fulfil, so that the baby's brain does not become impoverished as if the parenting were not good enough.

   There is even a promising psychodynamics of infancy. This changes how a child psychotherapist sees and responds to an autistic child. There is less emphasis on interpretations of parents' problems and more on the secret motives or sensibilities present in the infant, together with an exploration of capacities and challenges: the capacity for symbolic thought and creativity and extending boundaries of the self to regain lost, split-off, and projected parts.

A baby's developing brain is damaged when exposed to neglect, trauma, or abuse or to prolonged maternal depression (or felt as such). The key message from recent studies of brain development is that "human connections shape the neural connections from which the mind emerges" (Seigal, 1999). "The link between emotion and memory can be especially devastating. For even though the child will never remember the specific events at any conscious level, his lower limbic system—and the amygdala in particular—does store powerful associations between an emotional state, life fear or pain, and the person or situation that brought it on. Associations may be indelible" (Eliot, 2001).

CHAPTER TWO

The dynamics of
the parent–infant space

The parent–infant space is complex. To walk into it is to walk into known and unknown risks. It is a seemingly endless walk in a seemingly never-ending maze of rooms and corridors, where the walls, ceilings, and floors can move and what is done in one part of the maze seems to affect what difficulties are encountered in other parts. Everywhere there are restrictions and constraints that can add to feelings of anxiety, fatigue, or hopelessness.

But the shape of the space and the dynamics of walking through it are not so complex. The integrity of the parent–infant space—what pulls, shapes, holds, and collapses it—is based on two triangles: a real relationship triangle and an internalized one. The points of the triangle are held together by invisible bonds. Although we cannot actually see these bonds, we certainly can feel them. They keep us together. Without them, we gradually grow apart.

Mother–baby–father are bonded in their inner, real worlds and imagined dynamics of attachment and separation. Development and relationships play out with anxiety and repression, and the parent's own memories of growing up—good ones along with long-held resentments and buried trauma—are important factors for the professional to consider. Without early intervention and a professional to provide a reflective space, these conflicts are replicated, renegotiated, or stay unresolved.

Psychologists tend to focus solely on the mother–infant bond in a child's early development. Certainly, the mother–infant relation ship is important. However, in my view there is also a triangular mother–infant–father bond. On the basis of my own clinical observations and from the observations and explorations by the likes of Melanie Klein, Ronald Britton, W. R. Bion, W. R. D. Fairbairn, or Thomas Ogden, it does seem that a type of relationship triangle is indeed present at least from birth, and quite possibly from conception. From the very beginning, an eternal triangle is present and active.

The call from inside

As a practitioner, I can usually tell when a woman is pregnant (or, if the person in front of me is a man, if his partner is). There is a certain change in the look, a distinctive "call from inside", that I can sense, an introverted, deep, protective, primitive attitude that cannot be rationalized away.

As we know, pregnancy begins when an egg is fertilized. A cascading chain of physical and mental changes is set in motion at both the conscious and unconscious level. While conception takes place at the moment when two independent entities—an egg cell and a sperm cell—unite to become a third entity, pregnancy is the period during which this third entity develops within the mother's body. This "third cell", or fertilized egg, grows into an embryo and then into a foetus whose primitive awareness, through hearing and chemical affective changes, becomes increasingly "conscious" of the people involved in the mother's life and the different degrees of closeness and intimacy that these people share with her.

The infant forms a separate and different relationship with each parent. Infant research and infant observation show how, from birth or even before birth, the baby relates to its mother and father in different ways and can form a closer attachment to one than to the other. Fonagy's research on attachment demonstrates this and shows how the baby can be securely attached to one parent and insecurely attached to the other (Fonagy, 2001). Observations show how, even during the first two months, a baby will be feeding quite happily from the mother but then fall asleep if the father or siblings come into the room. The presence of siblings complicates the baby's relationships from birth. On the other hand, a baby may only sleep comfortably when the father is singing or playing an instrument, or may be consoled only by the father's voice.

From infant observation, it has become increasingly clear to me that two caregivers are vital for development. In my experience, a mother who feels alone with the baby may tend towards depression and the development of pathology. At the same time, I do not find that a multiplicity of caregivers is helpful. But when the principal caregiver is in a close relationship with one other person, this provides an environment in which the baby can experience anxiety—about being excluded or included, shared or left alone—in the security that it is capable of momentary separation from the main caregiver. Where there is an ambience in which the infant can have manageable anxieties in its mind, the organ that sustains it—the primitive , or emotional, brain—can deal with the different inputs of stimulation and not feel overwhelmed. Panksepp (1998, p. 206) mentions that, contrary to traditional thinking on the topic, which taught that fears simply reflect learned anticipation of harmful events, it now appears that the potential for fear is a genetically ingrained function of the nervous system. Even though learning is essential to the effective utilization of these ingrained fear systems in the real world, learning does not create fear by pasting together a variety of external experiences. The emotional experience of fear appears to arise from a conjunction of primitive neural processes that prompt animals to hide (freeze) if danger is distant or inescapable, or to flee when danger is close but can be avoided:

> Where in the brain is the area of the fear response? . . . [It is] in the lateral and central zone of the amygdala, the anterior and medial hypothalamus. . . . This highly interconnected network interacts with many other emotional systems . . . especially RAGE circuits (which contribute to the balance between fight and flight reactions). . . .
>
> It makes good evolutionary sense for FEAR and RAGE circuits to be intimately related, for one of the functions of rage is to provoke fear in competitors, and one of the functions of fear is to reduce the impact of angry behaviours from threatening opponents. . . .
> [Panksepp, 1998, pp. 206–207]

As a consequence of this evolutionary topography of the brain, a baby is born with an innate fear of being alone. The human baby is dependent and helpless for a long period, as maturation of the brain and development of independent, capable behaviour takes even longer than in most other animals. The extended closeness with the mother during this early experience leads to the development of a complexity of feelings—primarily of being loved, cared for, protected, stimulated in his senses, emotions, cognition, sexuality, played with and understood—which is called upon, in memory, by the baby when it is left alone. Feelings also develop in the child, though, not only of love and security, but of possessiveness, jealousy, anxiety, desire, making the baby want more of the caring beloved mother and initially resent the father's special relationship with the mother and giving rise to hate and anger, grudges, and vindictiveness towards the father and others close to the mother. The degree of coherence in the protection provided by the mother and father determines how these conflicting feelings are assimilated. So the baby is emotionally related to the caregivers, and the quality of this relationship—the way of life experienced by the baby—will enhance or damage this assimilation of feelings related to these emotions.

Psychoanalytic theory refers to this triangular dynamic as the Oedipus complex and considers it to be the central conflict of impulses, phantasies, and defences in the human psyche. Relationships with the two parents promote the growth of emotions and feelings early on, helping the process of consciousness through containment, shared experience, understanding, and verbalization. In Antonio Damasio's sense (2000, p. 37), it is through feelings that become conscious that emotions, which are body reactions to experience, have an impact on the mind.

Within the family, two aspects of the Oedipus complex are at work simultaneously: while babies are involved in their oedipal reactions, the parents may be having difficulties resolving oedipal, triangular conflicts from their own childhoods. This dynamic interplay is crucial in the development of either a satisfactory bonding or disturbances between members of the triangle.

Whether the caregivers must necessarily be of a different sex, I am not sure, but respect for the idea that the male is the provider of the other half for reproduction is important, almost as if the myth of hermaphrodite conception or immaculate conception are ideas that do not allow space for relationships being lived differently, from different angles. For survival purposes, the relying on more caregivers than just the mother or the feeling of security that the mother is helped or supported by "a village" of friends or family is important. Jealousy is an important dynamic in the relationship. In the light of current controversies about single-parent families and about homosexual couples adopting babies, it is hard to know how to accommodate these findings, but my observation is that there is an embedded pattern of two parents that is innate in the infant and necessary for its psychological and physical security.

As the foetus develops it becomes increasingly capable, and from the fifth month its sensory and motor capacities are evident. Parents are usually aware of their baby's emerging individuality while it is in the womb. They talk of what their foetus seems to prefer in the way of music, its manoeuvres in the amniotic fluid, what food it likes the mother to eat, and its response to her emotional states. From the baby's perspective, birth is a passage that transfers to the outside world a life with two primary humans, the father always having been present to the foetal child either in reality or symbolically. The father's actual or symbolic presence is important: it is my view that, without it, pathology develops.

The eternal triangle

The classic, healthy primary relationship is baby–mother–father (see Figure 2.1). Role substitutes can safely take the place of the biological mother or father—for example, it may be that the father role is assumed by the mother's current partner (Figure 2.1); also, even if the baby's father is not present, the mother may well hold his presence in her mind (see Figure 2.2). However, difficulties arise if a mother refuses to believe that the baby's father is important to her relationship with her child, acting as though the baby is solely her own creation (see Figure 2.3) or, at best, a part of the baby's father which she could never tie down (see Figure 2.4).

Another scenario might be that both the mother and the father have fragile or weak ego structures and hence have difficulty in accepting the individuality of the child (see Figure 2.5). Alternatively, as a result of infantile conflicts or trauma, they may relate to what Lebovici (1988) calls a phantasmatic child (see Figure 2.6). (Lebovici's concept of a phantasmatic child is discussed later in this chapter.)

The importance of the father's role in the triangle was highlighted for me during consultation with a mother over breastfeeding difficulties with her 10-day-old baby. She told me that, from birth, each time their baby girl heard her father play the piano, even if his playing was on the radio, she would stop crying. The father had practised regularly

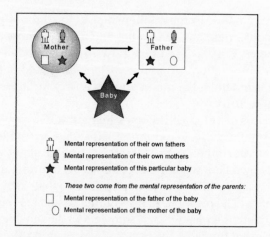

FIGURE 2.1.   The classic version of the eternal triangle—the basic model of relationships [mother–father–baby].

during the pregnancy, and the infant was able to recognize him both inside and outside the womb.

Psychoanalytic thinking about the Oedipus complex

According to Melanie Klein (1945), sexual and emotional development starts from birth. The child has a primitive ego capable of having needs and fantasies. The child's libido is intimately fused with aggressive-

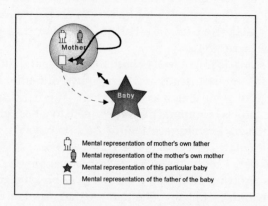

FIGURE 2.2.   Another variation of the (healthy) classic version, with father absent [mother–(no father)–baby].

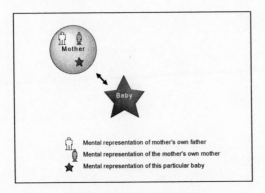

FIGURE 2.3.   Mother thinks baby is her own creation
[mother–(no father)–baby].

ness, and, therefore, children feel anxiety because the force of aggressiveness may destroy the source of gratification of their needs.

Klein further states that both the breast and the penis are primary
objects of attachment, giving the infant a sense of belonging to two
different parents. As the baby matures, the parents become clearly
differentiated. According to Klein, this occurs at around 6 months of
age when the baby is able to understand experiences with each parent
as resulting from a relationship with each one as an individual.

These relationships will have both negative and positive aspects
that are specific and predictable. The fear of loss of the child's loved
objects (the parents) as a consequence of aggression causes the child

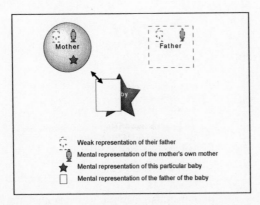

FIGURE 2.4.   Mother thinks baby is part of the father [mother–(father)–baby].

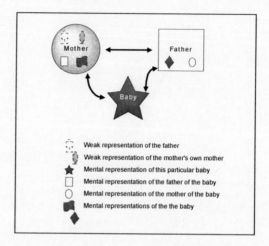

FIGURE 2.5.   Fragile parents have wrong representation of their baby
[mother–father–baby].

to desire reparation, to restore goodness to the phantasized injured object. Klein (1945) notes: "In dwelling on the infant's fundamental relation to the mother's breast and the father's penis, and on the ensuing anxiety and defences, I have in mind more than the relation to part objects. In fact, these part objects are from the beginning associated in the infant's mind with his mother and father". This awareness of the

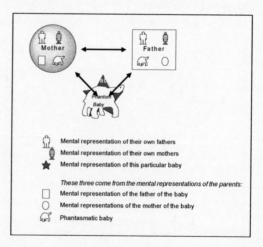

FIGURE 2.6.   The parents' phantasmatic baby [mother–father–(baby)]

different natures of mother and father generally coincides with the start of weaning. At this stage, babies suddenly realize that they are separate from their mothers. They also realize that their mother and father have a sexual relationship from which they are excluded, and this forms the basis of the oedipal conflict.

More recent research further defines the primal triangle relationships. Ronald Britton (1989) concludes that babies are linked to parents in two different ways: to the parents individually, and to the parents as a unit with their own relationship. If the parents' relationship can be tolerated, a child gains a third position where object relationships can be observed. This third position allows a baby space for reflection. Britton states, "*It creates what I call a 'triangular space'* . . . it includes, therefore, the possibility of being a participant in a relationship and observed by a third person, as well as being an observer of a relationship between them" (p. 86). Britton adds further that "the initial recognition of the parental sexual relationship involves [the baby] relinquishing the idea of sole and permanent possession of the mother, and leads to a profound sense of loss which, if not tolerated, may become a sense of persecution" (p. 84).

It is debatable whether Britton's sense of loss and persecution is the whole story of early emotional development, or whether infant reactions of this kind are a result of pathological development. Let me put forward another line of reasoning: *the child's attitude to a relationship is coloured by the child's specific phantasies, which, in turn, originate from that child's individual responses to and tolerance of frustration.*

According to Wilfred Bion (1959), the mother's function is to translate her child's needs and intolerable feelings into tolerable ones. That may be true. But what function does the father play in Bion's model? Why is it that a child's success in integrating experiences is so weighted towards the relationship with the mother and that experience with her becomes the basis of all other relations, including the relationship with the father?

W. R. D. Fairbairn (1952), in his work on child development, ventured a theory: he writes that repression appears before the Oedipus complex emerges and that overly dependent children direct it towards their mothers because the mother is the only significant object in their lives. When oedipal relations become established, children's relations with their fathers must be adjusted, because up until then, whether the infant–father relationship is accepting or rejecting, fathers are experienced as mothers without breasts. Hence pre-oedipal relationships are experienced only on an emotional plane. At a later stage, children come to appreciate the physical differences between parents, to acknowledge their parents' special relationship, and to realize that they are excluded from it.

This idea that babies perceive fathers as mothers without breasts puts the babies' relationship conflict with their parents into an entirely different perspective, according to Fairbairn:

> Fathers create emotional relationships with their children before the babies realise genital differences and that they are excluded from their parents' sexual relationship. This conflict occurs in the development of fantasies and feelings that result from the baby's perception of the father's penis as equivalent to the mother's breasts.

Thomas Ogden (1987) described a transitional oedipal relationship. He writes that female babies develop transitional oedipal relationships with their fathers that are similar to early relationships with the transitional object described by D. W. Winnicott (1951). In Ogden's view, the girl child experiences the mother in this transitional relationship as both male and female. The mother, having an unconscious identification with her own father, seems to allow the girl to discover her father untraumatically as an external object encountered in the safety of the dyadic relationship of the parents.

This concept of fused gender identity suggests the fundamental bisexuality of human beings implied by Freud. We can imagine that a woman and a man will reproduce in their relationship internal dialectical negotiations with their own oedipal figures, reactivated by the wish and reality of having a child. Again, we have a triangle.

In my view, the "eternal triangle" is the best place to start thinking about the basic premises on which we build our lives and relationships. From the moment of conception onwards, we encounter frustrations in getting what we need. Relationships are the first psychic structure—and therefore one of the most primitive—that is activated to get what we need. It is precisely because we actually use the eternal triangle to satisfy ourselves that I see it as a psychic structure that is a given in the same way that Klein sees the unconscious phantasy of the instinctual drive as a given, or innate process.

This understanding of the eternal triangle as the best place to start is true generally, not just for psychotherapists and psychoanalysts, who understand how unconscious and habitual modes of behaviour, expectations, wishes, and fears arise from infancy and childhood experiences, but also for others in related professions, for parents, or for any person who seeks an understanding of self to help others.

Phantasmatic child and imaginary child

Lebovici (1988) distinguishes between what he calls the phantasmatic child and the imaginary child: the phantasmatic child is the unconscious construction that parents make of the child, derived primarily from the oedipal conflict; the imaginary child is the conscious construction that parents make out of characteristics that they perceive or wish for (or from) the child. The phantasmatic child and the imaginary child are different from an actual child.

A *phantasmatic child* is the unconscious construction parents build up in their minds. But the phantasmatic child is not based on their child's actual behaviour. Instead, this unreal child is a product of the parents' conflicts with their own parents. Because thoughts of this phantasmatic child may influence the way in which their baby will eventually bond to them, it is important to identify this process, as it may well be the cause of difficulties.

The creation of the phantasmatic child in the mind of the parents could come from the unconscious construction of unresolved aspects of the Oedipus complex. For example, a parent may hold the wish to be an only child, or to possess the mother. On the other hand, the phantasmatic child could be constructed in response to a traumatic event that occurred before or during the pregnancy or as the result of a death or an accident that happened to a close relative. The phantasmatic child is not known to the parents and can usually only be reached and identified by a skilled psychoanalytic psychotherapist.

Many parents cover their baby with their own expectations, creating an *imaginary child*. For example, parents may imagine that their child is a gifted musician because they would dearly like him to grow up to be a concert pianist. These are conscious thoughts and, depending on how far from reality these thoughts really are, they are quite normal. It is when the poor child does not manage to live up to expectations that problems may arise. However, the fact that parents can recognize these inner desires makes them less likely to interfere with the child's actual development.

The negative thoughts provoked by the imaginary child may jeopardize the actual baby's normal development. For example, a mother might think that her baby loves strawberries because her own mother, who had died while she was pregnant, had a preference for strawberries. This idea is projected onto the new baby and interferes with the mother's interpretation of what foods her baby really enjoys. The therapist, however, through detailed observation of reactions and emotions, can identify such a problem and address it.

Current observations

My own experience in parent–child consultations leads me to suggest that, from the very beginning, the mother's mind offers a triangular space in which the child develops. Not until the mother's own oedipal conflict has been satisfactorily resolved by holding her own mother and father as a couple in her mind can she allow a space for the child's father to exist, whether he is actually with her or not. This suggests that the boy or girl child comes to know the father through the quality of the parents' relationship, perceived within the third dimension of the mother's mind. If she is able to create such a mental dimension for her child, she will be able to fulfil the function of mothering.

Donald Winnicott (1958b) has beautifully described the mother's "reverie" as a state in which she appears absent from the world around her, perhaps even mentally unwell. Her reverie emerges from intense thinking about her baby during pregnancy, and it helps her to identify with her baby's needs after birth. I have observed a father's reverie as well, a similar state of seeming mental unwellness in which he is absorbed in wondering about the growing child inside the mother. Who would expect such distracted paternal behaviour? In today's culture, fathers are seen only as providing material and emotional support to the pregnant mother.

Sebastian Kraemer (personal communication 1994) says:

> It is now clear that many of the qualities that were traditionally regarded as belonging exclusively to one sex or the other can be shared, but in a way that varies from couple to couple and from time to time even in the same pair. The father's participation not only liberates the mother, important though that is, it also has a direct effect on his perception of himself as a real man, not a mere performer, and on the infant's experience of being looked after, wanted, and loved by both parents.

Perhaps this father/motherhood role-sharing will open new ways for children to develop and resolve their Oedipus complex. A more equal paternal/maternal reverie may also help each parent to resolve oedipal conflicts from their own childhood. New role-sharing relationships allow for renegotiations with the parents' own mental representations (internal objects). As both parents become active carers, infants develop the capacity to handle feelings of attachment to and separation from each parent, to tolerate the parents' relationship, and to identify with the parent of the same sex.

Another mental process seems to hold promise. If the mother allows a space in her mind and her heart for an inner stage on which she can rehearse her relations with her internal parents and think about these scenes in relation to her child, many difficulties can be avoided or will simply vanish. The imagined dialogue between the internal mother and the baby's actual mother can either help and support or serve to criticize the mother's actions. The actual mother will develop her own style of mothering, guided by the demands and needs of her baby. Her own mothering style will be defined by her staging and resolving of conflicts with her own internal mother and father. When the actual mother admires her baby daughter, this may be the result of identification with her internal father and therefore may allow the real father in the baby–mother–father triangle a separateness from her own internal objects. When the actual mother admires her son, she identifies herself with her own internal parents and learns to free herself from them in the relationship with the baby and the father.

These intergenerational dialogues with internal parents can be reactivated in relation to the grandparents—and perhaps even the great-grandparents—when each child is born into the family. We may hope that there is a renegotiation of values in these relationships that spiral upwards and downwards in the oedipal situation as it is experienced through the generations. In diagnostic terms, it is in the relation to the dialectic with the father and with other members of the family that we may foresee an outcome that avoids severe pathology in the child or in the parents.

Case studies

CASE 1: SHONA—MOTHER DREAMT OF PREGNANCY

Shona wanted to have a baby but had not conceived. She was 23 years old and lived with her boyfriend in a stable relationship. Shona's mother was visiting her from another town, during which time the mother kept waking with clear dreams about her daughter walking hand in hand with a 2-year-old girl and the child's father. These dreams continued for five days, but when the mother told Shona about them she was rebuked and told that none of this was possible because Shona had just had her period. The mother continued to be preoccupied, and kept on warning Shona about the difficulties involved in having a child so young, all the time compulsively discussing contraception methods. Shona kept telling her mother that dreams were about oneself, not about others, and suggested that perhaps the mother had difficulty in accepting Shona as a grown woman and wanted to keep her as a baby.

A month later Shona missed a period, and her pregnancy was confirmed by a positive pregnancy test. The mother could not bear the idea of the daughter being pregnant and tried to make her abort, with all sorts of threats and reasoning, until Shona stopped talking to her. Shona started feeling the subsequent morning sickness as persecutory. The pregnancy became a nightmare of physical symptoms, and eventually Shona wanted a late abortion. This did not happen, and the baby was finally born after a long and painful delivery. Nurses in the maternity ward noted the lack of interest and bonding between mother and baby, and I was called.

In our first interview, Shona seemed to be inattentive to her baby's signals. When I asked about her mother, she started sobbing and said she had to end their relationship, given her mother's strong opposition to the pregnancy and her own unmarried state. After talking for some time, it became clear that Shona had been trying very hard to separate and be different from her mother. She was an only child and had always wanted to have siblings. It was not clear whether the baby that Shona initially thought about having was a wanted sibling or arose from a genuine wish to have her own child in a mature way and develop having her own family.

The conflict between Shona and her mother had interfered with the pregnancy and her ability to relate to her baby. The father of the baby had now married Shona, and he was very concerned. Her preoccupation with her mother's negative reaction had numbed her emotionally, and she had not been able to think. I suggested that I have joint meetings with Shona and her mother.

They accepted, and we had three sessions, during which I learned that the mother herself was 23 years old and married when she had

Shona, and she was suddenly left by her husband and ended up in *her* mother's house with her baby. She couldn't love Shona because of the overwhelming rage and anger she felt with the father. She felt humiliated within the family because of her poverty, her anxiety, and her depression and because she was dependent on her parents while living in their house which she had to share with other siblings, one of whom was severely disturbed.

As a baby, Shona was cheerful and grew up pleasing and entertaining others, always submitting without protest. After a year of dating, she moved in with her boyfriend at the age of 18.

Therapist's observations.   In this case, it was the dynamics of the family that had to be expressed and understood. This case is closest to an example of a mother who thinks the baby is her own creation (Figure 2.3). The father was made redundant emotionally and so was unable to help in any way to alleviate the tension and conflict between the two women. In therapy, his role had to be discussed with the mother and Shona, and then between Shona and her husband, resulting in a new experience for the four of them.

I have started with this example because it illustrates the dynamics of pregnancy and the immediate hormonal and family changes that occur. The intergenerational dynamic, with its conflict and shock, made the pregnancy a traumatic process rather than a joyful one. (Had the prenatal professionals been sufficiently sensitive, they could probably have picked up the emotions in the mother as a result of the common symptoms of pregnancy becoming aggravated and the tension that subsequently builds.)

Of primary importance here are the family dynamics and how they influenced the pregnancy and outcome in both a positive and a negative way. The charged atmosphere surrounding Shona and her mother spilled over and affected the relationship between the father and the baby. This case could easily have resulted in a continuing intergenerational transmission of pathology.

The treatment process was straightforward. The therapist gently unfolded the narratives and displayed them to the different actors in Shona's real-life drama. Because in this case an unresolved past was destructive, the therapist helped each member to close their respective narrative in the most appropriate way. Their lives could now open up to new experiences and possibilities, which helped each member renegotiate their relationship to their internal objects. Finally, by helping them bring their unconscious narratives into consciousness, the therapist integrated each member's experiences into a healthier scenario, removing unconscious defensive barriers and promoting true attachment.

CASE 2: MR E. — A FATHER'S REVERIE

Mr E. asked for a consultation because his girlfriend was pregnant and was proceeding with the pregnancy. He did not agree with her decision, but had accepted the fact that he was going to be a father for life.

I saw this father-to-be for weekly sessions over ten months. He showed a great deal of insight into the process of foetal growth. He himself had been born after his mother had lost two babies to cot death. His reverie included fantasies from his past and fears and wishes about what might happen to the baby he had fathered.

Mr E.'s own parents had given him up for adoption to a homosexual surgeon who had promised financial assistance to the family. Subsequently, Mr E's parents had several children. His concerns centred around his fear of conflict between the future child and the mother and of being stuck with the care of the baby. He continually expressed concern about gender identity. He had a real desire to become a thoughtful, supportive father to the child and partner to the mother. They were married three months after the baby was born.

After the birth, Mr E. experienced difficulties because he felt excluded from the lovely, suckling relationship between the mother and baby. He felt left out as the father, and later on he felt excluded from the rest of the mother's family. He expressed his desire to contact his own biological family, which he did, and this gave him the opportunity to talk over his feelings with his biological parents. Mr E. had a deep need to feel included as part of a family.

Therapist's observations.   In this case, unsettling problems of fatherhood had their origin in Mr E.'s traumatic, unresolved past. By allowing his reverie to guide him in exploring these issues, Mr E. came to a resolution.

Many layers of this case could be peeled back for examination. One of the interesting lines to follow is the transmission of thinking in pregnancy. Were Mr E.'s mother and father troubled and discussing the future of Mr E. while Mr E. was in the womb? Mr E. was raised by two homosexual men. Even though he never questioned his gender, he must have queried unconsciously his upbringing—by two men, rather than by a man and a woman—and how best to bring up his child.

Mr E.'s unconscious seemed linked to his need to revisit his own childhood development and seek understanding. While we can only speculate on the perfectly natural reasons his girlfriend wanted to have the baby, it is possible that she inwardly trusted his capacity to review his conflicts and be a good father and companion. If this were the case, the basic model of relationships would apply (Figure 2.1), although it would then be important for Mr E. to renegotiate his two sets of parental figures in his inner world, along with all the negative and positive feelings attached to them.

In most cases, however, "paternal reverie" is not brought about by problematic or pathological upbringing. I hear it constantly in the comments of husbands whose wives are expecting a baby. Paternal reverie creates in the father an internal floating attention to both the mother and the baby, revisiting the past and imagining and planning the future.

Helping fathers to develop this state of paternal reverie, with its internal floating attention to a developing family, can help generate a flexible and sensitive approach towards building "new family" relationships.

CASE 3: RONA — FATHER AS MAIN CARER

Rona, 15 months old, was having sleeping difficulties. She would wake five to ten times a night. Her father was the full-time carer. Although at weekends the parents shared responsibility for comforting her, during the week the father was in charge, and he was exhausted.

Both parents came to the first and last interview. The four sessions in between were held with the father and the baby, with the father bringing the mother's comments as a result of discussions between them at home. In the first interview, the parents described the pregnancy and birth, the first three months of Rona's life, and the mother's difficulty in separating from her child on her return to work in the fourth month.

Therapist's observations. The father had a gentle nature. When he was employed, his work was in the caring professions. He now felt he had no personal space, not even to read a newspaper, given the demands the baby imposed on him. Rona slept through all six sessions on her father's chest, held in his arms.

The father was the sixth and the last in a family in which there had been no personal attention from the parents. As a result, he had promised himself that he would be personally involved with his own children. I commented that perhaps he went to extremes. He agreed, and he asked me if I could help him find the right balance.

The mother felt guilty about not being able to come to the meetings, but she was concerned about losing her job. However, she suggested that the father might benefit from having time just to himself.

Rona's father discussed with me his fear of not being a good father. He had to explore his feelings about his own mother and father in order to become flexible and aware of his daughter's needs as separate from his own needs as a child. His anger and resentment about his parents' ways of treating him, linked as it was with intense jealousy of his siblings, was jeopardizing his parenting of Rona. He was responding to his mental representation of a deprived infant rather than to her actual needs.

We explored the meaning of cries and tantrums and ways of separating during the day and setting appropriate limits. When the right routine for Rona was finally established, there were no further problems.

In Rona's case, the relationship of mother–father–child was appropriately triangular and accepting of each other's needs. However, the father was unable to set limits and allow the baby to grow because of the high level of his internal competition with his own mother. The phantasmatic child of the father was the one that he would like to have been, a child receiving the care he wanted, in an idealized way, from his parents, as if that would have made him happy. We talked about his view of the ideal and compared it with the possible and best. We had first to liberate him from reacting to his internal objects before he could establish appropriate care for Rona.

This was an example of "*father* thinks baby is *his* own creation" (a variation of Figure 2.3). In Rona's case, the father behaved as if *he* were the child, enacting what he felt he had not received from his own parents. In a way, it seemed that the position of primary carer suited him well. In fact, it could be said that this was unconsciously planned. He chose a wife who would accept his being in charge and understand that he longed to re-live an experience of having his own father close to him. Thus the child-care arrangement suited both parents.

CASE 4: NICHOLAS—SLEEPING WITH MOTHER

Nicholas was 11 months old. He was sleeping with his mother because he would cry all night if he was not sucking on her breast. He had not yet separated from his mother or started crawling, and they were referred to me by her GP. In our first interview, the mother held Nicholas very close to her and continually patted him, although he looked around the room as if wishing to be freed. He was carelessly dressed and without shoes.

After listening to the mother's concerns, I inquired about the father. She told me she had had an eight-year relationship with him, but that he was now working abroad and was unreliable and she never knew when he was going to be around. They had once had a very passionate love life; however, this had turned into a painful experience because when she discovered, to her delight, that she was accidentally pregnant the father stopped seeing her completely and had seen the child only once.

I asked this mother if perhaps the child was fulfilling the father's role, always staying in bed with her and sucking her breast as he pleased. At this, the mother began to cry. She said that she liked the idea of having part of the father—the spermatozoid that had given her the baby—and that indeed she might be using the baby as a surrogate for the father. She became annoyed with me because I had put her in contact again with her pain.

The baby gently moved out of her arms, tried to crawl, and then came back to look at his mother. I mentioned his need to move away from her with her blessing. The mother then explained that she was one of five girls and that her mother had been very possessive of them. Her father had been in the navy, travelling for long periods. Over three sessions, we talked about her feelings about her mother and father and her longing for them. In her mind, her father seemed like a ghost, with nothing substantial that she could relate to.

These negative aspects of her father were important in her choice of a man for herself. It seemed she was exploring her own father/ mother relationships in her relationship with the baby's father and was internally punishing her own mother for the fantasy that her mother was continually sending her father away. She was trying to show her mother that she could eventually hold on to a man. She was compulsively overcome with joy at having a boy—of having, at last, a penis around all the time.

Therapist's observations.   This was a case of a mother who treats and thinks of the baby as a part of the father (Figure 2.4). The mother reacted to an imaginary child representing an idyllic situation of eternal companionship between mother, father, and baby. The mother's phantasmatic child had the significance of omnipotent control of her absent partner and of her own father's absences in childhood. This perspective blocked her view of the baby. She could not see the individuality of her child, and, as a result, the development of both mother and baby was being stunted.

During the infant–parent therapy, we revisited these issues together, and the mother was able to enter into an inner exploration of her ideas and feelings during the sessions.

The baby was brought to subsequent sessions wearing shoes and appropriate clothes. He calmly played by himself with the toys, as if allowing his mother to work on their separation and issues related to her past that were relevant to the difficulty in separating and individuation.

In the fourth session, the mother realized she had personal problems that needed further investigation in relation to her choice of love object, and she began individual therapy.

The overall difficulty in this case was the mother's inability to separate from her baby. This problem is difficult to identify during pregnancy unless questions are asked about the father, his presence, or (as in this case) his absence. The therapist must keep in mind the quality of the mother's parental relationships. In recounting these to the therapist, the mother is enabled to release the hold she has on her baby as her childhood emotions release their hold on her.

CASE 5: DANNY—A GRANDMOTHER'S CONCERN

Mrs S contacted me because she was very concerned about her 15-month-old grandson, Danny, who was hitting and biting everyone and then looking vague and withdrawn.

We agreed that she would come and talk about the child, but that if a consultation with Danny were required, the parents would have to ask for it. Both parents did decide to come with Danny, who behaved just as his grandmother had described. The parents were overprotective and concerned. Yet they seemed distant, and the mother appeared to be very controlling. It was difficult to discuss their concerns in any depth because they both avoided introspection.

In the second interview, the mother became very irritated, expressing great competitiveness and hatred for her own parents. In the third interview, the complaints and annoyance continued. It was impossible to establish any insightful relationship between the mother and her child, and Danny's hitting, biting, and withdrawn states became alarming.

I set up meetings between the mother and the grandmother. They started shouting at each other about which of them knew better how to deal with Danny's situation. The grandmother was desperate about her daughter's suffocating love for her son.

The story began to unravel. The grandfather had left the grandmother when Danny's mother was only 18 months old. The grandmother cursed him and devoted herself to raising her daughter alone. The word "father" was forbidden, as was any expression of feeling about him later on.

Danny's mother needed to scream at the grandmother for this, and in the shouting match it became clear that the grandmother held a profound hatred and pernicious jealousy of her daughter because her daughter had succeeded in carrying on a relationship with Danny's father for fifteen years.

Therapist's observations.   My role as therapist was one of facilitating the dialogue—or, rather, the fight—between the two women. My purpose was to reconnect the lost links between past and present. It came out in the family sessions that Danny's parents had married in secret, and other secrets were exposed as well. The mother's fear, aroused by her family's myth of the abandoning husband and father, caused her to act accordingly. Danny's father felt redundant and excluded; all decisions about the child were made unilaterally by the mother. The mother was horrified to see her own mother in herself, and she talked as if she were "possessed" by her and acting out an intergenerational conflict of revenge.

It was now clearer that Danny was biting and scratching at eyes that were too close to him, eyes that were not really seeing him, eyes that were blinded by ghosts from the women's pasts. In both generations, the mother regarded the baby as her own creation (Figure 2.3) while the father figure was absent and not to be thought about.

After revisiting her past experience and verbalizing her feelings, the grandmother was able to renegotiate her role in the family. She could link her new insights to an understanding of her past and accept her frustrated marriage as merely a very bad stage in her life. In time, she found a new love relationship.

I wondered whether the grandmother's preoccupation and re-accommodation in her new role constituted a kind of reverie as well: a state of inner preoccupation and concern about the grandchild coming and her experience of her own child becoming a parent.

CASE 6: ANA—WITHDRAWS INTO A CORNER

Ana was 3 years old when she was referred to me from her nursery. They told me she was withdrawing into a corner, rocking, sucking her thumb, and not wanting to talk to anyone.

Both parents were extremely shy self-employed professionals, working from home. They didn't think there was a problem with Ana at school, and at home they considered her behaviour quite normal. Ana had two older siblings who were in a special school because they were autistic. I later learned that the parents themselves had been diagnosed as autistic in childhood and had also received special schooling. Apparently, the parents were not surprised by Ana's behaviour, because to the parents Ana was just like them.

In a family meeting, I suggested to the parents that Ana had managed very well to get the attention of the nursery staff as well as mine, indicating that there was a part of her that would like to be different from her shy, withdrawn family. I asked whether the family wanted to help her to behave differently, and they agreed that they did.

Another therapist and I proposed family meetings to alternate with parents' meetings, and we had ten of these. This schedule allowed time for the parents to review their own personal histories, to try to understand their extreme shyness, and to help them to become more aware of the individualities of each child. For example, Ana needed to draw attention to herself in order to express the frustration and anger she felt at being denied normal social contact.

Since the parents were able to acknowledge that Ana had a problem, it made an open discussion about their own difficulties easier. However, they did not want to change themselves but were prepared to accept Ana's need for social contact, allowing her to have friends at home and letting her go to visit others. They allowed the nursery to make all the arrangements, and Ana's emotional development resumed a normal course. She became talkative and friendly towards her teachers and the other children.

Therapist's observations.   Ana had to fight to get help. Despite her young age of only 3 years, she had the strength to find a way of getting the attention of her parents, who were not responding to her needs.

This is another example of a phantasmatic child, except that this time the parents made Ana into a child after their own image. The situation was compounded because both parents were unusually shy and withdrawn. The case of Ana's family resembles the "fragile parents have wrong representation of their baby" scenario in the relationship model (Figure 2.5). Such parents might have an unconscious wish that their child should resolve for them the cause of their own problems. Or, conversely, they might try to hide their problem because they realize that it is their own damaged personalities that have damaged their child. They hide it under rationalization and by managing to marry someone similar, thus creating a "normal" world within the family that is not threatening to their fragile integration.

Ana was different and wanted to be sociable. At the nursery, she saw how other people related. Comparing it to the model she was receiving from her parents, her frustration emerged. The family *had* to accept that Ana was different. They *had* to integrate her into their environment so as not to leave her out by unconscious rejection. Without therapeutic intervention, Ana would almost certainly have had to go into care in order to develop normally.

There was a reason for setting up alternate meetings between the family and the parents alone. The parents needed space so that they could look at each child's individuality and to express any of their own frustration and rage safely and intimately. Ana, on the other hand, needed a family setup so that she could learn how to express herself verbally to them. They, in turn, needed to learn how to accommodate her needs, frustration, and capabilities. It was in the family meetings that her parents changed their "phantasmatic and imaginary" child into a real child.

The other two children continued without change because their parents were unable to see any need to change them. The parents reasoned that the children had accepted their withdrawn behaviour without frustration.

CASE 7: ARCHIE—AN IN-VITRO FERTILIZATION

Archie was referred to me at age 18 months for gaze avoidance, hyperactivity, little and patchy sleep, walking on tiptoe, and being interested only in boxes and hard objects and not at all in people.

Archie's father brought the mother and baby to the consultation. Much as he was concerned about the baby, he was even more concerned about and preoccupied with a drastic change in the mother's personality. After six miscarriages and twelve years of trying to conceive naturally, the parents had decided on an in-vitro fertilization. In treatment, the mother was unduly quiet and uninterested and seemed depressed. Although the father was a doctor who worked long hours, he was prepared to participate in the sessions because he wanted his wife back.

Therapist's observations.   I felt that the mother was exhausted. She was deeply frightened about her relationship with the child and about his strange emotional development. She felt alone with her concerns and cut off from her husband.

Watching the baby, I observed that he was avoiding gaze and contact and preferred moving around incessantly by himself and rocking. I commented on this, and the mother agreed with me. She expressed her loneliness when she was with him and how impossible it was to "get through" to him. She had expected a child who would react like a human being; she felt she had got, instead, a machine and that her husband did not understand what she meant by such a comparison. Because she was unable to conceive naturally, she felt she was a bad mother. It had been such hard work, so many tests, and now it seemed that it had all gone wrong.

I asked her, "Exactly *what* has gone wrong?" and she answered by trying to pick up her baby, something he obviously did not like. In fact, the baby fought against most things that she tried to do with him.

When I asked her who would say that she was a bad mother, she replied, "My father and grandfather". As a child she had lived with her parents in her grandparents' house. The grandfather was very domineering, judging and punishing her all the time. He felt that boys were good and girls were not. Therefore she could never be good enough. She adored her father, but he never spent any time with her. He was either working or in the pub. Her mother was sad and bored, and Archie's mother grew up feeling inferior as a female, good for little except to bring children into the world. So if she could not do that, she reasoned, then she was not good for anything at all.

Archie's mother's past was negating her capacity to be creative with this admittedly difficult child. I pointed out that now she had a man in her life who cared for her and was worried about her. The father was beginning to realize that the baby was difficult and that Archie's development was in jeopardy.

The reality that Archie's development was in jeopardy reinforced a negative self-esteem in the mother. I asked her if she would like to explore with me her child's likes and fears and help Archie connect with her, with his father, and with the world in general. She seemed reassured by the opportunity to reappraise her self-esteem and be trusted to develop her own creativity.

For ten sessions we explored together the child's likes and dislikes, and she continued this exploration at home. The father attended two of the sessions. In the last session she attended with her husband, the mother said that my positive statements had shaken her out of being stuck in the memory of her depressed mother trying to cope with her fate. My pointing out her husband's love and concern for her, and that he could help her fight the world if necessary, had made her feel very attached to me. She felt that I had allowed her to be my child emotionally and that through these new mother–child feelings and experiences, I had helped her experience a model of mothering she could continue to use with her own frightened child.

With Archie's mother, we see how the internal model of her own mother left her static and paralysed. She was persecuted by her internalized parental figures and frightened of having an exploratory relationship with her "strange" son. Her internal father reassured her at one level that she could have a child but undermined her capacity to produce a child naturally. It was as if she could not relate properly to her parents, and Archie, as an uncommunicative child, had reactivated her negative experiences with them.

The mother may also have been ambivalent about having a child. Repetitive miscarriages can produce a state of mind that often leads to the child born subsequently feeling too precious to be reprimanded or questioned about his goodness. Such ambivalence might have been shown in a fear of the repetition of the past that did not allow her body to react appropriately. She needed to identify with me, and with the father in me, in order to have a safe space in which to play, to feel good about herself, to feel welcomed and beautiful, to recognize difficulties in everyday life, and to explore the growth of her individuality.

The repeated miscarriages, *in-vitro* fertilization, and a fragile baby reactivated Archie's mother's traumatic past. She was convinced that it was her own damaged personality that had damaged their child. He was credited, being a boy, with a sense of rightness and goodness, forcing the mother to give up her acquired positive outlook.

Archie's father, or relatives, or friends could perhaps have resolved this situation had they been made aware, as here, of how parent–child interactions are often based on how our real children interact in the inner world with our past experiences and internal objects.

Archie's case is a variant of the parents' phantasmatic baby (Figure 2.6). The imaginary child built by the mother was almost not allowed to exist, given the strong fear and anxiety about her reproductive capacities and the difficulty in keeping a baby growing inside her. The father seemed to deny difficulties in his wife and maintained a positive outlook about Archie's growth and development, regardless of the reality of the baby's unrelated behaviour. The influence of Archie's mother's childhood experiences crept in and undermined her mothering capacities and ability to act. Instead of asking for help, she identified the baby with her father and grandfather (the phantasmatic baby) and herself with her depressed mother.

CASE 8: SASKIA—FEEDING DIFFICULTIES

Saskia was brought to a consultation at age 11 months with extreme feeding difficulties. She would only have milk and took very little in a disorderly way. She was a classic "failure to thrive" baby, and all the professionals involved were concerned.

Saskia was born prematurely. The parents thought that she suffered from post-traumatic feeding disorders because during her first three months she had been fed by tube in a premature baby unit.

She was born prematurely because of a wrong scan diagnosis: at an 8-month routine examination she was diagnosed as suffering from a condition in which the organs are outside the skin. Immediate surgery was organized, and within twenty-four hours a Caesarean section was performed, with paediatricians on standby.

To everyone's surprise the baby was born normal, although too small to be breathing by herself.

Therapist's observations.   My question shocked them! The parents had been telling me the story of Saskia's birth in an automatic, matter-of-fact way, but I made them slow down and remember carefully. What did they feel in the twenty-four hours before the Caesarean? It took them several attempts to put into words their fragmented and frightened feelings. In those twenty-four hours, they went from paradise to hell. At the end, birth of a normal baby brought relief, but they never regained paradise.

Their happy and calm pregnancy had suddenly been interrupted by the results of the scan diagnosis. Images of baby monsters with different deformities were nightmarish. Talking to me, they recounted their anguish and revulsion, with tortured expressions and voices full of distress and fear. To their horror, they came to see that the way they were looking at their normal baby girl was as though she were a realization of those hours of anguish. They had not been able to separate the shock they had experienced during the pregnancy from the reality of having a healthy baby, albeit one who was a bit small. The traumatic stress disorder was as much theirs as their daughter's!

Saskia's parents had been seen in the premature-baby unit by a child psychotherapist, but they had not looked at their feelings of shock and anger, nor had they realized that the baby's confused state could be connected with their own unresolved feelings. The hospital's original mistake—the wrong diagnosis—was totally denied, and everyone was busy helping the baby to thrive. But neither the parents nor the baby could come together in sorrow and set boundaries that could be caring and protective.

We arranged sessions to integrate the shock, relief, and sorrow into a programme where Saskia and her parents could acknowledge, handle, and finally accept the full range of emotions that their traumatic experience and the hospital staff had put them through. Individually, and as a family, they had to reconstruct their mental representations of each other to be able to devise a secure attachment and, eventually, a coherent routine at home.

This case is a variant of the parents' phantasmatic baby (Figure 2.6). A normal pregnancy was interrupted by a trauma. Even though Saskia was at home with two nice, mature, and thoughtful parents, the trauma had changed them. With monster babies mentally blocking a real view of Saskia, they could not find a way to relate to her. This serious disturbance, which had the effect of cutting off the parents from their child, could have had even more serious consequences.

Tube feeding, which Saskia had undergone, is a sort of continuation of foetal life in a different setting. Spitz (1951) describes in detail cases of neglect occurring due to lack of individual attention in a hospital setting—a syndrome that he called hospitalism—where attachment does not occur, limbo prevails for far too long, and babies do not form object relations or have representations of an ever-present mother or caregiver, becoming "hospital babies" and subsequently failing to thrive.

Because of the trauma, the normal mother–father–baby relationship did not exist. Saskia was left with no objects with whom she could develop enriching mental and physical relationships. Without these objects, she could not relate to her parents, and the parents were paralysed by disturbing mentalizations of unrealized monsters. This paralysis halted any further awareness of their real baby's needs and desires, making them so mentally inflexible that they could not meet the demands of normal new-family functioning.

CASE 9: INAM—INCESTUOUS PREGNANCY

Inam came to me at the age of 16 years and pregnant, referred by her health visitor. She was living at a hostel for adolescents with babies because she had been thrown out of her parents' home. Inam was drinking heavily. She did not want to come to our meetings and was brought after several missed appointments by an older man. He said he was a professional, a Muslim with three families, one in the Middle East and two in London.

Inam seemed annoyed at being recognized as an alcoholic. She also seemed to be hiding something. The man who brought her seemed concerned that her drinking would affect the baby. I asked him to leave so that I could speak to Inam alone, and she wove a story about the father of the baby disappearing when it was too late to have an abortion. Inam was angry that her Muslim friend had brought her to me by force, and we explored what this meant. She talked about sexual abuse in her childhood by her own father and other males in the family. We set up a number of sessions in which I talked to her alone.

After a couple of sessions, Inam telephoned me, disclosing that everything she had said to date was a lie. I explained to her how I saw her story and that I suspected that the man who had accompanied her was not only *her* father but also the *father of her child*. She accepted this without comment and came to the third session and confirmed my hypothesis. She was not only feeling bad about the abuse she had suffered, but terrified about the kind of baby she would have as a result of her alcoholism. She added that she did not know whether the father of the baby was her father or one of her brothers, who had also abused her. Inam also disclosed that she was illiterate, and this made her feel as if she were learning disabled.

The individual sessions that followed explored the pain and neglect she had experienced in childhood. With her permission, meetings were set up with Social Services and her health visitor to find appropriate help for her. She attended evening classes in English and went to live in another borough in a mother-and-baby home where she could get help and support. She then asked for individual psychotherapy, which she continued to work at successfully for several years.

Therapist's observations.   Inam was caught in a cul de sac. Only my guessing at the truth eventually led to a way out for her.

She was illiterate, in an alien culture and country, and totally dependent on an abusive father and siblings. She had had a neglected and abused childhood and no supportive models with whom to identify. With alcohol, she could drown her anxieties and desperation.

Inam became a good mother and had a good relationship with her son. There was no further contact with her father and no genetic difficulties with her child. From a clinical standpoint, she was stuck in a complete mess of maternal and paternal identifications, and her own identity was blurred by abuse, neglect, and lies within the family. In a case like this one, it is important to take cultural background into account. Her fear of losing her father and brothers for good was painful as well as frightening. Yet her pregnancy brought her new hope, and, through it, she was able to move away from her old life and into a new one. She needed a lot of professional help throughout this process, during which she was terrified of losing her baby to Social Services.

Inam's case is a variant of one where parental figures are so blurred that it is difficult to identify them (Figure 2.5). The case took up a great deal of professional time and thought. It is an extreme example of a baby at risk. Only as a result of the therapist guessing at the truth was it possible for this vicious circle of incest and abuse to end.

Conclusions

I have found in my clinical experience with pregnant women, mothers, fathers, and babies and in my work with disturbed children that answers to important "first questions" will best determine next steps. These answers frame the context of central relationships and outline the broad features of the dynamic underpinnings of the central characters in the case. It is important always to ask about:

1. family relationships;
2. past experiences of pregnancies;
3. ideas about pregnancy;
4. the process of becoming a parent;
5. the family reactions to pregnancy, since these become imprinted patterns of authority or the elders' reactions to their own wish to procreate;
6. the actual circumstances in which the baby is developing.

The role of the mother and father in the mother's bonding and the emotional development of the child are intimately related to the internal interrelation of the mother and father figure in each parent. In other words, an internal triangle is present and constitutes a working model for each parent (Figures 2.1–2.6). How the mother uses her own resources and those of her partner to discover and enhance the personality of their child may be a matter of chance for some, a struggle for others, or a matter of close observation and constant exploration for happier parents.

Parents often have expectations that are unrealistic or simply unacceptable to their child. To persist in such expectations can jeopardize the child's natural development of its identity and self-esteem.

Mothers or fathers left on their own to bring up a child or children still need the support of a partner. It is possible for this support to come from the internal presence of a partner through the resolution of the parent's own Oedipus complex. If such an internal partnership is not possible, a support network of friends or relatives is necessary to assist the parent and to act as the reflective, or "digestive", apparatus for undigested feelings in the parent and baby.

When pathology or disturbance occurs in the child or in one of the parents, usually the mother, the reliability of the other parent or support network is needed to carry out a consistent routine for the child, regardless of disagreements, divorce, or other crises. Where there is evidence of early problems in the mother–infant relationship, the dyad or the threesome has lost the capacity for thinking as individuals and for digesting the primitive feelings that are activated or reactivated in day-to-day encounters with each other.

Pathology in early bonding often seems to be difficult between two persons when a third is not allowed into the relationship because of conflicts in the parents' past or because of a natural fragility in the baby which elicits the mother's total identification. If there have been conflicts between the parents in the past, help at an early stage is needed, otherwise inflexible intergenerational factors will re-emerge through the parents' dialogue with their own internal objects.

It seems to be extremely important that a parent's individual difficulties in integrating certain experiences be reviewed, explored, and renegotiated if pathological development is to be avoided.

Recommendations

Pregnancy often turns out to be an ideal time to set up a healthy change in the family. Medical check-ups should be accompanied by psychodynamic interviews with parents-to-be. As important as the containment of disease, or preparing for the baby's arrival, is a way for parents-to-be to contain and hold primitive experiences, anxieties, and fears and to help the powerful processes of nature, rather than leaving the healthy upbringing of the child to chance or luck.

Information leaflets talk endlessly about folic acid, proper check-ups, diet, the intake of calcium, and other physical preventative measures. However, it is rare to see guidelines that refer to the psychological state of pregnancy, conflicts within the family, new feelings aroused, explanations of why physical tests are necessary, the function of scans, or the delivery of bad news. More information is needed about how to get counselling in regard to both physical and mental disabilities, as well as about how to recognize and deal with normal symptoms or cope with the potential chances of genetic abnormalities. Misdiagnosis is not unknown in pregnancy, even with the most sophisticated technology.

It is well known that no money is allocated for preventative psychological medicine. However, there are ways of looking at this whole area that make sound economic sense. What is the cost, for example, of having a properly trained prenatal psychotherapist (such training is now available) as against the cost of treating the entire family at a later stage, plus the maintenance of special schools, hospital units for suicidal teenagers and drug users, psychiatric units, units for eating disorders, and so on? Most of these problems are not physical: they stem from a lack of experience in prospective parents, or from the inability of the parents to form a proper attachment to the child or to separate and mourn figures from their own past, or from imposing their expectations on their innocent child.

A hospital setting may not be the best place to start a family, but it might be the very place to provide an example of proper care, particularly for those families for whom previous neglect, abuse, trauma, or deprivation inevitably lead to an inability to trust the mind to prepare the family nest for the new arrival.

CHAPTER THREE

The psychodynamic approach, observation, and interaction time

In this volume, we consider babies who are mentally troubled, at risk, or suffering from physical disabilities, and through case histories we examine various conditions and ways of minimizing the attendant emotional complications. But first some basic concepts must be outlined. Though the language we use may be simplified, the method and aim are complex: to define a prevalent psychic dysfunction and personal structure and determine how this can be modified in subsequent development.

We start in this chapter with an overview of the research in developmental psychology. With this background, we are better able to think about "derailed" development, about responses and integration in development, and about the normal ways of adapting to the world. And, with psychoanalytic tools from psychoanalysis—transference, countertransference, a clear setting, and free-floating attention—we can form a picture of our patients' troubled internal worlds and think with them about aims in the consultation and what is the best therapy available for them to move forward emotionally. Accompanying this is another essential tool—the infant observation technique—through which we can learn to observe our patients in a passive, receptive, and attentive manner. Finally, interaction time—where the therapist deliberately engages with the child—may provide a means for discovering how communication processes within a family work and can be therapeutic in itself.

THE PSYCHODYNAMIC APPROACH

There is now general agreement on a theory of mind in which an infant—with the help of innate forces—integrates outside experiences.

Since Freud discovered the unconscious and the roots in infancy of later pathological development, a great deal of psychoanalytic understanding and theorizing has been made of the "reconstructed clinical infant" in adult and child psychoanalytic treatments. Research in infant psychology has confirmed and enriched these early working hypotheses and intuitive approaches, demonstrating that babies have rich and sophisticated mental and emotional capacities from birth.

Developmental psychology

Babies are born with the ability to suck, to turn their head, and to look. We have learned from the work of developmental psychologists that with these three capabilities, infants are shown to have:

1. a predilection for the mother (confirmed in experiments, by McFarlane, 1977, on recognizing the smell of mother's breast milk);
2. an individuality from birth (observed and described in the classification by Middlemore, 1941, of types of sucking and sucklings);
3. control in engaging and disengaging at a distance and organization of cycles and rhythms such as sleep–wake/alertness (Sanders, 1977; Sanders, Stechler, Burns, & Julia, 1970);
4. a thinking apparatus, with abstract capabilities, that:
   a. seeks stimulation when they feel bored, e.g. moving to another object of visual interest (Klaus & Kennell, 1976; Meltzoff & Moore, 1977)
   b. evaluates constantly and changes behaviour accordingly (Gewirtz, 1965, 1969; Lipsitt, 1966)
   c. seems pre-designed for cross-modal transfer of information that permits them to recognize a correspondence around different

senses (described by Meltzoff & Borton, 1979, in an experiment with 3-week-old infants who were given a dummy when blindfolded but could recognize the specific dummy, out of three different dummies, when the blindfold was taken off); babies take in information through one of the senses and encode it into a representation that can be recognized in any sensory mode; these abstract representations seem to show the more global qualities of experiences that provide infants with a perceptually unified world;

5. the capacity for connection between mother and child by mutual "tuning in" (Klaus & Kennell, 1976);

6. the ability to distinguish between acts, based on feelings, e.g. the soothing action of mother when baby cries (variety of affects and affect proclivities: Ekman, 1972; Izard, 1978; Tomkins, 1963);

7. an expression of emotions—already described by Darwin (1872) as innate patterns that would evolve as signals to be universally understood for the survival of the species (this has since been confirmed by experiments with blind babies by Fraiberg, 1971, and others: newborn and blind babies do show, until the age of 4 months, all the affective facial responses according to their affective state);

8. motives in their complex brains that lead them to learn through communicating about intentions, interests, and feelings with trusted companions, and to interpret with them a common reality.

The initial integrative capacities of the newborn are seen to be enriched by the increase in neurophysiological organization, which completes the picture of the process of assimilation, accommodation, identifying invariants, and associative learning—babies learning to assimilate what is pleasurable, to gradually wait for food, to differentiate known faces from unknown ones, to pull and move a mobile, and so forth (Brazelton, Koslowsky, Main, 1974; Emde, Gaensbauer, & Harmon, 1976; Stern, 1974a, 1974b).

Response and integration in development

It is well documented that infants are capable at birth (or shortly thereafter) of organizing in an adaptive fashion. They can respond to pleasure and displeasure (Lipsitt, 1966); change behaviour as a function of its consequence (Gewirtz, 1965, 1969); form intimate bonds and make visual discriminations (Klaus & Kennell, 1976; Meltzoff & Moore, 1977); organize cycles and rhythms such as sleep–wake/alertness states (Sanders et al., 1970); and evidence a variety of affects or affect proclivities (Izard, 1978; Tomkins, 1963).

The newborn experiences at birth the loss of the intrauterine life with:

1. a sudden and dramatic difference in the stimulation of all senses;
2. the experience of hunger: new internal sensations in the stomach, of pain, when empty, colic, etc.;
3. the need to express wishes, to communicate;
4. the need to wait, thereby developing a sense of time;
5. the need to adapt to the environment;
6. the need to exercise abstract capacities of the mind;
7. the experience of fear of the unknown.

Thus the primitive ego of the infant perceives, thinks, and feels according to innate predilections and experience. We do not know directly the form of these capacities; they can only be inferred from the feelings transmitted by the baby to the mother (or to the interviewer). This transmission occurs through the mother's emotional reactions and awareness, in principle, and is then thought about, understood, and "returned" in complementary actions or verbalizations to the infant.

Therefore, the way the baby responds to internal and external experiences will depend *not only* on the sensitivity of the mother and the adequacy of the environment, but on the basic endowment of the baby. That is, it will depend on:

1. the interplay of the baby's loving and aggressive tendencies, e.g. in food intake, its basis attitude can be observed, ranging from absence of greed to great avidity;
2. the baby's natural personal strength, which depends on its innate tolerance of frustration and plays an important part in:
    a. its positive integration of experiences, e.g. again in food intake, greed or inhibitions can show an imbalance in the capacity to wait, with pain reinforcing discomfort and increasing anxiety (conversely, early habits of playing, and developing a relaxed, pleasant feeling while sucking, show that such pleasant feelings

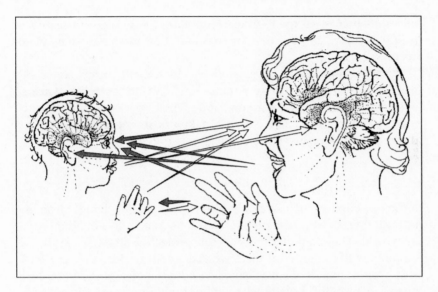

FIGURE 3.1.   The many interactions between mother and baby (drawing
courtesy of Colwyn Trevarthen).

can override the unpleasant ones and in this way become integrated as a positive experience)

b. the baby's ability to communicate successfully with the mother
or caregiver.

Figure 4.1 illustrates the multiplicity of interactions between the
mother (or caregiver) and baby. The look, the smell, the voice, the talk,
the signalling, and the touch form an important complex yet mysterious field of enrichment in the knowledge of each other and stimulate
development of the baby's brain, emotions, cognition, and neurobiological and immune systems.

The mother has many internal objects—mental representations of
her mother, father, husband, baby, others—with and through which
she relates to her baby.

The baby has preconceptions of what is going to satisfy its needs,
including maternal ones that in the interchange with reality will become proper internal objects—conceptions of the good and enriching,
time, and waiting.

There are circumstances where the mother cannot send these communications, or only a few of them, or the child cannot send commu-

nications that reach the mother or they are too weak; or, because of hospitalization of one kind or another, this interchange may not occur.

A mother's previous depression, psychiatric difficulties, abusive or neglectful attitude, or a traumatic pregnancy and/or delivery are all obstacles, especially with certain babies who find mood changes in the mother intolerable, or have a fragile make-up, or whose individuality is difficult to fathom, given their special sensitivities.

Ways of adapting to the world

If the newborn can perceive pain, discomfort, fear of changes from the intrauterine to extra-uterine life, then it also has ways of adapting to the world. These adaptations and self-protective strategies at the beginning of life mainly introject what is good, useful, and gratifying and project outside what is experienced as unpleasant, persecutory, intrusive, or painful. At times the infant will unconsciously split and deny what is increasingly painful, creating an internal representation that comforts him. For example, if a baby is tired of crying because it wanted to be held, it might calm down by relying on memory and creating an internal representation of such comfort. With increasing maturity, the ego of the infant is better able to find such inner balance and to integrate the experiences of pleasant and unpleasant. The infant gradually becomes aware of both loving and hating the same person simultaneously and, also, that his actions have consequences. For example, if the mother disappears after the baby kicks her or had a tantrum, it may feel guilty and may wish to repair their relationship.

The process of adaptation is intimately linked with the capacity to integrate internal and external experiences in the individual self and in being able to stand states of varying integration when needs arise.

Psychoanalytic background

Melanie Klein's theory postulates psychological object relations from birth, with the notion of a rudimentary ego able to perceive anxiety and to react to it defensively. The concept of unconscious phantasy is seen as particularly relevant in shaping psychological functioning. Unconscious phantasy may stem from the interplay between the infant's psychological reactions and response limitations in the mother's understanding. Evidence of the infant's early mental and emotional functioning is to be found in observational studies carried out by Esther

Bick (1964). W. R. Bion's (1962b) concept of container–contained—the mother's capacity to contain, understand, and give back the infant's projections—is also of great importance in the field of early psychological development. Bion pointed out that from the beginning of life there seems to be a desire for knowledge in the infant which is to some extent independent of emotional and bodily needs. He suggested that the mind needs the experience of getting to know someone as much as the body needs food and terrible consequences for the growth of the mind result from thwarting this need.

In her 1937 paper, "Love, Guilt and Reparation", Klein mentions that the child wants love and understanding in addition to nourishment. Her insights into the early external and internal relational modes of structuring emotional development are in accordance with later research in developmental psychology.

D. W. Winnicott, in thinking about the creation of the subject in the space between infant and mother, which involves several stages of tension through which the identity of the baby is simultaneously created and derived from it, has articulated the following stages:

1. attachment/separateness in the primary maternal preoccupation;
2. recognition/negation in the mirroring role of the mother;
3. discovery of "me" and "not me" in the disillusion by mother of not fulfilling all infant's needs;
4. creation and destruction in object usage of the mother, and the baby's concern about it.

Winnicott (1960b) was the first to place the psychological state of the mother on an equal footing with that of the infant: "'There is no such thing as an infant', . . . without maternal care there would be no infant" (p. 39n). Winnicott's idea of the creation of the subject in the space between the infant and mother involves several types of dialectical tension of unity and separateness, of internality and externality, through which the subject is simultaneously constituted and descended from itself. Thomas Ogden (1992) notes that each of Winnicott's four stages represents a different facet of the interdependence of subjectivity and intersubjectivity.

Defensive behaviours

Defensive behaviours in the infant have been studied by René Spitz (1961) and Selma Fraiberg (1980) and systematized by Henry Massie and Judith Rosenthal (1984). Defensive behaviour is transitory, a response to temporary conditions. Likewise, primitive defences are a step in normal psychological organization. Pathology will always be considered when there is a fixation to these mechanisms or later regression to them. Such defences can be indicators of difficulty in emotional development if they become permanent. As we know, defensive behaviour is initially a protective strategy that helps the infant to cut off from internal or external stimulation that is experienced as overwhelming—for example, falling asleep as soon as a sibling comes into the room. Some very early defensive behaviours that can be seen are withdrawal to sleep, including somnolence, gaze aversion including inattention, or a blank gaze. Any other defensive behaviours tend to be avoidant, not only of gaze, but of motility or body proximity—for example, moving away, avoiding holding, pushing the other way. Other motility-avoiding behaviours are protest and fight, or a shutdown of individual sensorimotor modalities. Another defensive behaviour can be the substitution of one sensory modality for another. Fraiberg (1980) described defensive behaviour in infancy as being, in general, avoidance, freezing, and fighting. Massie and Rosenthal (1984), in their studies of early psychosis in the first four years of life, make a parallel between defensive behaviour, primitive defences, and symptoms that can be seen in the first two years of life. The clarity of these parallels is interesting. While defensive behaviour is something that can be seen, the primitive defences are a mechanism of protecting an adaptation that is completely internal and can only be inferred. The primitive defences in the first two years of life are introjection, projection, denial, splitting, displacement from one body function system to another one, de-animation, transformation of affect, and undoing and isolation of affect. Massie and Campbell list the numerous symptoms that can appear in the first year and that are warning signals of serious emotional disturbance.

Assessment and diagnosis

We need to differentiate between detection, assessment, and diagnosis. "Detection" is learning to see warning signals of emotional difficulties. "Assessment" is about forming a picture of the internal world of the infant in trouble and the parents, and thinking with the parents about how to help the infant in the consultation. "Diagnosis" is the possibility of classifying according to agreed parameters the pathology in the infant, in the parents, or in the relationship.

In "A Note on Normality and Anxiety" (1931), Winnicott's first paper in his *Collected Papers: Through Paediatrics to Psychoanalysis* (1958a), he points out that anxiety is normal in childhood. He places great importance on finding out when anxiety is not normal and its impact on emotional development. Winnicott devises a systematic method to evaluate anxiety in the paediatric consultation, and this is described in his *Collected Papers* in a paper called "Paediatrics and Childhood Neurosis" (1956a). He says: "We diagnose illness and abnormality only if the degree of disturbance is crippling for the child, or boring for the parent, or inconvenient for the family. In the prevention of neurosis we try to give what is needed in the earliest stages of infancy . . ." (p. 319).

Ernest Freud devised a baby profile in a study at the Hampstead Child Therapy Clinic following the idea of pre-stages of libidinal distribution and forerunners of conflict (W. E. Freud, 1967). Even though the guide for infant observation and metapsychological analysis is interesting, his profile leaves out the valuable diagnostic tool of the observer's own countertransference and the rich interplay of the baby's instincts from birth, with object relations and defences.

Fraiberg's (1980) method of assessing an infant and its family considers the baby from birth and includes all the variables present at the time of referral. The assessment is carried out over five sessions and by different infant clinicians. Members of a team meet and discuss their opinions on the case to design the plan of intervention. It is possible to rely on an infant observer for the assessment of the emotional interplay if he or she is experienced enough, as sometimes a therapeutic intervention takes place during the process of observation.

Stanley Greenspan and collaborators undertook an in-depth study of normal and disturbed developmental patterns in infancy in order to develop a systematic and comprehensive classification of adaptive and maladaptive infant and family patterns (Greenspan, 1992). They describe stages in emotional growth from ages 0 to 2 months as the search for homoeostasis, internal and external, and from 2 to 4 months as the "falling-in-love" period, when the mother–infant relationship develops. However, it is the first two months that require further detailed observation and explanation since the newborn exercises its individuality and predilections according to other forces, which is a need not merely for homoeostasis, but for clear object relations with its mother (or other attachment figure).

Massie and Campbell (1984) created a scale of mother–infant attachment indicators during stress. This was an outcome of their Early

Natural History of Childhood Psychosis Project. The scale was devised in the context of their study of pathology in an effort to reliably quantify studies of the pre-pathology interplay of the mother–infant relationship. It is a one-page guide of standardized observations of components of mother–infant interaction for the paediatric clinician or mental health worker. The scale is composed of succinct descriptions of key parameters of mother–infant bonding, touching, infant clinging, maternal holding, and physical proximity. These are graded for the intensity of the interaction or avoidance between mother and baby, as indicative of the adequacy or not of the mother's and baby's mutual responsiveness (cf. Figure 5.2 herein). The principal purpose of this scale is to assist the practitioner to identify early on the need for a therapeutic intervention with the family, with evidence of a parent–infant interaction, so as to avoid a crystallization of pathological patterns of behaviour. The scale can be used from birth to age 18 months, and it has the advantage of early assessment of mother–infant interplay and follow-up. It shows clearly the newborn's capacity embedded in the mutual bonding process. The critical finding in the project was that the relationship between a mother and infant who later became ill was often disturbed as early as the first few weeks of life in terms of the recorded reciprocity, synchronicity, and intensity of the parameters of mutual bonding mentioned above. In some cases the primary contribution to aberrant interaction seemed to come from the child, in some cases the parent. Even though the purpose of the scale for use in this study was to detect difficulties as early as possible in paediatrics, it is simple and is based on a profound study of the prevailing psychodynamic processes that can be shown in specific behaviours in infancy. The professionals who use the scale learn to detect, assess, and refer the baby for treatment, but not to intervene further. When Massie and Rosenthal speak about the diagnoses they make, it is more complicated, being based on all the data available to them, the observation of longitudinal film data, histories and medical records of the children and project questionnaires, accounts of the therapeutic process, first-hand therapy in some cases, and first-hand interviews with families and patients in others. The problem that becomes evident in this lengthy process of assessment is that it does not cover crisis intervention and it requires considerable technology and information to develop an assessment.

On the other hand, in "Infant Psychopathology" (1983), Kreisler and Cramer give guidelines for examination, clinical grouping, and logical propositions for children. The authors start with a physical examination, continuing with an observation of a mother–infant interaction, and then consider certain clinical groupings: somatic expression, developmental disturbances, motor expression, and mental or psychic expression. These categories are not linked to specific courses but can result from various influences. Each category has its own characteristics, but there may be associations between them. This is a very integrated psychodynamic way of looking at the child, and it is possible to use it in the first interview of any disturbed infant–parent relationship. Kreisler and Cramer note that infant psychopathology has the potential for innumerable variations and that the role of family interactions is fundamental and usually does not appear clearly in this classification. They add that psychodynamic explanation of disturbances cannot be included in this nosology.

What is not included in any of the assessments described above, although it is implicit in Fraiberg's work and in Kreisler and Cramer's, is the important role of the transference from the infant (as well as from mother) and the therapist's countertransference as technical elements to describe the dynamic processes that are unconscious in the mother and infant at the time of the interview.

Psychoanalytic technical instruments

There are two main psychoanalytic instruments that one has for work with parents and infants: transference and countertransference.

Transference

The transference is, according to Betty Joseph (1975), re-enactment in the here-and-now of past experiences, bringing what has hitherto been repressed to consciousness into a condition regarded by the patient as better. It is the basis for analytic work: to know about the repressed past by re-living it in safer conditions.

Three main elements were designated by Freud in "The Dynamics of the Transference" (1937): first, the repetition of infantile clichés; second, the libidinal need; and third, the resistance. By definition, it must include everything that the patient brings into the relationship— how the patient is using the analyst, alongside and beyond what the patient is saying. Much of our understanding comes from how our patients act on us to feel things for many varied reasons—how they try to draw us into their defensive system; how they unconsciously act out with us in the transference, trying to get us to act out with them; how they convey aspects of their inner world built up from infancy and elaborated in childhood and adulthood. These are experiences, often beyond the use of words, that we can often only capture through the feelings aroused in us—through our countertransference, used in the broad sense of the word.

In diagnostic terms, the transference is an important piece of actual information as to how to proceed. In a mother–infant consultation, it is important as a source of information and not as an object of study in itself. Fraiberg (1980) mentions the clinician's need to utilize the positive transference of the mother to help in the process of exploration of the baby's and her own difficulties, and to confront the negative transference of the mother to clarify her relationship with the therapist. I would like to add that, if the baby has clear *object* human relations from birth (in Kleinian object relations, either *partial* if it is with a part of the mother such as the breast, the voice, the holding, and so forth, or *total* when it becomes more integrated as a consequence of experience) with capabilities in active use and development, the baby can also re-enact and communicate in the consultation through transference, using the same elements in a more primitive form. The therapist has to be able to stay with the very primitive communications of the baby, which are shown in his body, hands, gaze, movements, transmission of affects, moods, or lack of them. In this way a picture is formed of the baby's internal world thus far, and whether the feelings and perceptions of the mother about the baby concur with those of the therapist. The therapist has to be able to form a picture of what sort of internal world the baby has managed to form thus far, and explore whether the feelings and perceptions of the mother about the baby are correct, and then decide on treatment. A number of sessions are used to help the dyad or both parents and baby to sort out the difficulty, in which case it is important to explore the transference onto the therapist.

The aim of assessment in the early intervention in mother–infant psychotherapy is to explore first and then to free the innate healthy potential for normal communication and development of parent and infant relationships. This need not be a lengthy process, since the difficulties in interaction have, hopefully, not become entrenched so early on.

Countertransference

As described by Heinrich Racker (1951), countertransference is the expression of the therapist's identification with the internal objects of the baby. According to Racker, "It is the totality of the analyst's psychological response" to the patient (p. 133); he sees "The analyst as subject and the patient as object of knowledge . . ." (p. 136).

In infant–parent psychotherapy, countertransference is the main tool for investigating the parent's and the infant's internal unconscious worlds and the quality of their (object) human relations, anxieties, and defences. Possession of this insight helps us to decide whether the focus of the work is mainly on the mother's or parents' psychotherapy, or whether the difficulty arises as a result of the parents' incompatibility in understanding the baby's individuality (which might require referral for marital therapy or work), or whether there are genuine difficulties in reaching an irritable or fragile infant.

Countertransference guides our understanding by giving us important clues and links. It will also guide the level at which we pitch our work and the way it is done. The kind of interpretation of unconscious needs, defences, and mechanisms that takes place in long-term psychoanalytic work is kept to a minimum and is only done to the extent that ghosts from the past or mental representations of the baby in the parents are perceived to interfere with the real perception of this particular baby's behaviours. For example, the sort of internal mother that seems to be forming and the baby's needs, wishes, use of primitive defences, ego functioning, structure of the self, and so forth will all be central in the psychotherapy.

Interpretations as to the possible causes of symptoms, quality of interactions, and maternal memories and unconscious projections onto the infant are made after their effects on the child have been clarified, and if the mother is able to accept the interpretations. It is the rigorous observation of the behaviour and body language of mother and infant reacting to the interpretations and the countertransference that will monitor the positive or negative effect of our comments.

The countertransference can suffer according to the degree and quality of the projections. Winnicott (1947) pointed out that both hate and the generous response in the countertransference are indicative of mental states worth considering (Ekman, 1972), and they demonstrate organized social responses in conjunction with increasing neurophysiological organization (Emde, Gaensbauer, & Harmon, 1976). From the early months, the infant demonstrates a unique capacity to enter into complex social and affective interactions (Brazelton, Koslowsky, & Main, 1974; Stern, 1974a, 1974b).

Racker (1951) states that even pathological countertransference reactions can be used as a tool "because it is the expression of the analyst's identification with the internal objects of the patient and has characteristics and specific contents, anxieties and mechanisms". According to Joseph (1975), countertransference is "The notion of our being used and of something constantly going on." Hate in/from the therapist towards a particular mother and/or baby could give an important clue as to the degree of disintegration and conflict present, because of chronic personality disorder, borderline psychotic personalities, or a present regression or confused state due to projective identifications between mother and baby.

The generous response is indicated when the professional gives the mother extra time or advice or help—for example, by getting other organizations involved, or by making him/herself available at all hours. This seems to be a reaction of the therapist who is trying to repair his or her own internal mother–infant relationship as a result of some particular aspect that has arisen in a given consultation. This kind of countertransference reaction occurs more frequently in professionals who have not been well analysed themselves, and it is therefore common in lay professionals treating mothers and infants.

Feelings of being rejected can appear when the wrong interpretation is given or there is a desire on the part of the therapist to refer to another professional colleague. This reaction is usually linked to an identification with internal objects in the mother or in the baby that results in a wish to get rid of anxiety quickly and/or to feelings of rejection; it is most important to raise this in the consultation and to explore to whom this feeling belongs and what has happened.

Another common reaction in the psychotherapist working in this field which can easily be rationalized is feeling so caught up in the parents' personal narratives and their internal world that the infant is left to one side, ignored and unattended. I consider this response to be an indication of denial of the baby's existence, and/or serious difficulties in bonding and/or attachment in the parents—as if the narcissistic structure of the parent binds him or her to the baby's individuality. The psychotherapist may collude with this and identify with this mechanism in the parents, which reactivates a similar situation in the psychotherapist's own past, and in this form rationalize that mother–infant psychotherapy is only a matter of exploration and working with the mother's mental representation of the baby. The reality is that the therapist has had to struggle with his or her own process of individualization, which has become concealed by a great deal of rationalization and resistance. The therapist's own need for psychoanalytic treatment is partly due to a need to *reconstruct* the infant in ourselves and to see our own infant–mother relationship. But, because we are reconstructing, we are not able to change what had happened, and an aspect of unresolved anger about not having been helped then and there obscures the fact of not being able to help parents and infant by conscious or unconscious choice.

The analysis of the countertransference in the therapist needs to focus on the individual and on the atmosphere of the interactions. The exercise of this insight into the internal world of mother, father, and infant helps us *to know* whether the mother needs to be referred for psychotherapy in her own right, or whether it is possible to help the present imbalance by working in an exploratory way in a few sessions.

It is important to understand the negative aspects of the identification with the internal object of the parents or the child. It is useful to mention Winnicott and his refinement of the meaning of "hate" in the consultation. When this feeling appears intermittently, it is important to evaluate the degree of parental internal conflict and/or degree of chaos and internal conflict in the infant and to be cautious about holding, understanding, and slowly incorporating in the dialogue what we think they should know or they could take. In this way we are exploring the phantasmatic child of the parents. Common in the experience of hate is fear of a flood of primitive experiences of feelings which needs containment.

Free-floating attention

Free-floating attention is attention that concentrates on putting together information received not only verbally but also by the sensory, visceral, cognitive, and emotional organs. It benefits from an indirect, parallel thinking of the trained mind which perceives sensitively the unconscious contents of the patient's mind. These may appear like a missing link that clarifies or explains deep-rooted traumas that have been split off and interfere with the proper mental functioning of the patient. On many occasions what is so perceived cannot be verbalized but needs to be contained and deflected by the psychotherapist to facilitate the assessment or psychotherapeutic work with the patient. This attention is free-floating, whereas conscious attention works on gathering information from or pursuing issues with the patient.

Infant categories in psychoanalytic literature

In order to clarify terminology, it is necessary to distinguish between the different kinds of infant that appear in the psychoanalytic literature.

1. *"Laboratory" infant:* the observed infant in developmental psychological studies and research. These infants are recruited usually by advertisement for developmental research. In general, the parents self-select and are likely to believe that their infants, and their own relationships with them, are good and strong enough to stand experimentation (e.g. as in the research reported in Acquarone, 1990). It is important to realize that such infants, recruited for studying certain hypotheses, are aware and accept the "experiential" situation. Therefore, they are only representative of the well-motivated and securely attached range of the general infant population.

2. *"Observed" infant:*

    a. *Infant observation:* this discipline consists of observing an infant from ages 0 to 2 years for an hour a week at home, making detailed notes afterwards, and discussing the observation in a small group. The purpose is to observe the development of emotions and interactions over a period of at least two years, inferring the psychodynamics according to different psychoanalytic theories.

    b. *Observed social infant:* this occurs in everyday "social interactions" of mother/parent and child or with other children in parks or nurseries or other situations outside the home. These are naturalistic observations of everyday life in different settings, and they enrich our knowledge of the range of normal behaviour.

3. *Reconstructed clinical infant:* in adult or child psychoanalytic treatment, this is the joint creation of two people: the patient, who has grown up or is growing up; and the therapist, who has a theory about that particular infant experience. This recreated infant is made up of memories, current re-enactment in the transference, and theoretically guided interpretations based on countertransference.

4. *Clinical infant:* the infant brought for a consultation by the parents because it is presenting a behaviour, or a physical symptom without physical cause, that is of concern to the parents or the profes-

sionals involved with the infant; it might also be that the parents are concerned at not being able to understand their infant.

a. *Imaginary child:* this is a conscious construction that the parents make from their narratives and expectations and from some interaction with the unborn child. At birth, the imaginary child is compared with the real baby and perhaps mourned. Conflicts arise in this natural process of mourning when stillbirth, malformation, or disability occurs, and the resulting shock of the trauma can paralyse, idealize, handicap, or make the baby seem persecutory. This dynamic might then become unconscious and exercise a negative influence on the family.

b. *Phantasmatic child:* this is an unconscious construction that parents make and is the intergenerational transmission of "ghosts of the past" from the parents or the family. According to Lebovici (1988), this relates to the Oedipus complex in the mother and its conflict or resolution. Other conflicts may be in relation to ideal projection of the self or different parts of it—ego, superego (internalized parents), needs, or wishes. The phantasmatic child is not known to the parents and has to be inferred from the mother's presentation in the consultation.

Summary

Infants are seen from developmental psychology and psychoanalysis to be capable of organizing themselves in an adaptive way. Their initial integrative capacities are enriched by their neurophysiological organization, which allows assimilation, accommodation, the identification of variables, and associative learning.

It is also possible to see how the baby is born with a primitive ego that has its own predilections and leads the perceptions, thinking, and feelings. Therefore, the way the baby responds to internal and external experiences depends not only on the sensitivity of the mother and the adequacy of the environment, but on the basic endowment of the baby: the interplay of aggressive tendencies and personal strength to tolerate waiting, frustrations, and so forth.

A review of psychoanalytic theories of development as an exercise in comprehending the complexity of emotional development leaves us with a sense that they all seem to be theorizations done retrospectively from different populations. However, infant observation shows us that all the psychoanalytic approaches are applicable at one time or another to explain different situations or reactions that the infant goes through in relationships during its emotional development. It is possible also to witness how the individual make-up of the child works together with the parents and the environment to create a unique relationship, and the parents likewise can enrich or damage the same process.

I have tried to specify some of the sources of information about the development of experience, senses, and emotions, treating behaviours not as fragmented data about an infant, but with a deeper dynamics that can be understood by incorporating the psychoanalytic tools of the transference and the countertransference, free-floating attention, and an appropriate setting. This manner of treating infant–parent difficulties requires the specific skills obtained through training and supervision.

INFANT OBSERVATION: LEARNING TO SEE

One of the first ways we learn is from observation. It is a skill as old as humanity.

Some people—like Charles Darwin—created whole new sciences from observation. He observed his own children and created an emotional theory of the newborn's facial expressions. At the end of the nineteenth century, Husserl and Brentano created a method of learning from observation in a philosophical way. Freud learned from detailed observation: simply looking closely at what is in front of the observer, as objectively as possible, restraining any effort to change the reality of what is observed. Other great observers—Melanie Klein, Anna Freud, and Donald Winnicott—all used observation to create different theories of the development of emotions.

Observing an infant from birth with the mother in their home, every week for an hour, is a valuable discipline and experience. The observer has to learn not to interfere with the process between mother and infant and to bear the strong feelings and primitive communications without acting out any of the anxiety these may produce. It is not as easy as it may sound—but it is an important experience for the professional who wants to understand early stages of emotions, how babies find their individuality, and how adults think about their roles as parents.

What is observed is:

• the growth of the relationship between the infant and the main caregiver, usually the mother

- the development of emotions, cognition, play, and selfhood
- the constructive and protective mechanisms for survival and competence
- everything that is displayed.

Observers must find a place in the room without interfering with the usual activities taking place between infant and mother (or father) and must not to fulfil any roles in the family. They must maintain an attentive, reliable, friendly, non-intrusive attitude and be able to follow different dynamics and be aware of their own feelings and ideas at all times.

They must later write down their observations in detail and then discuss them in a small group of up to six persons, with a leader. In the group session, each observer presents this written material and, in the period of an hour, they discuss what they have seen, perceived, and felt during a particular observation, and what might be beyond. The exchange of experiences in the different observations, and following the infant development presented by five other observers, provides a rich background for understanding the wide range of the normal ups and downs of growing up. Their comments provide insights into the unconscious roles and expectations that the family places on them. These expectations about the observer may be related to the real capacities of the observer, or they may be the mother's expectations projected into the observer and more related to her inner world. (See Figure 3.2.)

In any case, the role of the observer—the impassive receptive listener—evolves as family and observer become familiar with each other and, through reliability and receptivity, a trust develops.

The purpose of the observations for the observer are many:

- to encounter strong and primitive emotions
- to observe development and also learn from his or her own responses
- to learn to see and describe processes such as the development of emotions and the different capacities of the family members
- to learn to understand unconscious processes and patterns of behaviour that might be transmitted from one generation to the next, patterns that belong to the individuality of members of the family and their inner world

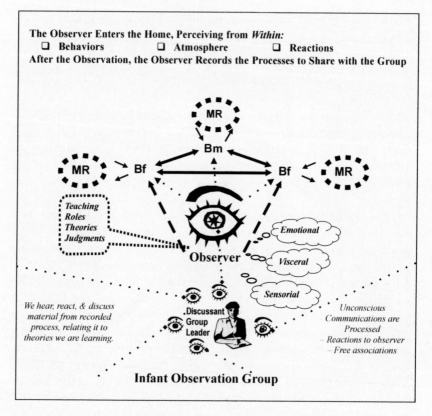

FIGURE 3.2.   The infant observation experience.

- to see the emergence of the infant's personality moulding the parents, as well as the parents' attunement to their baby.

The observation sessions themselves hold different kinds of anxieties.

- Some anxieties originate in the inner world of the observer, because the observer is new in the intimacy of other people who are not his or her own family. The observer must struggle to accommodate his or her past experiences, whether personally as a baby or with bringing up his or her own children. In this process, the observations helps the observer heal him/herself.
- Some anxieties arise simply from the novelty of the experience.
- Anxieties arise from the infant—they too face an uncertain world.

Yes, infants have their mothers, but the mothers have anxieties, and even though these anxieties may be modulated by experience, they reverberate with the shadow of death or damage (e.g. when a child is born after a previous cot death in the family, or when one of the parents has had a stroke or been diagnosed as chronically ill).

Overall, the observations are based on the "ordinary family" so that observers can be exposed to the wide spectrum of what is considered normal. All concerns about feeling intrusive are analysed in their entirety:

- Sometimes this intrusiveness is related to the fear of perverting the perception (the observer may feel that he or she is judging the parents, or finding emotions where they do not exist, in order to progress in his or her careers) or idealizing the mother and not being able to contemplate her ambivalence, for example.
- Sometimes the excitement at observing particular behaviours, depression, sexual management of siblings, or other themes can be intrusive.

The problem to be avoided is observers witnessing neglect, abuse, and/or serious mental illness. Every effort should be made to choose normal healthy families. The regularity of the visits makes the observation a focus for seeing the interplay of transference and countertransference reactions outside the consulting-room—therefore, any changes in the routine have to be made with a great deal of care and not often. Holiday times or disruptions have to be incorporated and preceded by a great deal of notice, otherwise a family that has become dependent or accustomed to accommodating the observer may feel as though they are not being treated with care themselves, and this can create resentment or even interrupt future observations.

The respectful observer will establish with the parents a clear time for the visits that suits both parties and will stick to this schedule without making any alterations. This is a part of the discipline that gradually allows the observer to see the unfolding of emotions between the newborn and the mother and to register his or her own unconscious responses to this process, exploring these elements as feeling states that the observer learns to discriminate from the mother's or baby's projections onto him or her. It teaches the observer sensitivity about the infant's mode of communications and states and about his or her own emotions, allowing feelings to be reflected and recognized.

One of the most important assets that an observer brings is a willingness to create a space in the mind where experiences can be reflected and anxieties can be faced. The observer learns to tolerate positive feelings—such as love, gratification, joy—and negative feelings—such as anxiety, frustrations, uncertainty, discomfort, helplessness, and many other feelings that particular infants may have. The mere fact that observers are passive, receptive, and attentive means that they learn to withhold acting out, giving advice, or performing roles, and in this withholding they face up to anxieties of all sorts, reflecting on them, building tolerance, and developing the free-floating attention that brings up lost links from the unconscious of the mother and baby or from aspects of themselves.

In general, closely observing infants and their mothers is to be present in the intimacy and accommodation between two new persons—one very vulnerable and ready to know, feel, and develop; the other more mature, who will protect, care, and attune to the baby's need. To witness this interaction for two years is an honour, and we should feel very grateful.

INTERACTION TIME

Seeing eye-to-eye during the consultation

During the clinical assessment, interaction time is the time that I dedicate myself to interacting with the baby and parents. This interaction might happen with the baby in the arms of the mother or father if it is too little, or on a big couch, or on the floor.

What toys or objects are used will vary according to age. A red or colourful ball is always present, because I make babies follow this with their eyes and watch their interest and span of attention. In addition, I have colourful mats with different sensorial noises and shades and materials, rattles, tethers, plastic rings, different kinds of materials in sizes and structure, a treasure basket, a family of big cuddly teddy bears, and other cuddly toys variable in size, softness, or firmness. I have boxes, two thin blankets, a box with animals, fences, cubes, paper, and felt-tip pens, and a simple doll's house with furniture and people.

The importance of this time is how the infant or toddler behaves with me and with me and the parents—what are the terms of engagement, what does the baby need to be engaged, can the baby attend and focus, is it easy and immediate or not, is there warmth and trust or smiles or fear? I try to see in child's gestures—and in the gestures of the parents—whether there is a willingness or a reluctance to engage.

It is important to see the baby's individuality—its personality and temperament—and whether the parents agree or disagree with this picture of their baby. Usually I try to see whether babies will lead me into their inner world so I can find out whether there are steps missing in the encounter—are the infants able to show boredom, do they need a great deal of entertainment, are they easy to reach? By talking to them, I find out from them about themselves. Their degree of attention and interest in what I am saying will help assess whether or not hypotheses about them are corroborated. A dialogue then takes place.

Interaction time is sometimes extended over a number of sessions. With the toys that it chooses, the baby or small child will guide me to the quality of its internal world and preferences it has towards maintaining this world, or changing it. Most of all, I allow the behaviour towards an active me to develop, and, as it does, I study the modality that appears. I foster attention and engagement, attunement, reciprocity, turn-taking, and the formation of representational or symbolic capacities, and I assess how the baby's memory works.

In this there is a sense of wonder and exploration. No two children are the same, but neither are they so different that is not possible to know about stages of appropriate or expectable development, though the individual rate of development will vary from child to child. It is important to note that while some children are quite like the norm, if there are considerable differences from the norm, then this should alert professionals and parents that something may be going wrong. It is for us developmentally orientated professionals then to find out whether there is a reason for this disparity.

During interaction time the parents are present, and their anxiety about the possibility of something being wrong with their child may be palpable. If in the interaction time I am able to make the child do more things or relate differently, my rule is to capture the parents' attention by talking about possible thoughts and desires in the baby. Parents will have seen my behaviour and heard us interact and communicate. I would like to awaken in them a sense of exploration and wonder similar to the one I have created with the baby. I help the parents to develop ideas, to be daring in trying new ideas with their child, even if it is very different from their traditional ways of interacting. I want them to comprehend play differently: to become playful.

The immediate problem may be the parents' difficulties in dealing differently with this child, or it might be the mother's anxiety about feeling that she might have damaged the child and why and how that happened. Some of these problems might have arisen from the way they were raised. Fathers who do not know how to be gentle with a baby boy who needs it, or do not know how to sing to a child who loves it, need to be encouraged as well. There is a fundamental necessity for the parents to become the parents this particular child needs, and they need help to do this. The parents themselves may also be having problems, which may be either apparent or subtle, and this will usually come to the surface at some point. I may pick up on the parents' relationship at any time: sometimes when I am on the floor with the child, sometimes when the parents are holding the baby, and sometimes when they are almost on the doorstep—then the important comment will come. For example, in a consultation about an 18-month-old "autistic" child, just as the parents were leaving, the mother said, "And do you think that the death of my mother on the delivery day has damaged him?" This was the first time that she mentioned this detail. When asked originally about the delivery, she had answered that the birth was a perfect water birth with no complications.

Sessions with the parents alone do occur, mainly when the child is a very active toddler or a small child. In order to allow them time by themselves and to digest aspects of the child or themselves, a calmer environment is sometimes needed. Insightful parents will do a lot of work by themselves once they are on the right track, but insight needs help, and links between thoughts that appear in the mind of the infant–parent psychotherapist may be transmitted to the parents. Often the child is demonstrating parental difficulties in its actions or is acting out the conflict in a way that is obvious for the therapist but unbearable for the parents.

When the baby is in serious difficulties of not relating, lethargic, frantic, or lost to the parents, in the interaction time I look for:

1. the attention span;
2. the motivational system of the child that does or does not allow it to have intersubjective experience, and the quality of this.

In looking at a baby's attention span, I explore the sensory modality, the quality of movement, and the maturity of the reflexes. What is the child's response to touch, smells, taste, sight, and hearing? I experiment with them in a playful way, exploring the extremes of the sensory continuum with play. I observe what is pleasurable and annoying or rejecting. I look for use of all the senses, different movements, and what movements the child expects—for example, different types of holding, quality of muscle tone, level of activity, and whether the baby is slow or quick to warm to a strange adult—and I share this with parents in "baby-ese" mode, talking for the baby.

In examining the intersubjective experience, I look for the interest that the baby shows in relating to people or objects, and what kind: whether they are soft/cuddly or hard, hollow, for wearing, for covering, and so forth. In this respect, I watch and listen for the emotional tone (normally the preferred one is "motherese", but some babies have other predilections) and rhythm preferred by the baby, which can be found by singing different tunes or playing music.

It is interesting in this respect to talk to the baby about expectations and modalities of the parents and therapist. Parents sometimes marry a person in the same profession or activity level (e.g. musicians or athletes) because they expect or like that type of person, and they may find it difficult to understand and sometimes may even dislike children if they do not follow in their footsteps. But we do not choose our children, and certainly it is not just a matter of education or nurture. So we have to enter delicately, with empathy, the depths of what is not allowing the child to relate; once we discover this, we corroborate whether the parents have a closed modality to relate to and whether this agrees with the one the baby would like or is able to tolerate.

Interaction time helps us discover how communication occurs: whether there is conversation (protoconversation in the case of babies); whether this fulfils the condition of being fun, telling something that is then being captured by the other party; whether there is turn-taking, expressiveness, gesturing, affects; and whether our experience of interaction with the child is different from that of the parents, which we will already have observed at the beginning of the consultation. Most important is to find out whether the preferred mode of communication is distal or proximal, and we share it with the parents.

When interaction time is part of the therapy, this helps the baby and the family to develop the experiences that they need together in order to replace missing or deficient facets of their relationship, and at the same time it helps the parents to find out more about themselves and about their child, pointing out what the obstacles may be to development and fun. Overall, interaction time is about moving towards a common and shared experience with corresponding emotions.

PART II

PUTTING THEORY INTO PRACTICE

CHAPTER FOUR

The assessment procedure

When an infant is referred, either the infant or the parents are experiencing unhappiness. To develop a professional opinion on the problem, we will need to explore the parents, the parenting, and the infant, why difficulties have appeared, and how and when this process started. Overall, the procedure works like this: a baby and a family are in trouble; we attend to the referral, exploring the meaning in the parent's mind of having been referred, and by whom and why. We create a suitable setting to work in, observe the individuals and the surrounding situation, and give ourselves time to reflect in order to evaluate the sort of help that is suitable and safe for this baby and this family.

This process will be understood through information that comes from infant research, developmental psychoanalysis, and the transference and countertransference, to reach an overall picture and respond with the appropriate help needed. Sometimes this procedure is therapeutic in itself; sometimes it takes several sessions and a team of professionals to gain a clear understanding of parental mental functioning and parenting capacities and to reach a plan of action possible in the community (or hospital) and safe and convenient for the infant and the family.

The clinical examples here are rich and provide material for widening the mind about the specific thinking when the consultation focuses on a nonverbal baby.

Psychodynamic assessment of infant and parents

The aim of our discussion of psychodynamic assessment is to systematize the thinking behind the observation of an infant and its parents when the infant shows developmental disturbances or the parents experience difficulty about understanding or providing for their infant's needs.

We may observe in the infant excitement or apathy, enthusiasm or depressive indifference, or no play activity, interest in objects rather than people, vocalizing or not. In order to avoid mechanistic information or interpretation of unmistakeable signs of unconscious phantasy, we must attempt to infer some psychological meaning in overt behaviour, not simply describing symptoms, but trying to understand their psychodynamic meaning. We need to remember that any symptom may be an expression of different mental mechanisms. Our evaluation aims to define prevalent psychic dysfunction and to determine a particular structure. To refer to a specific psychic structure in infants it is necessary to underline that what we are observing is the present mode of mental functioning and that this can be modified in subsequent development. Elasticity is the predominant characteristic of early psychic function, and developmental forces are at play, restructuring and facilitating this process. We can then examine the interplay between the infant's needs and those of the mother. We can also observe the current functioning and characteristics of the primitive ego of the infant and the infant's way of dealing with pain, fear, and anger through protective strategies. We can also note the main tendencies—whether they be love, hate, or aggression—that these mother–infant couples have as modes of interaction. We should also observe the unfolding of the self in the infant and mother and whether they relate to each other with their "true-" or "false-self" aspects (Winnicott, 1960a).

Since we have to infer unconscious processes from the observation of what we can see and feel, we can be guided by the principle that helped Freud to discover the unconscious: "I learnt to restrain speculative tendencies and to follow the unforgotten advice of my master Charcot: To look at the same things again and again until they themselves begin to speak" (1914). The objective of infant–parent observation, therefore, is to watch closely the interplay of emotions in each individual, or in the couple, or in the family triangle. The infant's behaviour is observed in detail both when it is with the parent and on its own; the observer also notes his or her own feelings and, when and how this emotional interplay occurs, and why.

The referral

The referral normally comes from an agency—institution, GP, developmental clinic, maternity ward, health visitor—though there may also be self-referral. Usually, the only information given is of the kind: "baby does not want to feed" or "mother and baby do not seem to be attached to each other" or "child does not sleep". An appointment letter is sent to the family.

Parents come with a child with whom they have problems, but they also come with their past experiences. In general, parents want something better for their children, but their bad experiences sometimes burden them without them realizing it. We have to be aware of this emotional impact from the parents and work with the hidden, unconscious, negative feelings that are activated as a consequence of the consultations.

What do we look for when a child is referred because of not sleeping? or not eating? or crying too much? We start from the first appearance of the couple—or the parent alone—and the infant. There is communication coming from their physical appearance and attitude, to the place they have been sent for expertise: our senses, organs, phantasies, the words, the spoken sounds or lack of them—these all tell us their story.

Experience with other cases comes to the fore, as does unease or ease with our knowledge. We allow the atmosphere to be created by the infant and the parents, the anxiety, guilt, annoyance, desires, despair that we feel giving us the true state of affairs. We receive, and perceive with interest and sympathy, allowing our organs, senses, knowledge, and free-floating attention to find in the tumult of information and feelings the missing pieces of the jigsaw. We contain our anxiety about the way the mother or father holds the baby and what they do or say to it, and we allow ourselves to experience what the infant is living, whether chaos, abuse, or prop feeding. If the abuse or neglect is very dangerous for the child, or for the possibility of think-

ing, we ask for or suggest alternatives, such as taking into consideration what the child might be feeling or thinking or developmental
issues.

There are various possible family situations that we might encounter:

- The family that identifies with each other so closely that they find it
  difficult to separate, to individuate. The mother cannot make decisions if they are not fully approved by the father, and vice versa. The
  child plays into this situation, paralysing growth and getting stuck
  in this syndrome of not hurting each other.
- The family in which the members are separate but are interested
  only in themselves in a narcissistic way.
- Busy parents who want their child to grow up quickly.
- Situations where there is a symbiotic relationship of the mother with
  the child, and the father is either absent or not interested.

In order to treat a difficulty, or a disorder, we need to start making an
assessment not only of the baby and the parents, but also of their
emotional environment.

The psychotherapist uses different senses or theories or tools to
understand the family. We look at the capacity to represent experiences internally and externally, since the family might be at risk.
Through mobilizing natural resources of the mind to try to understand
why they are stuck, we can provide a good model for them to use in
resolving future difficulties. In this respect, the use or knowledge of
dramatization is worth remembering. An important stage in early
childhood is the playing of pretend games and representative play. It is
important to reactivate playful encounters or create them as a situation
that helps transitions, both for infants and for their parents.

The importance of observation

From birth, the infant has feelings and perceptions and is naturally
disposed towards reacting. These are transmitted to the human
caregiver to help the infant in the necessary process of translation of its
needs and adaptation to the outside world. The vitality and interplay
of this process are inferred through close observation of the infant
alone and with the mother, based on psychoanalytic concepts and
technique.

In such observation, the therapist has to:

1. be able to experience the particular emotional impact of the infant
    and in the interaction with his mother—it is particularly important
    to observe:
    (a) communication or lack of communication on the part of the
        baby, without the mother, as this is an indicator of the capacity
        for and speed of recovery
    (b) discrepancies in behaviour and reactions
2. have an attitude that is responsive and reflective but not reacting
    and without theorizing prematurely, and with no expectations or
    ambitions;
3. notice the feelings, ideas, perceptions, and impressions aroused in
    himself as well as in the infant and mother.

The feelings so transmitted, and the emotional reactions in the therapist during the infant observation, create a field of fragmented data
that, with tolerance and intuition, can be assimilated and synthesized.

A part of the psychotherapy training is to undergo personal analysis of our mind and emotions. In this aspect of training, we are able to
learn how not to be affected by our own personal problems and what
is evoked from our past, and to be affected and aware of our countertransference reactions to what is observed. As explained earlier,
countertransference reactions are our emotional reaction to what is
manifested by the patient, made as an instrument of knowledge of the
patient. It is useful to check with the mother whether her perception of
the baby's behaviour and interpretation of its feelings is in agreement
with the therapist's view. If there are discrepancies, it is useful to
explore these with her.

The setting

Since the reality we need to understand is emotional reality—psychic
reality—and this was not originally perceived by the sensory apparatus but by our psychic emotional apparatus, it is important to talk
about the setting for such work.

Where do we intervene?—wherever our workplace is. If it is in a
hospital, the therapy setting should be a quiet place, free from inter-
ruptions of any kind. We can choose an office or a corner where there is
some feeling of quietness and where intimacy can develop. If it has to
be in a special-care baby unit or an intensive-care unit, where the
sound of monitors cannot be avoided, we can still undertake the work

with an observing eye. We can see or feel whether the parents are there, and the quality of the feelings. Words and anxiety need a container, and our presence may provide the first indication or hope for the parents that something that is felt as unbearable can be safely experienced, reflected upon, and talked about. Relief comes from the knowledge that professionals are prepared to be with them and to hold their hands while encouraging insight about what is behind their sorrow and despair.

Usually, psychotherapy in a hospital setting goes along the lines of witnessing, accompanying, sharing, and offering a supportive arm (physical as well as psychic) for the tormented mind to hang on to and experience the security of feeling held. Such experience might recall previous ones, or be totally new.

In these situations, I believe that the primary task of being psychotherapeutic is not about putting into words an understanding of anything, but being really present and aware, and offering general sympathy and containment for a while. When I hear interpretations of unconscious states of mind in regard to the needs, wishes, and defences of a mother crying next to her deformed neonate that will not survive, I understand that the experience has overwhelmed the psychoanalyst as much as it has the doctor who delivers a prognosis of death and leaves immediately afterwards. The importance of specific bereavement training applies to both.

Returning to considerations about the appropriate setting for assessing behaviour and emotions in the baby and parents, this could be in a family's home, if parents are very disturbed or the baby is too fragile to go out. Both situations are extremes where the psychotherapist will need special professional support. The home setting is difficult because the traditional psychotherapy training is based on working in a consulting-room. Home visits are generally made by other professionals who are primary health-care givers, and they are therefore the ones who sometimes need the input of a psychotherapeutic approach.

The training in infant observation helps the psychotherapist to take in a home environment with ease, observing the growth of relationships and normal crises in development. The experience of at least one home intervention gives a psychotherapist a more grounded understanding of the family's reality: the overwhelming power of the home—personal elements, talking, as well as the words and emotions being expressed. The professional will need to determine the best space and time for a psychotherapeutic intervention. On one occasion, I asked a mother (who was extremely depressed) and the father to turn off the television and CD player and unhook the telephone, and to get the children to bring their toys and stay in the room. In that way, it was possible to hear as well as observe, to concentrate and experience free-floating attention, and so understand the problem.

Other places for working are a safe room for seeing babies and children. This could be in a health centre, nursery, a room in a GPs' surgery, or a private consulting-room. It should be possible to sit on the floor and conduct the interview there, with toys and play materials appropriate for a baby's use; it is best to use the baby's own toys, if available.

So, the interviews take place in a room where is no telephone or answering machine. If it is in the special-care baby unit or at home, it is useful to create an atmosphere with as little interference from outside influences as possible. It is very important to feel the atmosphere created by the mother, and the baby's attempt to deal with this or to create his own. Simple age-appropriate toys are provided, such as soft pieces of material, rattles, sponge balls, plastic teething toys, an unbreakable mirror, and colourful and cuddly toys.

If the baby being interviewed is crawling, it is necessary to keep all the doors locked to allow complete freedom of movement and to observe what then takes place. Electric switches, devices, and windows are special trial points, to see how the parents deal with disciplining or letting the child handle them or not.

In general, an interview lasts fifty minutes; however, in cases of crisis (as when death is imminent), the interview may last for an hour and a half. In this time and space it is possible to observe the emotional impact that the baby and mother have on each other and the therapist and to pay attention, minute by minute, to the resulting interplay of emotions. It is important to distinguish the information communicated in all various areas of external and internal functioning. The number of interviews may vary between one and five. This depends on the need to assess how the mother uses the help she receives and whether the baby is able to respond adequately. The spacing of the interviews will depend upon the needs of the family and the availability of the therapist. In general, the first three interviews are either weekly or fortnightly, and the last two are monthly, in order to see how the mother uses the new insight in her relationship with the child and whether the infant has benefited from a new understanding of the difficulty it presented. After each interview, notes are made that serve as material for further thinking and to reach the conclusion and recommendations of the assessment. These must be discussed with the parents.

Clinical case studies

CASE 10: TOMMY, AGE 4 MONTHS

Tommy, who was referred by the health visitor and medical officer, cries a lot and is easily frustrated; he does not smile. He has had all sorts of complaints since he was born. Mother had been to the health clinic twice a week, worried about one thing or another, and had made frequent telephone calls to the health visitor.

I became conscious of Tommy crying in the waiting-room. He had enormous blue eyes and seemed to be looking for attention. He always looked very serious, or annoyed. I accepted the referral.

Mother came with baby and sat him on her lap. He looked at me intensely. I held his sight, and we all waited in silence. After a little while he started smiling, and I held his sight longer. I felt that he knew he was the centre of attention, and I wanted to observe, in detail, how he reacted to a new situation, how sensitive he was, and to what. I feared that as soon as I spoke, he would cry. I did not know exactly why.

Mother is a young woman with a soft appearance and understanding attitude. She started to speak calmly about her reactions to his behaviour. "At the beginning, when he was a newborn baby, whenever he would cry, I thought I was doing the wrong thing but I realized that he did not like to wait and I seemed unable to find the way to help him to wait." She explained that, at the moment, he was teething and was biting everything—the dummy, the sooth-ers—but he seemed so short-tempered, and she wondered if he was always going to be like this and how she could help.

The baby began to feel uneasy and started to cry. Mother then said, "That is exactly how he is: content if you look at him or hold him and if he can look around all the time; if not, he becomes frantic and his crying continues, making him really upset."

I thought that the mother was genuinely concerned and was moti-vated enough to explore with me what was happening. The child seemed to have a regulatory disorder; he was hypersensitive to some things we could discover, and the mother felt pleased to hear that she could be helped.

The mother talked to the baby nicely and comforted him, and he burped. He was placed on her lap, and he was looking at me and around the room in a very persistent, focused way. It seemed as if he was exploring the familiarity of the room.

The baby was transmitting to me a fear of falling apart if not held by my eyes. I also felt that he was jealous when the mother and I were engaged in conversation, which made him anxious, requesting again to be soothed. I had the impression that the baby had not developed emotionally in his four months of life and that he seemed as insecure as a newborn child in a world where being alone is experienced as being left completely alone, without the internal representation of an understanding mother. He had difficulty in introjecting a good-enough mother (Winnicott, 1960a).

We talked about the mother's feelings of being so understanding and her possible difficulty in waiting and accepting limits. I asked the mother how she had limited his constant demands. She answered that she could not, because he seemed to fall apart. I asked the mother whether she herself had siblings, and she answered that she had six and they lived in the countryside and there were no particular problems. She had a laid-back attitude and almost everything was acceptable for her, so she was not used to being firm. The baby became uneasy again, and mother soothed him again. She explained that she played games with the baby and had to move around with him all the time.

I asked about toys, whether he had any that he preferred. The mother said he had cuddly toys but he did not entertain himself, or show a preference for any. Again the baby became restless and cried very loudly; the mother patted him on the back gently, and he burped. He was uneasy and so upset that he vomited a little. I remembered the continuum of his symptoms: colic, diarrhoea, constipation, aches, and so on.

The baby seemed to become more and more anxious as the interview developed. I began to feel guilty for making the baby sick and for being of no help. I understood the mother's feelings of inadequacy and the baby's primitive mechanisms of clinging and adhering to mother in a desperate attempt to survive. His intolerance towards discomfort and pain were transmitted with an intensity that made it difficult for mother originally, and then me, to do anything about it.

The mother asked me whether I would go to their house and see him more naturally, and she mentioned that the baby did not like to be on his back or on his tummy or being held tight by a seat-belt or baby-seat. I remembered having seen him hanging from a bag on mother's chest while coming to the clinic. At the first interview, the baby was trying to touch my hands and things from over the table. I felt puzzled by the fact that the mother continued to hold the baby tightly to her chest, restricting his movement to such a degree that it made it impossible for him to look around.

I felt that Tommy's individuality seemed completely different from that of the mother. They were both sensitive, but in different ways—she liked him tight against her chest, he did not. I wondered to what extent this clash in expectations was occurring, and how confused were mother's identity as a person, as Tommy's mother, and as an explorer of Tommy. I talked about this to the mother, who revealed her feelings of anxiety at this confusion.

Second Interview

Tommy smiled at me straight away. The mother expressed her amazement, because he never smiled. I mentioned that perhaps he was very sensitive to her moods, that perhaps she was happy to be able to share with me her baby's anger, and this created an atmosphere that he perceived. The mother, amazed, said it was true, that he might be sensitive to moods, and that was the difference between them. Mother and father were artists, visually sensitive, but baby's sensitivity could be to moods. She felt quite frightened of him when he awoke in a bad mood. I looked at the baby, who was searching around the room with his eyes; he smiled, and I asked him, "and when did Tommy wake in a bad mood?" Mother said, "during the week, and I find it unbearable on Mondays". I tried my interpretation of the situation in order to observe the reactions. "Daddy goes to work and baby becomes the boss, eh? And perhaps baby likes the idea of being the boss, but on the other hand he might like to be shown that he has a strong mother who can deal with his wishes and needs, his hate and anger." Mother said that she never thought of that possibility. The baby moved down between his mother's legs and sat on the floor, looking at me and smiling. He would make noises with his mouth or bang the legs of the table and laugh, looking for my attention. I moved the chair, and he looked in panic and continued looking around, serious and frightened. I thought that he was showing some fear of losing control of his activity, as he experienced the scratchy noise of the chair moving as something threatening to him. His eyes were the main way of feeling secure, in charge.

Mother had mentioned several times that both parents used their eyes in an artistic way. I observed that Tommy did not seem to find beauty with his eyes but used them as a way of finding inner balance when he was overcome by anxiety and fear. It seemed to me that he was trying to push out—and leave there, away from himself—the discomfort he felt inside. Tommy's quick change of mood, his fast reactions to panic and power to dominate the adults around him, were transmitting to me a certain fear of being confronted with his own anger, on a person-to-person level. He gave the impression of having the need to change moods, being able to escape in that way onto safer ground where tolerance could restart and anger be delayed again.

I gave him a teddy-bear to watch his reactions, and he bit it, pulled it, hit it, and laughed. We laughed too. I mentioned that he seemed to like showing his anger without danger of destroying. Tommy wanted to sit on the table; mother was frightened, but she helped Tommy, who then lay on his tummy on the table and pushed himself forwards with his arms. By lifting his head, he could still keep control of what was happening around him. The mother said it was amazing—he never smiled, stayed on his tummy, or touched a teddy. What did I do? I said I thought that the two of them seemed to be different personalities. Tommy seemed to me a strong-minded boy with a weak capacity to tolerate frustration. He was protecting himself from his own annoyance—which upset him greatly—by expelling it into mother, sometimes making her feel uneasy, or onto his body, by causing more than expected physical concerns—for example, crying, burping, and so on. If that was acknowledged, channelled, and limited by her understanding, it would help him. He might need to cry, become frantic, and see that that at the end of it the world was not going to fall apart for him or for her.

We arranged to meet once more to see whether she might need further help, and if so, what kind.

Two weeks later

Father, mother, and baby came for the third interview. The father seemed a very pleasant young man, who was very relaxed with the baby in his arms and loving towards Tommy's mother. He had come on this occasion because he had heard some interesting comments about Tommy from his wife. They had put Tommy on his tummy on their bed or on the table for five minutes, then seven minutes, then eight minutes, slowly increasing the time. Mother said that she had learned to go slowly in specific situations, now more aware that these might be frightening to Tommy.

The baby was laughing a lot; I tapped my nails on the table, and he stopped laughing, looked towards the noise, and almost started to cry. I then realized that he might benefit from being spoken to in a very low voice, and he smiled again. So we discovered the over-sensitive hearing of this baby, which, together with the difficulty in coping with anger and frustration, was painful for him. As we were talking quite excitedly, because the parents then linked that information to situations in which he had started screaming, the baby started crying and did so for twenty minutes. We stayed in silence until he had finished, and then he started smiling again and did so until the end of the session. It seemed important to allow this experience to happen, given the parents' lack of experience in tolerating their baby's expressiveness.

Conclusion.   My conclusions were that Tommy might be one of those children who are born with a low level of tolerance of pain, an absence of what they need to cope with immediate discomfort, and a weak personal ability to try things, or take risks, for fear of disintegration. His level of anger seemed to override his good experiences, so he felt full of bad things. He then tended to rid himself of these feelings by manifesting symptoms of illness. He tried in an omnipotent way to control with his eyes what he felt to be out of control—for example, his over-sensitive hearing. He was feeling insecure at present, as if his mark of reference was his mother and not himself. His identity seemed to be blurred, and he adhered to his mother's person rather than to a mental representation of her and some idea of himself—with thumbs and feet, with teddy-bears to soothe him, and so on.

Mother said that both her ability and her husband's to tolerate Tommy's crying were very important to her. It seemed to me that I was standing in for her adult self, which can stand anger and discriminate between her personal troubles and those of the child. My recommendation was for mother to continue trying to find Tommy's individuality and to strengthen it. Mother asked me if I would help her in that process, and I saw her twice more, where I actively intervened in helping her to acknowledge her feelings and those of her baby. We were careful always to speak very softly.

In a follow-up session four years later, Tommy had started to learn to play the violin successfully, showing a good ear for music.

Discussion.   In the process of assessment of the psychology of this infant, several levels were unfolded in each interview, leaving material for research into his potential, such as his intellectual capacities.

I explored the emotional interaction that I felt might help in the understanding of Tommy's unhappiness and continual angry moods. These really seemed to belong to the strength of his aggressive tendencies, which made the mother unable to understand him, even though she was responsive enough to do so.

CASE 11: SARAH, AGE 4 MONTHS

Sarah's mother, a chronic depressive, did not feed or clothe Sarah properly. Every caring agency was concerned. The mother did not attend clinic appointments or take her medications regularly. She complained that nobody cared about her; "they" wanted to take her children away, even though she said she could manage. She could not understand why people were concerned about her baby—she knew how to bring up her children, as she had done it with her eight siblings. She was just tired all the time.

First, we discussed her hate and anger at having to look after her siblings, and towards her mother for being a drunk and gambler; also, her hate towards me for providing fortnightly interviews that focused on her daughter and not on her. She showed some understanding of her resentment at her past deprivation and need to be properly mothered, thus allowing her wish to do something more positive for herself and her daughter in the present to become operative. This assessment took five interviews, which she attended, and she duly followed my recommendations.

I was asked by the paediatrician to help Sarah's mother to relate to her baby. Mother was an endearing 26-year-old woman, married, with a 3-year-old son. Sarah was underweight and not responsive when mother talked to her or changed her, but she did pay attention to my voice and my eyes and face. Sarah's body did not show much vitality, nor did her movements. She was never in the mother's arms or on her lap—always in the buggy or being changed on the table.

At the first interview, mother talked about her previous experiences of depression and her despair that, having brought up eight of her brothers and sisters, she could now not bring up her own daughter. Her depression kept her in bed for days, and her daughter was fed with a bottle. At that moment, she handed the bottle to her daughter: the baby could not hold it properly, and it fell. I was suffering in silence, as I wanted to observe their relationship in a non-judgemental way. The baby complained, and the mother rocked the buggy. The baby continued to complain faintly and then fell asleep. Mother lifted the bottle from the floor and left it by Sarah's side. The baby awoke and moaned, as the bottle was too far from her reach, near her legs. Mother rocked the buggy; the baby's moaning remained faint.

Mother talked about her sad adolescence and the breakdown she had suffered when she was 19; she had had a second breakdown after her son was born. At the time of this consultation, she was on medication but was not taking her tablets regularly because they were not good; I read her file and saw the name of the psychiatrist, and I asked for her permission to contact him.

I had the impression that she was giving me her pathological background in order to enable me to help her internally to come out of it. I thought that I had to work with the strength left in her ego, to engage in personal work, and I wanted to see what she would do with my help.

I learned that even though she had been a patient of this psychiatrist for seven years, she never attended follow-up appointments or remembered to take medication. A psychiatric nurse was allocated to visit her at home but was never allowed in, or mother did not answer the doorbell.

Second interview

They were on time, waiting for me. The mother came eagerly and talked positively about my calming influence on her. I felt she was calming me and stopping me from worrying about Sarah. I felt it was important not to lose sight of Sarah. I wanted to continue assessing her. Mother put her baby self in front of me all the time instead, actively requesting my attention for herself. She seemed desperate to find a responsive mother. She told me her own mother was a drunk who played bingo daily. Baby Sarah was less lively in her way of communicating her needs. She looked so pathetic and helpless, and she did not move in her buggy; even though she was a month older than in the previous interview, she appeared very small and crouched.

I tried to describe how I saw the baby, and I sat with mother on the carpet. Mother insisted on seeing me more often and acknowledged her tremendous need for my daily and constant support and the anger aroused in her and feelings of frustration that she had had to wait for a fortnight to see me. The mother was not interested in the baby—she wanted to get better without tablets, but she did not have the energy. I told her that we were going to look into this matter and asked if she would attend the next appointment with the psychiatrist.

The health visitor was very worried about Sarah and telephoned me; the baby was losing weight and she was also worried about her emotional development.

Third interview

The baby came, with almost no warm clothing on a very cold winter day. The interview was a month late, as the mother had cancelled the previous fortnightly appointment because she had flu. I felt overwhelmed and worried. I had heard from the psychiatrist that she had failed to keep her appointment with him, and the baby looked in such a pitiful state. The health visitor was right to be concerned. I spoke to mother about the feelings of concern felt by the professionals involved with her, and of my awareness of the immense despair they felt. She had nice, caring people concerned about her—what could we do?

I felt also that the baby did not have enough mothering but still had potentially good possibilities. I started to pick Sarah up to see whether she would react, and slowly she did. She made eye contact with me, and her body stiffened.

The illness of the mother was so deep-rooted that it was difficult to help Sarah to develop—but they were still together and alive, and there was a bond that somehow was important to maintain. In a case conference I put forward my recommendation (checked with the health visitor and with the sister from the day unit) that the mother should attend the day unit, and if medication was necessary, she should be given it at the day unit, and that baby Sarah should have an experienced childminder. Both needed basic mothering care; in the absence of a mother/baby unit, something similar might be a possible solution. I advised on the importance of the link between mother and baby when baby went home. Two hours every day over a cup of tea, the childminder would tell mother all about what baby had done that day, and the responsibility would be handed to the father when he came home, who would check on the safety and feeding situation while he was there.

My intervention thereafter was as consultant through the childminder and the health visitor.

Follow-up at six-monthly intervals over the next two and a half years showed Sarah developing well in all areas—sensorimotor, affective and cognitive, social—except eye-to-eye contact with mother, which in this case is understandable, given the time it took for the establishment of a good home situation.

Discussion.   I took longer to assess this child because the mother tried to convince herself and me that she had the strength to use psychotherapy. The overwhelming nature of her psychopathology made me lose sight of the deteriorating state of the baby, who was helplessly becoming a passive sufferer of the depression and in danger not only of not developing emotionally and of becoming very disturbed or disabled but of dying of cold and hunger.

I felt that the baby's response to me expressed some hope that the problem could be tackled if only the system was prepared to support it. The health visitor found an unusually caring childminder, who would phone me and discuss the baby, setting limits, when and how, and so forth, and the sister in the day unit was equally caring, supporting, and unobtrusive, allowing mother to develop internally.

CASE 12: JANET, AGE 5 DAYS

Baby Janet was referred by the sister at the hospital because although she had been born normally and sucked happily from the breast soon after birth, she suddenly stopped feeding, refusing any food at all. She was losing weight, and on examination it was found that there was nothing physically wrong. She was going to be put on a drip as she was such a small baby. The message then became urgent—how do you find out what is wrong with a newborn baby?

I accepted the referral: the mother came without the baby, and I felt that she was indicating to me that she had the problem and not the baby. She was interested to know what nationality I was, as if she were trying to find out whether or not I could understand her. I wanted to hear her problems, and I let her know that I did. I then realized that my intellectual wish was interfering with the trans-mission of the state of the mother's internal paralysis. I was also emotionally paralysed, trying to hold on to an intellectual position. I mentioned the difficulty in knowing what was happening and that perhaps the baby should be brought in. She agreed, and the baby was brought into the room with her eyes half open and expressionless. The baby was lying flat, with none of the typical movements. I looked at the baby, and a thought spontaneously occurred to me: "What a sexy face!" I tried the mother's reaction by mentioning this thought to her, from which time the whole inter-view changed in quality. The mother allowed herself to express her strong sexual feelings when breastfeeding, to think about her fears and anxieties, and to express her anger about the situation as a Muslim woman and her forbidden wishes.

We now turned to Janet, who was lying there in a lethargic way, not interested any longer in her mother, who I now knew had reacted to feeding her new baby in such an intensely sexual and angry way. The baby seemed unable to smell, hear, or feel hunger. I wondered if the experience of satisfying these inner needs with mother had been experienced as an electric shock, which had left her motion-less, without wish or need. I could see no signs in her of sucking rhythms, quality of movement, sleep attitude—nothing. Fear was in the air. I said to mother that I wanted her to feed the baby in front of me, even though she felt it to be frightening. After an initial refusal, the feeding took place, and the vicious circle was broken: the mother recognized the need to be honest with herself about her feelings, and she recognized the vulnerability of her daughter, who felt overwhelmed not only by her encounter with the world but by such an angry unconscious reaction from her mother.

Discussion.   It is possible to see in all its strength the state of paralysis that instinctual forces, unable to find expression, can create in a child whose mother is unable to respond and contain them, perhaps—as in this case—because of a personal difficulty in dealing with her sexuality. The child seemed to be invaded with the raw state of her own needs, and tension built up with no possibility of resolution in the outside world. The increase of the different needs at the same time (hunger, to be held, warmth, and positive reactions with mother) at such an early stage, and the negation by the mother, who was unable to receive or gratify these needs, had made Janet's primitive ego unable to cope and to give up. There was nothing outside her in which she was interested, nothing that could calm her. The fact that the mother could satisfactorily restart her relationship with Janet showed the baby's determination to hold on to her mother for gratification as the object she had expected, that she wanted, and that had shocked her enough to mistrust any substitute.

CASE 13: JOHN, AGE 4 WEEKS

John was referred by the health visitor because of "lack of bonding between mother and baby". He was the third child in the family. The two older children were girls, and the mother had had no difficulty with them.

During the observation in the first interview, John presented himself as unresponsive to noises, changes of light, hunger, voices, bell ringing, the mother's proximity, or physiological needs of physical discomfort. His sleeping states seemed to show no differentiation: it appeared to be light sleep all the time, without any expression on his face. His whole body seemed to lack any holding or reflex activity. He appeared to be like a rag-doll or a sack of potatoes. He had been seen by the paediatrician when in hospital, and nothing was found wrong physically except weak reflex responses, which became weaker, until there were none. The mother was losing interest.

I observed also that mother had the capacity to respond emotionally to her other children and that her concern for the baby was almost rational. I felt the sadness. The surprise and bewilderment caused by this situation was striking. I felt the despair and bewilderment when faced by this unresponsive baby. I felt unwanted, and anger began to take the form of wishing to withdraw from the case. The baby seemed to be wrapped in his own state of self-contentment or self-nothingness. Could John be reached?

I tried first to see whether mother, or any other member of the family, had tried to achieve responses from John. The parents seemed to expect a baby who responded, as had their first two. I wondered whether this baby was providing the family need for a doll.

Discussing the mother's past experiences, her childhood, her relationship with her own mother, and her present marital and personal situation did not seem to help in understanding the situation.

In the second interview, the father was present (as were both daughters) and was clearly worried, but no different behaviour was shown towards the baby. On this occasion, the mother was showing, and transmitting, a wish to be helped. She sounded desperate. I decided to pick the baby up and try to reach him through his body or his senses to see which one might be operating and how long it would be necessary. He opened his eyes after about ten minutes of my gentle touching of his hands and cheeks and talking to him.

I felt, in the meantime, that he was there and reachable if only I knew the way. I found myself thinking that I needed patience and determination. I felt hope in the parents, and I feared to let them down. I proceeded in my interaction with the infant. Once the baby opened his eyes, I felt that the process of communication could start. I believe in the power of the eyes to connect with the outside world, coming out of the enclosed walls. From there on the process continued, observing how much longer he needed to maintain the connection, to put affection in it, to expect responses, to use it to orient himself in a situation. It was important to see whether he became interested in the connection by being and becoming stimulated. I felt I needed to use all my skills, sensitivity, and knowledge and an enormous amount of patience to encapsulate and continue the enriching communication process that had started.

Once the eyes, mouth, and body were engaged with me (which took about forty minutes), I thought it was important to continue with the mother in the enriching of his experience.

I took the eldest daughter first as a bridge to connect with the mother. I asked her to tell John about her school. When the turn came for the mother to hold the baby, I had to help her by sitting behind her and stimulating the baby by touching his feet and hands and talking about the new experience.

When I came back a week later, the mother talked about overwhelming feelings of death and loss when breastfeeding. I commented that talking about it might help her to communicate with the baby, who might be transmitting to her his difficulty in having left her womb.

The intervention was designed to help the mother know John's individuality and to discuss with the mother her feelings and ideas that overwhelmed her, either by awaking in her the baby's transmissions of his discomforts and primitive reactions or by the wish to explore further her own feelings.

Discussion. I realized that this baby needed to be reached actively, in an exploratory way and persistently, and then to be kept attentive and stimulated more than did other month-old babies. Even when he was holding on to me, I had the feeling that it was necessary to be active in reaching him. I talked aloud about this in order that mother would hear that this was a peculiarity of her baby and that she would have to treat him specially and not feel discouraged if she was not stimulated by John.

Usually babies have brief periods of attention seeking or showing boredom. This was not in John's nature. It seemed as if he was weak in his connecting attempts, and it represented too much effort. But obviously the continuous stimulation would engage him. It seemed important for the sadness of having lost the womb to be worked through with his mother, who was feeling it but was unable to deal with it actively with John, given the passive resistance he was presenting. The assessment consisted in describing how the baby was reacting and to what, and his peculiar way of reacting to his family. The content of the conversations I had with his mother seemed to make John more lively. I had the impression that he was unburdening himself.

CASE 14: FIONA, AGE 9 MONTHS

I will briefly present this case of head banging. The health visitor was concerned because of the continual bruising present on Fiona's forehead. The hospital had already investigated all possible medical causes.

I saw the mother and baby on two occasions for fifty minutes. The child was crawling on the floor quite happily until she wanted to climb out of the window or play with the electric switch; she would then start furiously banging her head. Instead of having a temper tantrum, this little girl had developed the habit of hurting herself. It gave me the impression, following detailed infant observation, that she had learnt to twist inwardly the aggression towards her frustration. The bigger the frustration, the bigger the reaction against herself, making mother and others panic and feel concerned about damage to her head. The compulsion showed some early traumatic experience, which I investigated. Mother explained that Fiona should have been born by Caesarean section, as the delivery had been extremely long and the baby was very bruised.

The continual damage to herself made me feel that I had to devise an interaction in which Fiona could develop her aggression and rage in various other forms. Her intelligence seemed to have been geared towards actively seeking frustrating situations, enjoying the emotional situation she was creating. She appeared to have a determined ego that presented a much more resourceful mind than her mother. It gave me the impression that she did not go through the formal stages of interacting with her mother, probably because of her aggressive nature and tendency to withdraw. I learned that she had been a placid baby for the first three months and never cried; she was breastfed until the age of 5 months, when for no apparent reason she began banging her head. Her tolerance to frustration seemed to have been contained while breastfeeding, although she had been experiencing difficulties already in acknowledging pain or discomfort which seemed to have been quickly put aside, in a severe split that did not progress to an integration in her personal ego. The weaning process revived in her the change from the inter-uterine life to the extra-uterine one. The separation felt then seemed to have become unbearable, as well as the loss of the breast. It was experienced as an insult to her narcissistic inner balance. Since she had no experience of separateness and selfhood, she developed the anger that was then turned against herself in a desperate need to rid herself of it. The mother seemed to be a person who, at the time of the consultation, found difficulty in acknowledging the danger the girl was in because of the head-banging habit, given her placidity in the first three months of life. The health visitor raised the concern and referred her for consultation.

SUMMARY AND CONCLUSIONS

The aim of this presentation has been to systematize the assessment of a disturbed pattern in the development of an infant. This systematization takes the view that there are forces called instincts that are pushing towards living, developing, and progressing and other forces that are pulling backwards towards death and giving up. The systemization is also based on the idea of a rudimentary ego with cognitive and emotional capacities that guide the quality of the development. Even though this assessment stands in its own right, it could be a valuable complement to traditional developmental approaches when there is a need of considering the psychodynamic reasons by which the emotional life has become obstructed or is showing signs of deterioration.

The outcome of the assessment must provide a picture of the structure of the ego, ways of functioning, use of the sensorimotor apparatus, thinking, the emotional apparatus, ways of protecting against pain and fear, and tolerance to frustration.

The prognosis will include an overall picture of resources available if help is found to be needed:

- from the parents or the agency, and what form it will take
- from the infant's potential.

In the case studies presented here, we can see that the design of the intervention or treatment differed considerably, depending on the capacity of the mother to sustain the process of the intervention and the degree of the damage to the infant.

I have tried to screen disturbed emotional functioning from the knowledge and experience of emotional functioning in the normal infant and from serious emotional disturbances in children under age 5 brought to treatment.

CHAPTER FIVE

Diagnosing troubled babies: disorders in infancy

This chapter chronicles the major disorders in infancy. Whereas diagnosis in early childhood has been studied from a medical point of view for some time, we classify disorders on a different basis: the child's personality, for example, or the origin of the trauma, or the regulation of inner and/or outer states, moods, communication, or habits related to sleeping, eating, and crying.

The four classification groups presented here—primary, relational, environmental, and medical—address the child, the parents, their personalities, and the way in which to treat the child. Examples are discussed and presented in order to promote thinking on various degrees of severity.

The classification aims at encouraging reflection in the psychotherapist in relation to possibilities in a distressed young child who has entrenched problems and developmental difficulties. It is of help, therefore, in positioning the "concern" or problem and remaining focused in a skilful way. Rather than leave the young child with a label, the aim is to design assistance around specific individual needs.

The importance of
comprehensive diagnostic procedures

Diagnosis can be described as the process of exploring and analysing all aspects of an infant's life—including the infant's endowment, circumstances, and parents and the quality of its relationship with them and with other people and/or objects—to arrive at an opinion about the infant's actual state and emotional development. A plan is devised for further monitoring or for intervention if needed. If the latter, the most appropriate intervention can then be designed.

It is important, however, for the professional to develop a sense of individual pride in becoming attuned with the family and the infant in order that the diagnosis can combine the art and the science of understanding the emotional, intellectual, motor, and sensory patterns in infancy, so making it possible to see which are the baby's adaptive capacities as well as difficulties in these areas. The diagnosis can then provide the basis for a containing space where doubts and anxieties can be displayed safely and overcome by appropriate action. In these instances, follow-ups will show whether the family and baby still need help, whether doubts about maladaptive or distorted reality were correct and problems indeed have developed, or whether the latter have resolved themselves through normal development.

A diagnosis can also be used in another way: as a magnifying-glass to help bring about optimal development in a particular child. By this I mean that sometimes the child needs an expert eye to discover its latent abilities and encourage its development or to find out about individual needs, which are not necessarily easily seen by the mother, the father, or other people around them.

It is important, therefore, to examine the areas relevant for this task. The classification outlined here fits well with the complexity of the task of assessing an infant's difficulty, given that the individuality of the infant is so strictly bound up with the family and its circumstances, society, and culture.

For use in clinical practice, I refer to four main areas:

- Group 1   Primary: the child
- Group 2   Relational: quality of parenting
- Group 3   Environmental: psychological/social stressors
- Group 4   Medical: illness/disability.

On the basis of these four areas and the categories within them, we have constructed an early intervention matrix (Figure 5.1). This provides parents and professionals with a robust frame of reference once the assessment has been made, allowing the distress to be located in relation to its most probable cause and its manifestation as an occurrence of a particular condition or event. The professional must also hold in mind a third and fourth dimension in the clinical session by assessing the degree of intensity displayed in the presenting behaviour and the strength of its roots in its probable causes. It is this interplay of four factors that makes the diagnostic matrix so robust. By having the matrix in mind during the assessment session and on reflection afterwards, we can follow some landmarks laid down by other professionals and examine the parenting space with confidence and precision, separating the infant's difficulties from the parent's difficulties and medical conditions from the non-medical conditions. Keeping the matrix in mind gives us a classification language allowing us to articulate our observations and conclusions.[1]

GROUP 1
PRIMARY: THE CHILD

Group 1 looks at the cause of the difficulty as being primarily centred in the child. This can be broken down into the following categories:

- traumatic stress disorders
- regulatory disorders
- affect disorders

---

[1] The categories of diagnosis presented in this chapter are based in part on the *Diagnostic Classification of Mental Health and Developmental Disorders of Infancy and Early Childhood*, by Zero to Three: National Center for Infants, Toddlers, and Families (Zero to Three, 1994), and in part on a paper, "Infant Psychopathology: Guidance for Examination, Clinical Groupings, Nosological Propositions", by Kreisler and Cramer (1983).

DIAGNOSIS

GROUP 1: Primary
THE CHILD

Traumatic stress disorders

Regulatory disorders:
> hypersensitivity • underreactivity • motor disorganization/impulsivity

Affect disorders:
> anxiety disorders • mood disorders • labile mood disorder • low-affect disorders • childhood gender-identity disorder

Reactive attachment deprivation/maltreatment disorders

Adjustment disorders

Sleep disorders:
> awakes several times • sleeps too much • awakes and wants to play or feed • does not want to go to sleep • lacks consistency in sleep pattern • sleeps with parents • exhibits extreme tempers at night • reacts to environmental stress • Sleeps on schedule different from parents'

Feeding disorders:
> feeding disorder of homoeostasis • feeding disorder of culture • feeding disorder of attachment • feeding disorder of separation and individuation • selective food refusal • feeding disorder of continuation • overeating • pica disorder • rumination disorder • post-traumatic feeding disorders

Crying disorders:
> crying at night • excessive crying during the day and no smiling • crying because of physical disability • crying as a response to family tension

Relational and communication disorders:
> fragile • isolated or islander • ambivalent • rejecting or avoidant • retreat • symbiotic

---

TREATMENT

GROUP 1

Infant psychotherapy

When the problem is mainly in the child, the therapy will aim to understand the child's communication at all levels and help parents to understand them too and be able to act accordingly. The lower in the following list, the more severe the difficulty:

> Developmental crisis
>
> Reactive crisis
>
> Psychosomatic disturbance
>
> Difficulty in integrating experiences:
>> crying excessively and not smiling
>>
>> visual, social, or total withdrawal
>
> Physically damaged at birth or soon after

FIGURE 5.1. Early Intervention Matrix for Diagnosis and Treatment

GROUP 2: *Relational*	GROUP 3: *Environmental*	GROUP 4: *Medical*
QUALITY OF PARENTING	PSYCHOLOGICAL/SOCIAL STRESSORS	ILLNESS/DISABILITY
Over-involvement	War	Special needs from birth or before
Anxious/tense parenting	Post-war	Congenital syndromes
Neglect	Refugees	Damage:
Angry/hostile relationship	Homelessness	neurological
Mixed relationship disorder	Eviction	sensorial deficits
Abuse:	Moving	Other complications:
physical	Bereavement	heart
sexual	Accidents	organs
verbal	Violence	malformation

GROUP 2	GROUP 3	GROUP 4
Infant–parent psychotherapy	**Infant–parent psychotherapy**	**Infant–parent psychotherapy (special)**
Depending on the degree of difficulty, insight, and concern:	As for Group 2, but with particular emphasis on crisis intervention	Help parents to understand their feelings about their damaged child and to understand the child's inner world, as early as birth, and the unique challenges the child faces
Crisis intervention		
Brief insightful work		
Paediatric support:		
feeding disorders		
disturbed mother		
Network support:		
psychiatric disorders		
Home visit:		
high risk		
insight		

- reactive attachment deprivation/maltreatment disorders
- adjustment disorders
- sleep disorders
- feeding disorders
- crying disorders
- relational and communication disorders.

Analysis of over 3,500 infant–parent consultations at our clinics (private and NHS) identified the most common disorders in infancy as sleep disorders (60%), feeding disorders (20%), and excessive crying disorders (10%). The remaining 10% was spread among the rest of the disorders listed above.

Traumatic stress disorders

The symptoms of traumatic stress disorder surface after the experience of a single event, or a series of traumatic events, or chronic, enduring stress. The trauma may involve the actual threat of death or threat to the psychological or physical integrity of the child or to others known to the child. Included in this category are children who have been abused physically, sexually, or psychologically or who have felt mal-treated. Legal cases involving parents who have been abusive previously, and children who have an accidental or non-accidental injury, show children who are unable to sleep properly, experience continuous flashbacks, regress to previous stages of development, and develop unrelated aggression. This disorder becomes aggravated by long legal trials or uncertainty about their outcome.

CASE 15: AMELIA, AGE 3 YEARS

The youngest of three children, Amelia saw her father being stabbed to death by her mother. The mother went to prison for a while before the trial, and the children were temporarily put into foster care. Amelia was able to tell a story about the argument and the stabbing, which she had witnessed while the other children were sleeping. She had been awoken by the sounds of a fight, left her bed, and through the open door had seen the attack. The mother was freed after the trial, and Amelia began to tell another story in which the father had disappeared and the mother had done nothing. A year later, Amelia had serious sleeping difficulties, flashbacks, crying outbursts, and the need to review the different versions in which she had usually been awake or had woken up and seen her mother being battered by an alcoholic husband and then finally witnessing the stabbing and losing her mother and so being forced to change her memories.

Amelia never fully recovered, even after psychotherapy. She became easily frightened and had a serious tendency to withdraw. The mother then formed a relationship with another violent man but saw nothing wrong with this; in fact, she did not want to talk about the incident of the killing, and she had certainly convinced herself she had not done it.

CASE 16: SHAWN, AGE 4 YEARS

Shawn was referred by a solicitor involved in an accident-injuries claim, because he was biting his mother as well as everybody in the nursery. Two years before this event, he was seated in the back seat of the family car, being driven by his father, when another car crashed into the right side of their car, badly injuring his father, who was trapped in the car, screaming. Shawn's nightmares and day games compulsively reproduced the accident, with no space for him to grow into other areas of his mind, relationships, and experiences. This was still the case two years later. The recommendation was to work with the child on the traumatic event both individually and with his family. The child could then reproduce in his therapy the incident and the feelings around it, making conscious the chain of sudden events and allowing him to react to this, in all the different ways that he imagined. In this way, he was bringing into consciousness various aspects of his feelings towards his father and his mother that were occurring as part of his otherwise normal development. Bringing to the fore the trauma experienced, coupled with his capacity to react and to integrate all of these events with the feelings related to his parents and stage of development, allowed Shawn to calm his uncontrolled aggression and proceed with his development along more normal lines.

(Parents who are involved in a legal case for damages may not realize that the protracted proceedings inevitably involved in claims for compensation reinforce a disorder rather than help it. It is therefore in the best interests of the child and the family to get

therapeutic help as soon as possible, in order to avoid the secondary consequences related to aggressiveness.)

It is important to differentiate traumatic stress disorders from the
next category of anxiety disorders—regulatory disorders—because the
former are focused on the events that generate them, whereas the latter
are inherent in the child.

Regulatory disorders

Under the category of regulatory disorders come babies who find it
difficult to regulate experiences because of:

—a physical sensitivity

—a physiological state (e.g. irritability, irregular breathing, difficulty in concentrating for any length of time)

—gross or fine motor disorganization

—difficult physiological patterns (e.g. sleeping, eating, defecating)

—behaviour organization

—extreme affects

There is growing evidence that constitutional and early maturational
patterns contribute to difficulties in infants. An integral feature of early
intervention is that it is based on a detailed assessment of the uniquely
individual integrative patterns of the infant, as well as its physiological, sensory, and motor make-up.

Regulatory disorders can be divided into: (1) hypersensitivity (fearful and cautious infants, or oppositional and defiant infants); (2)
underreactivity; and (3) motor disorganization/impulsivity.

Hypersensitivity

Fearful and cautious infants.   These exhibit overreactivity to noises,
touch, or bright lights, and their behaviour is characterized by excessive caution, fear, clinging to mother or father, inhibition from exploring, and dislike of change (e.g. in routines, toys, faces, others). They
show worry or excessive shyness, and their internal world seems to be
formed from persecutory images and lack of trust. Easily distracted,
they show disappointment in most activities in which they engage. The

behaviour seems to be dominated by overreactivity to even minimal stimulus, making them difficult to be understood. They complain readily and transfer the irritability felt to any caregiver or professional involved with them.

CASE 17: TOMMY, AGE 4 MONTHS

Tommy was referred by the health visitor because he never smiled, looked at his hands all the time, banged his head, and cried constantly. The parents were concerned about his unhappiness and his not wanting to be in their arms, nor anyone else's. After assessment of the parents, who introduced themselves as artists working at home, with a nice normal background, Tommy demonstrated overreactiveness to noises, voices, and changes of light, body position, and people around him. He would startle easily and cry, looking suspicious. By exploring and discussing with them the timing with which actions should take place and how to reach him calmly in a few sessions, the parents and Tommy became able to reach a compromise between his hypersensitivity and their management of it.

Oppositional and defiant infants.   These children show stubbornness and defiant behaviour with their parents, thriving on the negative of whatever is requested. They seem to form their identity around issues that are the opposite or negative. At times they are considered strong personalities; parents tend to give in to them when they are babies and then find it difficult to change them afterwards. Parents feel overwhelmed and exhausted, and their self-esteem suffers as they constantly lose battles with the child. Such parents need to be helped to recover their identity, rescue their values, and develop a firm, separate identity from the child and to maintain it. Unfortunately, these babies seem to be more greedy for attention than other babies, and they manage to get it in their first period of life; naturally, they then want total control of their mother/carer forever thereafter. It is unbearable for them to accept anything less than total control during the period of separation, as well as afterwards. It is important to understand this and to explain it to the parents, but it is also very important to help parents to handle it early in order to avoid becoming slaves to their children and giving their children a false model of society. These children are control freaks in reaction to greed or, in other cases, to assault on their identity because of an unpredictable or uncaring early environment. They may fear losing themselves if they give in.

CASE 18: ILONIA, AGE 4 MONTHS

From birth, Ilonia was eating non-stop. By age 2 years and 3 months she was very fat and defiant and would scream easily if she didn't get what she wanted or in competition with her sibling. Her need to control her mother was extreme, and this had to be worked out in several sessions with her mother. It was necessary to explain to them how Ilonia had picked up her mother's vulnerability (the maternal grandmother had recently died) and felt the need to keep the mother around by feeding constantly and being oppositional.

Underreactivity

Babies who are underreactive are in a lethargic state most of the time, or it takes a long time before their need for change is acknowledged. Although the cause could stem from an undiagnosed physical disability—such as hearing or sight deficit—there might also be other mysterious sensibilities that need to be explored, or an already-quiet baby may not be being stimulated enough in a busy household. The difference between these children and those with low-affect disorder (discussed below) is that children who are underreactive have a basic lack of reactions and their normal state is lethargic, whereas in those with low-affect disorder the level of affects is constantly low and is there all the time.

CASE 19: JOHN, AGE 4 WEEKS

John is an example of a child with underreactive behaviour. Referred by the health visitor, he was third in a family of children all under the age of 5 years, and from the age of 15 days he slept all day long. In the home visit, he was unresponsive to the whole family, and it took forty-five minutes to awake and interest him with faces and conversation. His mother needed help to be with this underreactive baby and to learn techniques of stimulation. At the same time, she needed three months of psychotherapy to overcome her already established pattern of negative thinking and blame towards him.

As the case of John indicates, parents need help in finding a specific way of contacting these babies to help them to join society as early as possible, in order not to miss out on social, emotional, and cognitive stimulation.

Motor disorganization/impulsivity

Babies who exhibit motor disorganization/impulsivity appear to be craving sensory stimulus while, at the same time, their motor behaviour seems reckless. Some professionals call them hyperactive, attention-seeking, and so on. If such behaviour is not linked to a physical disability, it is very important for professionals to encourage parents to help the baby from the time this behaviour presents itself. One early sign is the difficulty the baby has in concentrating on an action, or in paying attention for a period of time when spoken to. This can show clearly even at the age of 1 month. Treatment is focused on helping the child to concentrate, to engage in an activity, and to keep its interest going. The child is helped to receive the attention that it so recklessly searches for, and to keep some knowledge of its identity and way of controlling its actions and thoughts.

CASE 20: THERESA, AGE 6 MONTHS

The mother, Mrs K., complained that Theresa was difficult to comfort and would never pay attention to her when she was talking. The Mrs K. was concerned that Theresa seemed to divide her attention among different interests at the same time: she would touch her mother in a kind of exploratory way, briefly, and look around at an object, move her legs, cry, caress her mother's hair, hold/suck her thumb. A paediatric examination confirmed the general good health of the child. The assessment of general sensitivities did not show a particular area of delicacy. Regulatory patterns were being established with difficulty. On observing her behaviour, it did seem difficult to find a focus in Theresa's behaviour, and the mother's attitude made the psychotherapist explore the mother's point of view and experience, to check whether there were patterns of disturbance in her that were being projected into the child. This was not the case, however. The little girl needed help from the mother to focus on any experience, and for that purpose the mother was asked to hold Theresa's face towards her whenever she spoke to her and follow her distraction in such a way as to remain the focus. It was important to engage Theresa and keep her engaged for a while. It was also important to hold her, touching her legs and arms, helping her to relax when being carried. In this way, Theresa was helped to focus and calm down, and her anxiety diminished gradually through feeling held in the mother's continuous sight and attention. While such behaviour by the mother might be experienced as intrusive by some children, in this particular case it was what was needed to claim Theresa's attention and to help the focusing, holding, and containing of the loose anxiety that Theresa on her own was not able to achieve.

Affect disorders focused on the child's functioning

Affect disorders can be divided into: (1) anxiety disorders; (2) mood disorders (prolonged bereavement and depression, including anaclitic depression and hospitalism); (3) labile mood disorder (chaotic behaviour and oscillating behaviour, happy elated to sad); (4) low-affect disorders; (5) childhood gender-identity disorder.

Anxiety disorders

Anxiety disorders should be considered where there is evidence of *specific or multiple fears* that are excessive for the child's stage of development. These include fears that do not have a precipitating cause and have lasted two weeks or longer. They manifest in small infants in states of agitation, uncontrollable crying or screaming, and eating and sleeping disorders. In general, the child transmits uneasiness to the interviewer, and this needs to be contained and understood.

CASE 21: TOMMY, AGE 4 MONTHS

Tommy was a serious baby who never smiled, cried easily, and wanted to be held continually. His parents were worried. On assessment of his individuality, he seemed to be extremely persecuted by his own greediness and incapacity to be satisfied by his mother. He was feeling continually insecure. His parents were laid-back artists who could not understand his difficulty in smiling. The specific treatment created a plan to help him that took into account the parents' awareness of the difference in needs, character, liking, and way of reacting of the baby. For Tommy to be satisfied and secure, it was necessary to observe him in the sessions to see Tommy's reaction to different changes in his everyday routine and in the relationship with his parents. Various fears appeared: to height; to not being able to see all around him and therefore not wanting to be on his stomach; to unexpected noises, because of auditory over-sensitivity making him jump; and to a "Monday morning" anxiety of the mother on being left alone with him. All these areas were explored together, and ways were sought of calming his anxiety rather than increasing it.

Mood disorders

The main difference between mood disorders and regulatory disorders is that in the latter there is a physical component that needs to be discovered in order to be able to help the child through increasing awareness and care, coupled with the child's ability to overcome the difficulty. In the mood-disorders category, the basic quality of the affects involved primarily requires exploration through attunement, close observation, and development of patience and a thorough understanding of what happens, when, and where, and which tactics will make moods more predictable and therefore easier to deal with.

Prolonged bereavement.   This is related to the loss of a primary caregiver, and, I would add, to the loss of the substitute for the primary caregiver, such as a nanny, *au pair*, childminder, or grandmother. Symptoms include protest, despair, and detachment. The child might insist on trying to find the lost person, show tremendous sadness, and be less active and seemingly detached.

CASE 22: RORY, AGE 1 YEAR

Ever since the *au pair* left, Rory had cried almost continuously, wanting to go constantly to her bedroom, not wanting to eat, and banging his head. Even though it was considered that perhaps the relationship with his mother and father might not have been good enough, it was evident in the general assessment that this was not the case and also that the *au pair*, who had been well incorporated into the family, had left suddenly without much notice. The parents were surprised and hurt; the mother was frantic. It is possible to hypothesize that the baby feared that such sudden disappearance could also happen with other members of the family. Intervention with the whole family took place, helping to reorganize the family. This was followed by work on the parents' mental representations of their family members and their own care when they were children. Rory's grief was acknowledged by greater closeness with his mother and father and other members of the family, and the replacement mother's help spent less time with him, making arrangements such as having the child take a long nap (2–3 hours) in the afternoon and stay awake later (until 9.00 p.m.), so that the mother and father could play with him. The bathing and dinner was already done by that time. It was also considered important to include a teddy-bear as his constant companion, which increased his feelings of constancy and security.

Depression in infancy.   This is a more serious demonstration of the drastic effects of an unresolved mourning, either for a caregiver or for the lack of caregiving. A child may stop relating properly or at all to people around him, or may stop eating or assimilating food or playing, as a consequence of having given up on attempts to recover its lost object.

René Spitz's films, which appeared between 1947 and 1952, and papers on "Anaclitic Depression" (1946) and "Hospitalism" (1945) graphically illustrate this pitiful state in babies, when after three months of personal care their mothers were imprisoned and had to leave them in multiple care in institutions. He talked about *anaclitic depression*, characterized in the first stage by weepy behaviour in contrast to previous happy and outgoing behaviour; after some time, in the second stage, the children's weepiness gave way to withdrawal and lack of interest in the surroundings, including people. Some of these children lost weight, suffered from insomnia, and had frequent colds and eczema. The third stage was frozen rigidity, and the fourth was death.

We have to differentiate anaclitic depression from "hospitalism". Hospitalism was the consequence of children living, from birth, in hospitals or foundling homes, with no first object or mother either to get attached to or to mourn. Again, we see in Spitz's films the devastating effects of a lack of a relationship in human beings, such as failure to thrive, retardation, autistic behaviours, and death.

Spitz began doing his clinical research on the high number of deaths in foundling homes, starting from data recorded by a Spanish bishop in his diary as far back as 1750. Statistics from the beginning of the twentieth century gave, for example, deaths of infants in foundlings homes in Germany as 71% in the first year of life. He also mentions, among others, Charles Chapin, who in 1915 said that in the United States, 31.5% died in the first year and 71% by the second year; another researcher, a Dr Knox in Baltimore, found that 90% died in the first year, and the 10% who survived did so because they were removed from the hospital; and other professionals, who reported that even though statistics had improved by 1947 and more children were surviving, these children were terribly damaged physically and were mentally beyond repair.

Sadly, even in this new millennium, we have orphanages in Russia, Bosnia, Romania, China, Bolivia, and many more countries, where it is still possible to find such disturbing conditions. Furthermore, in developed countries, cases of failure to thrive remind me of hospitalism, whereby babies do have mothers but they are felt as absent from the beginning. In some cases of postnatal depression, infants will produce a milder reaction, but still problematic, in which they become depressed and, in a few cases, retardation sets in, as has been studied in Cambridge by Lynne Murray and colleagues (Cooper, Murray, Wilson, & Romaniuk, 2003; Murray, Cooper, Wilson, & Romaniuk, 2003).

In this mood disorder, children can usually be described by their developmental quotient as delayed, with plastic expressions, grimaces instead of smiles, undifferentiated social contact if any, and lack of muscle tone. These babies and mothers respond very quickly to appropriate psychodynamic intervention if treated jointly as soon as possible, not leaving it beyond 6 months of age.

Labile mood disorder

Chaotic behaviour.   Here it is possible to think about chaotic behaviour *by children of chaotic parents,* in which it is difficult to find out what the mode of responding for the infant is because the infant switches from one kind of response to another. Parents sometimes find it annoying, feeling that they are "no good" or do not know what the child likes or dislikes.

These children have a history of different caretakers or sometimes of mothers with bipolar disorders or drug addiction. It is difficult to help them within the family because the mothers also suffer deep disturbances that need a system or network that would help as well as motivate the mother.

CASE 23: VALERIE, AGE 8 MONTHS

Valerie came to the consultation because the mother was anxious about not getting the right answer. She had two other children, apparently without problems. The baby had been irritable from birth, and the mother, Mrs G., found her more difficult to deal with than the other children. Valerie often seemed to be in different moods, but the other two children had "adapted" to her mothering, which she described as generally caring.

She could not remember the pregnancy and birth of the baby, and she seemed to rely totally on external clues for remembering—for example, if a child cried, she would feed or change it, otherwise she assumed the children were all right. However, because Valerie sometimes did not cry at all, she was not fed or changed. At times she would cry and protest even when she had been changed several times and fed in the same way. The lack of connectedness of the mother had not helped Valerie to learn a reliable system of communication. In one session, for no particular reason or in response to a specific activity of mine, Valerie would smile at me all the time. At other interviews she would constantly change behaviours as if she were testing something; or it seemed that a mood overcame Valerie and she would go along with it. At yet another interview, she would be serious, and nothing would take her out of her low mood. This state could last for the whole session and be maintained sternly, or it could change suddenly. The moods would oscillate between Valerie being overly nice and smiley to drastically low and inattentive.

Treatment was lengthy because the *mother had urgently to deal with her own until-then undiagnosed bipolar tendencies and moods*. The baby was, in effect, moulding herself in the image of a mother with an undiagnosed serious mental disorder. The other two children received more care from the husband, who managed to provide a steady pattern of behaviour that helped these children to respond and behave in a predictable way. These children most probably also did not have a labile mood.

Oscillating behaviour.   This relates to babies who present a tendency from early on to oscillate in the mood of their behaviour with parents who are stable, well-adjusted, and caring.

CASE 24: SKY, AGE 2½ YEARS

Sky was brought to the consultation because her parents were totally disconcerted about how to handle her moods and feared her when she was in a negative one. Three months before the consultation, a baby sister had been born, and their concern was related to the effects of Sky's moods on her behaviour towards the baby.

From 3 months of age, Sky would exert her character by stiffening her body if she did not want to be held or fed or go in the car, and she would scream non-stop at night. Her birth had been wonderful, in water in a private hospital; she was breastfed and established a three-hour feeding cycle quite quickly. However, there were days when the parents—mainly the mother—would find it difficult to get Sky to do anything; she would end up in tears, giving in to the obstinate, contrary behaviour of the baby. There were other days when the baby would be amiable and do anything requested and be smiley all the time, and extremely active.

When Sky grew into a toddler, her moods continued to influence her activity. She would get overexcited, laugh, and do things that were obnoxious, but her parents did not know whether to laugh at them or punish her. The actions included pulling off a whole roll of toilet paper, dirtying walls, tugging at curtains, pushing furniture around in a compulsive way, or singing loudly. When Sky was over 2 years of age, she spoke in such a rapid way that it was not possible to understand her. When her baby sister was born, she was 2½ years old and regarded the mother as a traitor. Sky had become extremely angry with the mother and totally involved with father. She would either kiss the baby non-stop, or push her around in a hurting way, and it would be imposible to stop her, or she would ignore the baby totally and talk and behave as if she did not hear or see her.

Treating Sky involved having both the parents and the infant present at the sessions, to see the dynamic in operation. I worked with the parents on the mental representation that they had of Sky and of important relatives who influenced them, and I studied the individuality of the girl. The mother also had a few sessions by herself to support the structure of the plan to help Sky and herself by acting consistently in spite of the mood changes of the girl.

Cases like this, which we also discuss later, could be confused with regulatory disorders. However, the swings in mood seem to be more profound, last longer, and are more difficult to switch than swings in affective states owing to difficulty in adapting to the external world or to the parent.

Treatment should follow these mood changes to find the causes and triggers that halt flights into non-stop activity that are mischievous and nonsensical, or the opposite—to find out the stimulus necessary to cheer the child up or to make the child feel content rather than guilty or persecuted.

Low-affect disorder

There are infants who show very little affect and also have difficulties in communication, even though in some cases aimless communication exists. However, this communication is felt by the parents and the interviewer as inexpressive or uninterested in affectionate returns. These cases are difficult to identify because a lot depends on the parents' background and culture. Families who are more expressive will experience low intensity in emotional reactions as difficult and will want to find out how to stimulate fun and relatedness to their level. Whether these tendencies are related to organic difficulties or to other traits in the personality, it is important to explore in each child the origin of this low emotional tonicity and see how it can be helped, both from the child's point of view and from the mother's. This includes observation of the mental representations in the parents and the child related to their expectations and realities. Afterwards, the parents have to be encouraged to accept the characteristics of their child and relate to what their child is, without resentment.

Childhood gender-identity disorder

Childhood gender-identity disorder entails disturbances in the acceptance of gender between ages 2 and 4 years. A change in gender is not only desired but manifested continually. This includes insisting on dressing as the opposite sex, selection of friends, play in fantasy always as the other gender, and so forth.

CASE 25: LORETTA, AGE 26 MONTHS

Loretta was brought to consultation because she did not want to wear skirts, only trousers, and would have a huge temper tantrum if she were forced into a dress or skirt. Loretta was one of twin girls, and the mother wished to know why her behaviour persisted. The mother and daughter came to the consultation without the father, who made a separate appointment; he did not agree with her on parenting issues, and, because the couple were divorcing, he did not want to criticize her in front of her.

Loretta was not as pretty as the other twin, and she seemed to want to attract attention in the interview by being rough, untidy, and moving constantly. She played with cars and a ball, totally uninterested in dolls or teddy-bears, in marked contrast to her twin and to the mother. Loretta's behaviour seemed to have been constructed in opposition to the sister and the mother, and/or in total identification with the father, as a lost figure that she wanted to keep present and around. It was timely that the mother consulted, since Loretta was engaged in an angry fight with her mother, whom she experienced as rejecting towards her father, at a stage when she had a great affinity with the father.

The treatment had to include the father and Loretta as well as mother and child separately. It was important to respect the parents' needs to have their different thoughts about the child not interfered with because of the ending of their marriage and the discord between themselves. The psychotherapist put into perspective Loretta's ongoing identification with the father in her view (projection of her ideal father) of him. Loretta felt partly that she identified with the mother in her criticism of the father, and she created a male model in the household which included her wish to be more active than what she perceived as "females" in the house, and partly that she would like to have a father liked by her mother.

The few sessions included the mother's reappraisal of what Loretta had been doing and for whom. It was evident that Loretta sensed that her mother felt more identified with, and therefore found it easier to understand, her twin sister. In Loretta's mind, she was trying to create and become the male role that she believed her mother had in mind, linked with Loretta's own phantasies about her ideal father. When the mother understood Loretta's mechanisms, she stopped being angry at the girl being so contrary about family life and tried to create a different relationship where both mourned the ideal male. The mother could help Loretta to develop her individuality in her own right and accept that the father is away and emotionally unavailable. The father understood that the end of the family was not the end of his relationship with each twin and that the best arrangement was for both parents to have time alone with each twin, to know them better and differently.

Loretta continued her preference for trousers, but she would accept wearing a dress for formal functions. The level of her activity, manners, and way of speaking changed radically, and Loretta became a thoughtful and expressive little girl.

CASE 26: JONATHAN, AGE 1½ YEARS

Jonathan surprised his parents when, at age 1½ years, he started to play with his sister's dolls, catering for them in a "motherly" way, and this continued for six months without stop. He did not like his "boys' toys", such as cars and trucks, and he even started to dress regularly as a girl. The anxiety that this created in the parents had to be explored, since the father had been an unhappy homosexual in his adolescent years, and only after a few years of therapy was he able to develop his heterosexuality satisfactorily. Jonathan had originally had a twin, but his twin sister was aborted.

Watching Jonathan's play, it was remarkable how it was centred on holding the doll, putting it in the pushchair and back in his arms. When asked about his loving and caring attitudes about his baby dolls, he demonstrated rage, anger, fear, and panic. This reaction was linked to the "reduction in the womb" of the other twin. The parents believed they could not cope with twins, and the aborted twin had been a girl. Jonathan had sessions on his own, given the level of anxiety awakened in his primitive mind about the reality and parental phantasies related to this foeticide.

Jonathan later ceased to feel imprisoned by guilt that he had survived and did not therefore need to keep repeating compulsively the holding and care of his dead twin.

Reactive attachment deprivation/ maltreatment disorders

Reactive attachment-deprivation/maltreatment disorders are demonstrated in children who are not inclined to attach to the parents but do so with other relevant caregivers. Sometimes they show a clear ambivalent behaviour, and at times they are rejecting and cry when in the presence of parents.

CASE 27: EMMA, AGE 6 MONTHS

Emma only cried when her mother approached, though she would happily stay in the arms of doctors and health visitors who referred her to me. The mother was extremely impatient and would shout and jiggle Emma energetically, showing no attunement with her. Emma remained expressionless or cried. The mother had a drinking problem. While there was no proof of abuse, unfortunately Emma had died of a cot death by the time that the second interview was to have taken place.

CASE 28: SILVINA, AGE 6 MONTHS

Silvina was continually crying and failing to thrive. She was very content in the arms of everyone except her mother, giving clues of possible maternal maltreatment. The mother, Mrs D., the youngest in a wealthy family, had a mild mental disability and was partially blind. Mrs D. did not want help from her own mother. Social Services put her in a hostel for mothers and babies, for observation purposes. Assessment of Silvina's needs demonstrated that Mrs D. did not cater for her crying, holding, and feeding needs. Social Services then placed Silvina in foster care for two months, until Mrs D. agreed to enter a programme of information and rehabilitation and live in protected social-services accommodation. An intense programme with the mother and the baby was planned: individual psychotherapy for the mother twice a week; infant–parent psychotherapy once a week, with ongoing monitoring and modelling from the staff to be discussed weekly with the infant–parent psychotherapist. Mrs D. was compelled to accept the plan, and, in the first session she began to cry and realized that she had a profound hate for her own mother for making her so limited, ugly, and defective. This was a breakthrough that linked the three generations in feelings of unspoken guilt from the parents, pity and rage from Mrs D., and overwhelming fear from her that Silvina could be defective as well. The individual psychotherapy took a year and half of weekly meetings, continuous monitoring of mother–infant interactions, and mother–infant psychotherapy. The latter was done by a specialist social worker, who was involved in the case at the beginning and wished to continue holding the case.

Adjustment disorder

I consider adjustment disorder to be a *reactive disorder* of another kind. An infant finds it difficult to adjust to a change in the environment or in the parents' routine and shows symptoms such as sleep and feeding difficulties, or persistent crying and lack of enthusiasm or inactivity.

Sometimes the difficulty in the child is due to a new setting that does not favour the child's general development—for example, moving to a flat or house that is too noisy or too quiet. There are anxiety-prone children who like or feel "held" by a busy road and constant noise, or the opposite can be the case. Aurally over-sensitive infants might feel invaded and disturbed by a busy road. All of this is worth investigating.

CASE 29: OLIVER, AGE 4 MONTHS

Oliver started day care with a very nice motherly lady. His parents consulted me because from having been lively and happy, he had changed to having an expressionless face and eyes that did not focus. By the time of the consultation, this behaviour had lasted a month. Observation of Oliver in day care showed a quiet baby who did not emit signals. The childminder was very attentive to the three other little children: a baby and a 1-year-old who were her own, and another 1½-year-old. They all needed attention and wanted to play. Advice given to the childminder about stimulating Oliver to communicate did not make her change. Oliver was moved to another day-care setting where the childminder was a younger person without little children, who observed the parents' culture and tried to act the same way as they in their absence, so helping Oliver and making him (and his parents) happy again.

It is important to act promptly if a drastic change is seen in the child, in order to help normal development to continue. An adjustment disorder in a child that is not sensitively treated may lead to serious difficulties in other areas.

Sleep disorders

Sleep disorders in children are a common way of showing uneasiness or distress. We think about this disorder as being separate or different from the anxiety, mood, adjustment, or regulatory disorders. The child presents disturbance in either falling asleep and/or in sleeping during the night. In some cases, it might be the parents who are the cause or who comply with the child's difficulty, and they always need help, whether the difficulty lies with the child or with them. The child's behaviour with regard to sleeping shows certain tendencies that are worthy of investigation:

- awakes several times

- sleeps too much

- awakes and wants to play or feed

- does not want to go to sleep

- lacks consistency in sleep pattern

- sleeps with parents

- exhibits extreme tempers at night

- reacts to environmental stress

- sleeps on schedule different from parents'.

Awakes several times.   The causes of anxiety could be valid and should be differentiated from anxiety disorders and traumatic stress disorders. It will be a sleep disorder if the quality of the anxiety is related to separation difficulties, or getting around parents and dominating them over sleeping issues. The baby is showing some anxiety with regard to separating from the parents, and the parents find it difficult to evolve with the baby, instead getting involved in rituals and behaviours that are uncomfortable and tiring. Such a tendency in babies may be because of an initial physical irritability and/or physical disabilities, as well as an internal feeling of insecurity. All these need to be explored, since some children learn to act frightened in order to maintain the parents' attention. Such behaviour can be easily identified by the parents. Parents should be helped to explore their own inner difficulties in understanding what it is that is disturbing the growing infant and preventing it from creating a secure pattern of sleep; this should allow them and the baby to separate *and* feel safe. Once parents know what is causing such anxiety, they can help the child to feel more secure through individual solutions—perhaps a quieter bedtime ritual or by introducing "transitional objects" (Winnicott, 1953) like a teddy-bear or other favourite cuddly toy, blanket, or other comforter during the separation from the parents at night.

CASE 30: NICOLE, AGE 1½ YEARS

Nicole would only fall asleep in the arms of one of her parents and would then wake up several times a night, needing the same ritual each time. The parents were taking turns in attending to her. Nicole was born prematurely and cried a great deal in the first two months; she was held in the parents' arms all the time as the only way she could be consoled. She put on weight steadily and carried on with almost the same ritual until she was a 1½ years old. The parents, on the other hand, still saw her as a premature fragile baby, and they feared for her life. Both parents felt guilty about her prematurity, since it occurred after a very nice (and passionate) lovemaking, and deep down they thought that this had led to her premature birth. Partly through guilt and partly through inexperience, the phantasy of fragility and damage did not allow the parents and Nicole to overcome a natural separation through sleep with trust on both sides. Once the possible causes for this night-time ritual and difficulty were explored, parents were capable of changing their routines and trusting that Nicole could cope with the change, which she did. Nicole felt the parents' trust and moved along to a different quality of sleep, internally secure that her parents could be caring and firm about her.

Sleeps too much.   When this occurs, it is important to inquire into the possibility of physical disability. Otherwise, it could be an early indication of difficulty in the child's integration of the external world. Some babies are observed as presenting difficulty in dealing with jealousy; having been born into a busy household, they lack a protective strategy to cope with mother's attentions being elsewhere.

CASE 31: ISKI, AGE 3 MONTHS

An example came from an infant observation in which Iski would fall asleep in the first two months whenever a sibling or the father came into the room and talked to the mother.

Awakes and wants to play or feed.   These babies show a manipulative tendency. It is important to find out what is the reason behind their waking in the middle of the night. There might be a reaction to outside changes, such as the mother starting work, a new birth, a child starting school, death of a relative, and so forth. The parents feel unable to stop the habit. It is necessary to get them involved in thinking about the cause and maintenance of the behaviour, so that they are able to play and talk about it during waking hours and allow the child to sleep through the night with a rested mind and without waking the family.

CASE 32: SAMUEL, AGE 7 MONTHS

Samuel would awake around midnight and play, laugh, and be adorable; his parents would take turns in attending to him. Samuel was not so adorable during the day; and his parents felt that his behaviour was irritating, but they did not wish to interfere with his "needs". The story that unfolded was that the parents came from different cultures, religions, and classes, and their fear about the child not growing up properly was due to their internal rivalry about which way was best. The parental couple never realized until they had Samuel how much they wanted him to be like them individually, and, in their wish to do the best for him, he was getting away with his attention-seeking behaviours at night.

Does not want to go to sleep.   These babies show a tendency to be contrary. This behaviour goes along with refusing to eat when food is offered and a general liking of doing what they want when they want, as if they need to assert their personality. If this behaviour perturbs parents or continues, the reasons (whether seen as a baby or a parent power struggle or simply inconvenience) need to be found. Some parents think they know what is best for their child but act in their own interests, since they might be preoccupied with other problems, or overwhelmed, and the infant feels out of their minds or deprived of individual attention. The baby's individual personality and experience and the parents' responses need to be explored.

Lacks consistency in sleep patterns.   These babies sometimes have a sleep pattern and sometimes not. Generally, with chaotic parents who themselves find it difficult to establish a routine with their child, the child cannot internalize a pattern and responds instead to whatever it feels like rather than having a pattern imposed on it. It is important to speak with parents about the importance of or need for routine and consistency for their child, in spite of their personal arrangements and beliefs. Some parents keep taking their children out late to dinner, or keep them up with them in the evening, but still expect them to understand when they should fall asleep and when they should not!

Sleeps with parents.   In Western societies, sleeping in the parents' bed after the age of 6 months appears as either a symbiotic tendency in both parents and baby, or the child being used in difficulties between the couple.

CASE 33: NICHOLAS, AGE 11 MONTHS

Nicholas was referred by the GP because he slept lightly and shared the bed with the mother, sucking her breasts whenever he wanted. At the first interview he appeared without shoes, held by the mother very tightly, and with his nappy showing, looking very much as though he were a 3-month-old baby. In the course of the interview, the mother disclosed her long, uneven, passionate, and tortuous relationship with the father of the baby, who disappeared when she became pregnant. The baby, however, was sharing continually the blissful relationship that she wished she still had with his father. In this way, the baby was not developing properly, and the mother kept her joy for herself. Three sessions focused on the infant's need and the quality of his personal traits, disclosing his mother's phantasies and her lack of perception of his individuality, helped her to become aware of the depth of her conflicts and seek individual psychotherapy for herself.

Exhibits extreme tempers at night.   This can include vomiting and is a psychosomatic or hysteric tendency. It appears very often as a major obstacle since parents feel frightened by the baby's continual vomiting if he is not attended to at once. As with any other behaviour, parents need to understand the mechanism and the individuality of the child and the child's extreme reactions, then dramatize the behaviour and play with different responses for a few days. The baby is allowed to negotiate and propose changes, and the arena of playing, dramatizing, and talking gets set up. Parents then can endorse the new policy, which may be protested against at first by the child but is accepted soon after. In these rehearsals of actions, the mental representations of behaviours and their malleability in handling them helps the resolution of conflicts in a symbolic way.

Reacts to environmental stress. Sensitive babies at times show sleeping (or eating and crying) difficulties in reaction to tension or even distress in the parents that the parents do not seem to be aware of or lack the energy to think about. These difficulties disappear as soon as an interview is set up and the parents are obliged to talk about their home situation. It is possible then to see from the background story, and through the calm and contained behaviour of the child, that the child is not the problem.

Sleeps on schedule different from parents'. This can be corrected when the rhythms of parents and child are studied and helped to match. Some parents complain that a child's waking hour is 5:00 a.m. (other parents may love it, because they start the day at 6:00 a.m. and they can all have breakfast and chat). Similarly, there are babies who will not sleep before midnight or later. The way to help includes a gradual slow moving of the unwanted timing towards the wanted one and then maintaining this new schedule.

* * *

We can fill all the categories above with many examples. Sleeping disorders constitute 60% of the referrals to our infant–parent clinics. The emphasis of the intervention is on understanding the personality and tendencies of the infant and exploring the parents' difficulty in setting limits and being firm and consistent. Issues of separation for parent and child need to be explored. The creation and use of transitional objects, dramatization, and other distancing techniques are helpful to both parents and infants. We have also successfully practised group psychotherapy work with parents and infants or toddlers with sleeping disorders.

Feeding disorders

The category of feeding disorders covers difficulty in the intake of food, or in establishing certain regular patterns, or in assimilating the food. A feeding disorder creates a relationship disorder that is secondary to the feeding difficulty and relates to basic intimacy and understanding of inner states in the baby and in the mother. Paediatric examination is the first step towards investigating the technicalities of the problem.

Feeding is a basic interaction that should develop into a relationship that is nourishing mentally, physically, and emotionally. The causes of feeding problems may lie in past trauma such as prematurity, prolonged surgical treatment, a fragile make-up in the baby due to unknown vulnerabilities, or unconscious pressures on the mother's mind. In any circumstances such these, a pleasurable, stimulating feeding relationship may fail to develop. The effect can be traumatic, frustrating, or sad, creating situations where monsters suddenly appear: in the eyes of the infant, the mother might have become the different nurses in the premature unit or paediatric wards where intubation and other painful procedures took place. The mother cannot appreciate fully all the distress that the baby has gone through and the mental representations that the baby has formed, and she tries to form a relationship without being aware of these monsters from the past. It is crucial, therefore, in these units or wards that the mother is present, so that she can foster a good relationship from the beginning. As one young mother commented: "I was there as much as I could, every day, holding his little hand—I feared that he was going to take in the nurses' management as his first love relationship, and therefore he wouldn't recognize me as his mother." That is why the continuous presence of the mother in such traumatic circumstances is so important—to ameliorate the effects in the mind of the infant.

In feeding difficulties, as with all other difficulties, we are confronted with observing and exploring the fit between a particular mother and a particular baby. Even though one may hear about previous difficulties of a similar sort in the family, perhaps in the mother or in her previous children, the referred infant needs as much individual attention as the parents because now is the opportunity for resolving the conflict that is causing the infant to suffer.

The baby might have a physiological or physical cause for not being able to swallow food, or for vomiting or not assimilating, or for other symptoms, so a thorough—preferably non-invasive—paediatric examination is imperative.

We also know that a physical symptom can develop as a result of anxiety that has not been contained or understood, and that possibility also has to be investigated.

Feeding is central for development because it:

—provides nourishment for growth;

—satisfies the painful experience of hunger;

—provides an opportunity for creating and developing other pleasant experiences such as affectionate contact and verbal and non-verbal communication with the baby and allows the baby initiative, management of time, negotiation, and so on;

—focuses the baby's attention on exploring and creating new strategies and moods;

—mirrors the baby's mental and physical states;

—provides a basis for attunement to each baby's needs;

—gives the baby, through being held by the mother, the experience (when all goes well) of discomfort changing into comfort and of adaptation to others' needs;

—organizes the different sensations and sets a time-routine for the day;

—secures a space and time for this meeting of bodies and souls;

—helps to lay the foundations for other emotional relationships and developments—neurological, immunological, cognitive, as well as social.

When feeding does not go well, these aspects of behavioural development are in jeopardy. To compensate, the baby has then to acquire such enriching encounters with the mother or carers through other situations in order somehow to develop its emotions. So, babies may be awake more, or may ask to be held more, or may try to play at odd times.

Feeding disorders can be divided according to the age at which they manifest:

In the first three months:
• feeding disorder of homoeostasis
In the first six months:
• feeding disorder of culture
• feeding disorder of attachment
After the first six months:
• feeding disorder of separation and individuation
• selective food refusal
• feeding disorder of continuation
• overeating
• pica disorder
• rumination disorder
• post-traumatic feeding disorders.

Feeding disorder of homoeostasis

Feeding disorder of homoeostasis, described by Chatoor (1989), is a regulatory difficulty in newborn babies and infants, with a contributing factor in the mother. Some babies are born irritable or are difficult to awake for feeding, or they tire or get distracted quickly; mothers may find this situation difficult or may not initially realize that their child is not putting on weight, and they subsequently become anxious or exhausted or guilty, setting up thereby a vicious circle. Some mothers may also have psychiatric illness and exhibit an overall difficulty in reading cues from the infant and in exercising patience.

The disorder manifests itself in the first three months as a difficulty in finding a pattern: these babies do not eat well, or take too long, or they feed either irregularly or too quickly and often. It is important to recommend to the mother early preventative intervention that includes description of the child's difficulty, asking for help from friends or relatives, and letting mother speak about her feelings, leading to awareness of this baby's specific needs. Any work done has to be descriptive of the interaction and understanding of the individuality of the baby.

Feeding disorder of culture

Feeding disorder of culture generally involves vomiting or pushing the food out with the tongue, leading to struggles overeating and to force-feeding. From a study (Acquarone, 2003) of 650 cases of feeding difficulties referred by health visitors and GPs in England, 350 involved foreign mothers whose babies presented feeding difficulties in regard to bringing up or not swallowing the food and pushing it out, so that mothers would enter into force-feeding, or uneven games, from as early as 2 months. These cases presented a conflict of cultures linked with the need of mothers to succeed with their babies while being confronted with the different eating and food habits of the host country. The mothers seemed to feel that they had lost their needed link with their own mothers, land, and culture. Deprived of family and culture, they felt forced to adopt new rules for bringing up their children in a way that was foreign to them. The mothers could not identify with the English culture yet saw their children as becoming English and different.

It is important when this disorder appears early on (i.e. before 3 months) to arrange an allergy test and paediatric examination. If the paediatric examination is satisfactory, there might be a difficulty in the baby in incorporating what is positive and good and in integrating experiences, with a corresponding difficulty in the mother in integrating new feeding habits. This may be related to conflicting advice that some mothers receive about not eating garlic or curry, or alcohol or spicy food, on the grounds that these might affect the breast milk.

Lacking second opinions on the advice received, such mothers might feel inadequate, depressed, or angry about being in a country with such different feeding habits, and they end up feeling confused and anxious.

After age 4 months, the baby and the mother might have established a *mismatch of eating habits*, the baby being slow to feed and the mother being a fast eater, or the *infant feels the food as persecutory* because it is linked with "ghosts" in the mother's mind (Fraiberg, 1980). Of course, it could simply be that *the infant doesn't like the taste* of the puree, or milk, or other food given and the mother does not like these either but does not acknowledge it.

Feeding disorder of attachment

Babies with feeding disorder of attachment (described by Chatoor, 1989, as anorexia nervosa) may or may not eat, but they do not put on weight, being known as "failure to thrive". Such babies seem to have no internal image of mother, and their faces resemble those of the babies suffering from hospitalism in Spitz's films. Either the mother is deeply depressed or she is engrossed in preoccupations that do not include the baby's mind or primitives states. The state reached of not wanting to eat, even early on after birth, indicates a serious difficulty in attachment to the mother and giving up on the external world. When babies eat but do not increase in weight, this might indicate a secret fear or horror of a relationship that, even though it is wanted, is greatly feared. This can happen in situations where the mother is chronically depressed and the father abusive or absent. Onset of this disorder is usually between ages 1 and 6 months (e.g. Janet, Case 12)

In the first three months, the baby may have difficulty in regulating internally and externally with the mother. A lot of emotional distancing occurs, and the baby does not manage to feed properly or enough so as to grow. Such babies might need to regulate their anxiety or might simply wish to explore different kinds of attitudes in the relationship. Some mothers or parents enjoy this exploratory behaviour, while others feel concerned, confused, or on trial. It is important to note the tone of the experience and to observe whether the baby and the parent need confirmation of the state of the other.

Fear and anguish are engendered in professionals by the child who fails to thrive, given the risk of damage to a developing baby and even of death itself. However, professionals often deal with such feelings with denial and employ mechanical distancing manoeuvres with these babies and parents. Such behaviours in the professionals may mirror the internal attitude of the parents with respect to the child, since it is the absence of a nurturing parent in the mind of the infant which does not allow him to thrive.

Feeding disorder of separation and individuation

The onset period of the feeding disorder of separation and individuation (described by Chatoor, 1989, as anorexia nervosa) is the time of separation (according to Mahler, 1975), disillusion (Winnicott, 1958a), or the depressive position (Klein, 1937). The mother–infant dyad has created a good feeding situation, but when the infant starts to show its individuality, its mother finds this intolerable and starts *conflict situations*: these refer to food battles whereby the infant picks up the mood of the mother but does not agree with her. The mother may be preoccupied with economic, emotional, or family difficulties or deaths. She needs help to sort out her negative projections on the food intake that are making the situation so problematic. Such cases are seen with adolescent mothers who form attachments with their babies but find it difficult to accept their babies' growing up and independence. Schizophrenic mothers, too, sometimes find it easy to form attachments to their infant, but when the infant begins to act differently from the mother's expectations, annoyance and irritability appear and a vicious circle is started, leading subsequently to failure to thrive.

Selective food refusal

With selective food refusal, the baby eats only one thing and may manifest an independent spirit, preferring to make up its own mind rather than feeling as being in the hands of "disgusting food". This could lead to a battle of wills between infant and parents. In some cases, though, the baby might be experiencing repetition of a traumatic feeding in the past that was necessary because of surgical operations or intubations. If so, dramatization is highly recommended, using objects of the traumatic feeding situation in the dramatization and including a transitional object to open up a dialogue about the repressed past. Selective food refusal differs from post-traumatic feeding disorders in that it is not generalized to other activities: the baby's sleep is good, behaviour is neither withdrawn nor aggressive, and so forth.

CASE 34: MEG, AGE 16 MONTHS

Meg was referred at 16 months because she only ate chips from McDonalds. She was extremely small, like her father. She had no other problems, but it was a battle to make her eat anything else. Exploration with the parents about their behaviours showed a marked tendency by the father to spoil Meg, and her enchantment with him created a bad relationship with the mother which she could not handle. Past memories of jealousy did not help the mother or the father to have a firm policy in management and meal times at home. Both parents were 35 years old and came from different well-educated and strict backgrounds, but they themselves did not want to have an "organized" family set-up. Consequently, their home culture seemed to be a kind of adolescent rebellion against their families, which made them totally laid back and unregulated, whereas Meg needed structure and a family to eat with. The parents had to understand their own difficulty in growing into adults and creating rules that, though not the ones they wanted, would take into consideration the needs of their child. At times they saw in their little girl their overpowering parents, and they had to learn to separate their projections from reality. The therapy was centred around the needs of each member of the family, helping them to reach compromises.

Feeding disorder of continuation

With feeding disorder of continuation, the child remains bottle- or breastfed only, even after age 2 years, walking around with a bottle and not wanting to eat solids or baby food. After a paediatric examination to ensure that there are no problems with mouth reflexes or the digestive system, the parents' attention should be drawn to investigating within the family the reason for the child's habit. Often some degree of neglect in the mother is indicated, and this needs to be explored and helped. Such mothers are reluctant to ask for help because they do not see a problem. The infant or toddler is not viewed in the eye or mind of the mother as a growing person and so is treated permanently as a newborn baby. There may be some degree of depression in the mother and home situation, which calls for intervention to produce a different outcome. Some mothers express a wish of keeping the child small for as long as possible, to meet their own narcissistic need rather than that of the child to evolve. (Nicholas,

Case 33, in the sleep disorder section, who slept in his mother's bed and sucked from her breasts whenever he wanted, is an example of this kind.)

Overeating

Greediness does not draw the attention of professionals, because there is no pathology or damage associated with it; on the contrary, in many countries it is regarded as a sign of health or of wealth. However, if a child is too fat and the mother is concerned about the child's greediness, this may need to be investigated since it could conceal an anxiety mood disorder. There are borderline cases of vomiting related to overeating, and these almost constitute cases of bulimia, where the child is seeking attention by eating until becoming sick. The infant does not make itself vomit actively but passively, by continuing to eat after it is full.

Pica disorder

The term "pica disorder" is used in the case of children over a year old who, for at least a month, eat anything that is not edible or is not nutritious. It is usually not applied to younger children, given the habit of small babies to put everything into their mouths either because they are teething or because they are exploring their world. Pica can be an indication of mental retardation or pervasive developmental disorder.

According to statistics provided by Chatoor (1989), 75% of 12-month-old children put non-food objects in their mouth, whereas only 15% of 3-year-old children did so. Therefore, it is considered that for such behaviour in a child to be qualified as pica, it has to be both persistent and inappropriate. (It is of interest that studies by Millican et al., 1962, showed that 63% of mothers of infants with pica had pica themselves, or a sibling in their family did. Signs of malnutrition or iron or calcium deficiency have been found in children with pica studied by Robinson, Tolan, & Golden-Beecher, 1990.)

Rumination disorder

Rumination disorder is described in the DSM-IV criteria as the regurgitation of food or re-chewing of food without the presence of gastrointestinal or other general conditions such as oesophageal re-flux.

Infants with rumination disorder are not discovered as such be-cause usually they are believed to have vomited. But sometimes it is possible to see children who roll or move their tongue rhythmically to produce the regurgitation of food, or put a hand in the mouth to the same effect. Infants seem to use this habit as a self-soothing mechanism and to relieve tension, calling attention to their sense of deprivation. Treatment has to focus on the aetiology of the habit and must be carried out with great sensitivity so as not to make the mother feel more guilty and tense.

Post-traumatic feeding disorders

Post-traumatic feeding disorders are linked to a situation of oesopha-geal and tracheal manipulations, to intubations in premature babies, and to any other traumatic situations that might have occurred around the mouth, throat, eating, and breathing. Some premature babies who had undergone intubation for a month, plus oxygen, were brought to consultation a year later because they were only drinking from the bottle and did not want any solid food in their mouth and so were almost failing to thrive. Some babies had undergone surgical opera-tions from very early on and became confused about the experiences of food by tube, pain, and surgery. Older infants might have had an episode of choking, and they then link food with pain and fear. The parents are only too well aware of their child's fear, and they feel worried and frustrated, so that both infant and parent feel anxious in anticipation of painful or uncomfortable feeding.

Crying disorders

Excessive crying disorder indicates a vulnerability in the infant and a failure to express the resulting sorrow or discomfort in any other way. It includes:

- crying at night
- excessive crying during the day and no smiling
- crying because of physical disability
- crying as a response to family tension.

Crying at night

In the category of crying at night, it is possible to consider babies who fuss at night and continue doing so after the age of 1 year. Investigation of the individuality of the child and the circumstances might show family changes or alterations to routines; particular likes and dislikes; and a high level of reactivity and irritation. For example, when there is prolonged absence of a parent or other major changes in the family structure have taken place, the child may show through crying of this kind its difficulty in adjusting to such traumatic change.

Excessive crying during the day

Excessive crying during the day and no smiling under 6 months of age combined with temper tantrums indicates an irritable infant who is finding it very difficult to make sense of the world around it and its parents. Integration of experiences might be jeopardized because of the level of inner fragility experienced by the child, who enters easily into panic and feels that nothing or nobody is containing enough. These infants grow insecurely and are deficient in trusting human relationships. They need help at once because of the disturbance generated by their behaviour.

Crying because of physical disability

The crying of babies who have a physical disability may be excessive and different because of their disabilities and fragilities but also because their parents have unexpressed confusion, anger, and disgust for them. This parental factor does not allow them to attune, presenting a barrier that their babies seem to recognize and complain about. The professionals have to focus on the child, however, and, in seeing the child's individuality, manage to share this with the parents. In turn, it is useful to understand and draw out hidden or secret feelings with the parents to help them to relax and come to a better understand of the syndrome and themselves.

CASE 35: ABIGAIL, AGE 9 MONTHS

Abigail had cerebral palsy. Her crying was constant if she was not hanging from her mother's left arm. At age 9 months, she had not developed a relationship with the mother, even though she was breastfed. The work took the form of mother–infant sessions where the mother and psychotherapist tried to understand her internal world or difficulty in actually forming an internal world. Another therapist had to work with the mother separately to help her with the trauma of pregnancy and birth. (See Acquarone, 1995.)

Crying as a response to family tension

Family tension causes some babies to cry constantly in an attempt to push the parents to get help to sort out the causes of the tension. Sensitive children who seem to find unbearable the tension so generated need help and soothing techniques.

There are some children who, when moving home or when there are difficulties between the parents or other problems around, cannot stand being forgotten about or not helped . They have no other manner of showing their concern than crying. It is important for such babies to learn other ways of coping, and for parents to understand and help the situation from inside rather than resort to external soothing methods.

Relational and communication disorders

Relational and communication disorders might occur because the ego of the baby is weak in its structure or functions, or the baby's innate cognitive, sensorial, motoric, or affective capacities are impaired. These disorders can be divided into the following types, according to presentation:

- fragile
- isolated or islander
- ambivalent
- rejecting or avoidant
- retreat
- symbiotic.

It is possible that the baby may have a reduced or uneven sensory spectrum in one particular sense, or in all of them. The deficit could relate to emotional attunement or difficulty in receiving, perceiving, or regulating emotional information. When assessing the child, we need to explore which specific area is affecting development and thereby conceive an idea of the type of individual the child is and the kind of parents needed. We need to remember that the baby will communicate its difficulties through its body—quality of movements, posture, muscle tone, accommodation when picked up, reluctance to be in physical contact with the caregiver—so it is through the body that we have to assess the baby's willingness for contact and to monitor its progress.

Fragile

The child might be too physically or mentally weak to receive or emit communications of different kinds and so finds difficulty in regulating emotions in communications.

Isolated or islander

The baby is lethargic and does not show interest in the outside world. When awake, the baby seems to pay attention only to its own activity, movements, noises, and senses.

Parents have internal objects of their own parents and representations of their activities and realize that the baby is not responsive to them or, usually, to anyone else. Such babies become seriously delayed in overall activity if not diagnosed early. The cause could be regulatory disorder: for example, underreactivity that turns into a communication disorder.

CASE 36: JOHN, AGE 4 WEEKS

John was 1 month old and the health visitor had became concerned. The mother had two other children under 5 years, and she realized that John was not responsive and slept continuously. On assessment in the home, the baby took thirty minutes to acknowledge a body signal. His spine started moving when different kinds of touch were tried. It took another thirty minutes to interest John in opening one eye, and, for a busy mother with three other small children, it seemed an enormous amount of time to find contact and communicate. However, it is important in assessment that ways of communication are found and specialized support is given to these mothers.

Ambivalent

The ambivalent infant seems to have interests that do not match those of the parents, and/or the infant responds to situations or makes requests inconsistently. It might be that the parents themselves are ambivalent or incoherent and are therefore giving confusing messages that are difficult for the infant to read, or that the infant does not pay attention or care about such messages at times. The infant confuses the parents because sometimes it manages to respond correctly. Usually the serious difficulties in communication eventually become apparent.

Rejecting or avoidant

There are babies who actively reject human presence and interactions. They seem to be born with a low level of tolerance to frustration and so find experiences negative. An inner fear of death, or a basic terror of the unknown, does not allow them to trust the mother or caregiver. Since they dislike human proximity, they build more negative experiences than usual; their positive experiences are relatively fewer and relate to self-interest. They manifest their rejection by crying when picked up, avoiding gaze, and being occupied with objects.

CASE 37: RIO, AGE 7 MONTHS

Rio was referred at 7 months because he rejected his mother and did not look at her. She was becoming severely depressed. I observed the parents' home-made videos from his birth, and it was clear from the start that Rio avoided eye contact. He arched his back when picked up and did not respond to his mother's voice. Rio's older brother (6 years old) also displayed the same avoidant behaviour.

At the assessment, Rio would move and crawl away from people and would show a capacity to relate only if safely distant, looking briefly at people. The therapist started a ball game on the floor with him and his mother. The purpose was to explore Rio's individuality, his likes and dislikes. In this way, many sessions were organized to help mother to find out what was helpful for him and discover the effect that so much rejection had caused in her mental representations of the child.

Retreat

Babies with intrusive or abusive mothers develop a way of behaving that is characterized by withdrawal and or flight (see Ms M. and Joanna, Case 73).

Symbiotic

The symbiotic baby grows as an appendage of the mother, and the mother allows this to happen. With no developed personality, the baby is totally dependent. On the other hand, when a child accommodates to the continuous holding or support of the mother, it is usually the mother who is narcissistic and treats the child as a teddy-bear, not helping in this way to develop her own needs and unable to deal with any other person or children.

Symbiotic babies develop behaviour that is totally dependent on receiving the mother's full approval. Usually these cases are related to a physical disability in the baby coupled with an incapacity on the part of the mother or father to rethink their guilt and anger about the situation. This becomes a way of not seeing the reality, indirectly attacked and overprotecting as a result of their parents' unconscious fear of further attacking the already damaged baby (see Abigail, Case 67).

Early signs of relational and communication disorders

I have constructed a list of clinical criteria for the early detection of the general spectrum of relational and communication disorders, including autism (see Baranek, 2002; Dawson, Ashman, & Carver, 2000; DiLalla, 1990; Greenspan, & Wieder, 1999; Hobson, 1993; Kobayashi et al., 2001; Maestro et al., 2002; Trevarthen, 1979; Trevarthen & Aitken, 2001; Trevarthen & Hubley, 1978; Volkmar & Cohen, 1985). These "early signs of alarm" criteria are based on infants' behaviours that the parents are concerned about (and which the clinician can observe) and on the parents' response to those infants (research on home movies shows that parents of an as-yet undiagnosed autistic child unknowingly communicate with this child in a slower, flatter, less affectionate manner than they would with a normal child: Massie & Rosenthal, 1984; Muratori & Maestro, 2004). We consider that if four or more of the following signs are present around the age of 6 months, then early, skilful intervention is imperative. *Deficit in primary intersubjectivity*: lack of immediate response and interest in adults' intentions; no attraction for mother's face; lack of anticipation of mother's intentions; interest in objects (object relatedness); lack of imitation; lack of babbling; lack of joint attention; gaze avoidance; no orienting towards the parents and no smiling. *Poor motor (psychomotor) skills*: hypo- or hypertonicity; lack of moulding to mother or caregiver's arms; lack of grasping; stereotypic movements and noises; grimaces; dislike of being picked up or held; lack of curiosity; excessive or strange interest in movement of the tongue in the mouth; general communication difficulties. *Deficits in the sensorial spectrum*: dislike of the tone/volume of voice, preferring whispers (auditory hypersensitivity); hypersensitivity to touch or to specific touches; visually, auditory, or speech impairment. *Deficits in the transmission of affect*: extreme defences (such as denial, rejection, and isolation); extreme anxiety or distress, or complete lack of them; fears; irritability.

In addition to these observable "signs" in the child, it is important also to consider the degree of difficulty the parents have in relating to their child (their flatter, slower, unaffectionate manner) and in finding pleasure and satisfaction in joint encounters. Parents are usually the first to feel that there is something wrong with their child; in fact, they can be the best mental-health radar for realizing from their baby's communications the need for help or attention.

GROUP 2
RELATIONAL: QUALITY OF PARENTING

Relational diagnosis is an evaluation of the emotional quality of the relationship between the mother and child, how many points of contact they manage to establish, and the significance of their relationship to each other. The categories here are:

- over-involvement
- anxious/tense parenting
- neglect
- angry/hostile relationship
- mixed relationship disorder
- abuse (physical, sexual, verbal).

We look mainly at the style of parenting, the coherence between feelings and verbalizations, and the quality of the physical and psychological involvement. The quality of the mother's holding is observed—

whether it is relaxed, containing, tense, distant, and so on—as is the gaze, quality of communications, touching, attitude towards feeding, and responsiveness to the infant's communications and actions. It is important to observe and feel at all levels the emotional climate of the relationship and the quality of attunement and responsiveness from the mother (and father, if present, or when he is mentioned).

A suitable scale for assisting observation of mother–infant interaction from age 0 to 2 years is presented in Figure 5.2. This notes levels of certain behaviour—for example, holding, gazing, babbling, signalling, touching, and comforting, as well as feeding attitudes—in the infant *and* in the mother, showing how each interacts with the other and what it is necessary to monitor in order to decide whether there is a difficulty or a disorder in their relationship.

The quality of these behaviours is especially important to assess, as is whether the characteristics mentioned are in the awareness of the mother (or father) and can be changed with a few interviews or whether they need psychiatric or Social Services help as well. The mother will transmit to the interviewer the accessibility of the subject to be introduced and also whether the reaction to any help will be worse than the actual behaviour. Fear induced in the interviewer is a countertransference transmission of the mother's internal panic, which the baby has to bear continually. Difficult as it is to talk about, it is an indication of the fragility of the relationship, and it is important to analyse the best way to go about this sensitively. The professional should discuss his or her reactions fully with other specialists in infant mental health to avoid transference/countertransference complications.

All of these disordered behaviours are triggered by internal or external stimuli and can vary in the degree of disturbance. As we will see in chapter six, treatment depends on the mother's desire and capacity for insight and on the degree of her recovery from disturbance.

Over-involvement

Over-involvement by parents and not allowing space for the individuality of the child interferes with the child's interests and development of self. The child may show submissive, defiant behaviour, or indifference.

CASE 38: NICHOLAS, AGE 11 MONTHS

Nicholas, sleeping in his mother's bed and being breastfed on demand, is an example of such behaviour. He showed submissive behaviour because it seemed he realized at an unconscious level that his mother would feel very hurt if he wanted any independence.

Anxious/tense parenting

Anxious/tense parenting is characterized by the posture of the mother's body and arms in holding the baby. This might appear as being overprotective and at times over-sensitive and with a poor temperamental fit. Out of anxiety, the parents may become annoyed easily, mainly when tired and exhausted—a state into which they get very easily, given the amount of energy they need constantly to use.

Neglect

Neglect shows as not giving of emotional and sensory stimulation, or not demonstrating genuine interest in the child. At times parents ignore, reject, or fail to comfort the needy child. Their relatedness seems to be undermined by obvious other interests—career, housekeeping, social endeavours, and so forth. There is a lack of synchronization in the motor and verbal communications, and movements that are not engaged or matched. Parents sometimes consider it fashionable to have a kind of laid-back attitude towards bringing up babies, but this contradicts the basic natural instinct of mothers and covers up a lax way of not committing to a responsible adult–child relationship.

Angry/hostile relationship

An angry/hostile relationship manifests as handling or treating the child in a short or abrupt way. Generally, the parents cannot see the individuality of the child because they feel persecuted by not being obeyed or satisfied fully. The handling is rough, and babies are frightened of them. The tendency is towards the inducement of rigid behaviour (see Ms M. and Joanna, Case 73).

Mixed relationship disorder

In the mixed relationship disorder, the parent appears incoherent and evasive at times and over-involved at others. In a moderate way, many conflicted parents behave in this way but, if given some insight, can

INFANT	Frequency of this observation in 1 hour				Observer reactions
	Never	Rarely	Frequently (> 2x)	Always	
HOLDING: The posture of the infant when he/she is supported in the arms of the mother (e.g. comfortable, floppy, rigid, restless)					
GAZING: The eye-to-face contact within a dyad and the maintenance of this contact.					
BABBLING: The making of vocal sounds for the benefit of the partner in the parent–infant dyad.					
SIGNALLING: Facial expressions, noises, or gestures that seek to produce an affectional response from the partner.					
TOUCHING: Skin-to-skin contact initiated by infant for play or affection.					
COMFORTING: Infant's ability to find relief from distress by him/ herself (e.g. thumb-sucking).					
FEEDING: Infant's attitude during the intake of food, including anticipatory behaviour (i.e. head-turning, moving arm, sucking reflex).					
IMITATION: Moving mouth, tongue, hands etc. in imitation of mother's movements.					
AFFECT: the body or facial expression of emotional states (e.g., grin, sadness, worry, anxious, bland, happy, others. Specify					
ATTENTION: focused awareness—looking, orienting, smiling or vocalizing—of people or objects (specify).					
ANY OTHER OBSERVATIONS NOT LISTED ABOVE:					

FIGURE 5.2. Scale for observation of quality of mother–infant interactions (adapted from Massie & Campbell, 1984).

MOTHER	Frequency of this observation in 1 hour				Observer reactions
	Never	Rarely	Frequently (> 2x)	Always	
HOLDING: The posture of the mother when the infant is supported in her arms or any other way (e.g. secure and tender, rough, balanced precariously).					
GAZING: The eye-to-face contact within the dyad and the maintenance of this contact.					
BABBLING: The making of vocal sounds for the benefit of the partner in the parent–infant dyad.					
SIGNALLING: Facial expressions, noises, or gestures that seek to produce an affectional response from the partner.					
TOUCHING: Skin-to-skin contact initiated by mother for play or affection.					
COMFORTING: Mother's ability to find relief, physically or verbally, for the baby's distress.					
FEEDING: Mother's attitude towards infant's hunger and need to feed: a. Does she anticipate behaviour and have meal or breast easily available? b. Does she pay attention, talk to the baby, and enjoy feeding? c. Does she interrupt with any excuse (i.e. talks to others and looks away)? d. Is she fearful, full of anguish, or has she any delusions? e. Is she apathetic? Insight into emotions: in herself, in the baby?					
GAMES: playful encounters, including songs and teasing					
AFFECT: expression of emotional states—sadness, worry, anxious, bland, happy, others (specify).					
ANY OTHER OBSERVATIONS NOT LISTED ABOVE:					

become more coherent. For the child, this kind of unpredictable behaviour on the part of the parent(s) has a more devastating effect on the child's mind and development of affects and functioning than does negative behaviour of one kind only.

CASE 39: VERA

Vera's mother is an architect who works from home; father travels and is not interested in the child. When the mother has much work, she is irritable and short-tempered; when there is no work, she is overindulgent and spoils her child. She does not understand why her child is anxious and demanding.

Abuse

Physical.   Parents subject the child to physical punishments ranging from actual physical harm—hitting, spanking, kicking, burning—to physical restraint, leaving the child alone in a room or a cupboard for extensive periods, and other extremes of deprivation such as denying the child food, rest, medical care, contact with people, and so forth. The attitude of the parents is always hostile or has a perverse quality of smiling and being carefree in the face of the worst maltreatment (see Emma, Case 27; Silvina, Case 28).

CASE 40: LOUIS, AGE 6 MONTHS

Louis was reported by neighbours as being left alone, crying incessantly, while his teenage mother went out shopping or to the pub. The police had broken in and found him in his cot with an empty bottle, banging his head. The mother promised to behave and ask for help, and Louis was left in her care. She was now pregnant again and gave birth prematurely the following month. The first time Louis saw his mother after the birth, she threw Louis onto her bed because he was crying non-stop. A recommendation was therefore made for her to live in a home for mothers and babies, with constant monitoring. At the home the mother received information and training about mothering skills. The psychotherapy had to put into words, for the baby in the mother and the real baby, the strong emotions surrounding them and help to construct a way forward based on talking rather than acting out the anger, frustration, and impotence.

Sexual. This involves use of the child for the adult's sexual needs or desires, including forcing the child to receive or provide sexual actions or making the child observe the sexual behaviour of others. The baby may manifest continuous illness, such as urinary infections, or become withdrawn, or, as a toddler, may be inclined to exhibit its body, take off all clothes, or want to perform sexual actions with other children, from touching to re-enacting past situations. Sexually abused children tend to lack imagination and are motivated by concrete, non-abstract thinking. They may experience some developmental delay, as there is continuous trauma at home. Sexual abuse usually exists alongside other types of abusive behaviour and attitude (see Ms. S. & Susan, Case 80).

CASE 41: GIORDANO, 2½ YEARS OLD

Giordano was referred from the nursery as he kept pulling his trousers down and showing his genitals, with a glazed look. He was also standing on the window-sill and showing his genitals to passers-by in the street. It was found that the mother's boyfriend was sexually abusing him in front of the other three siblings. Individual treatment included the involvement of Social Services and weekly meetings for two years.

Verbal. This may seem to be a *milder* form of abuse when it appears on its own, because there is an attempt from the parents to restrain themselves from producing physical pain. It is important to consider cultural issues, since in some cultures there is more shouting and swearing and threats than in others. We are referring to parents who blame, attack, over-control, and are over-protective, producing either a frightened baby or one that acts out. The parent's tone is always negative and hostile, and there is a tendency to misinterpret the behaviour of the child as an attack on the parents or done on purpose to undermine or bother them.

CASE 42: SAMANTHA, 2½ YEARS OLD

Samantha was referred by her nursery because she retreated and actively withdrew within herself when approached. She was born to a depressed mother who was the daughter of a depressed mother. Samantha could never do anything right, and she was expected to be quiet or to sit in front of the television.

GROUP 3
ENVIRONMENTAL: PSYCHOLOGICAL/SOCIAL STRESSORS

It is important to consider in the category of psychological or social stressors the specific circumstances that the mother, the father, the child, or other family are undergoing—for example, death in the family, illness, disability, birth of a sibling, a stillbirth, a premature child in neonatal intensive-care, and so forth—as well as wider external circumstances such as war, earthquake, floods, or epidemics.

Special circumstances such as these can lead to the development of symptoms. For example, following a house move, starting nursery, or the birth of a sibling, a particular child might feel this too much to cope with and so does not sleep properly, or withdraws, or becomes aggressive, and so on. Once the situation is understood, it can be helped by showing the child and the family members the impact that this is having on their emotions and life.

Other social factors could include:

—the life and order of the city where the child and parents live

—the economy of the city and country

—the parent's job (or lack of one)

—security or insecurity

—problems with immigration, eviction, housing, fraud, and so on

—physical health of parents, grandparents, and siblings, especially if they live in the home or nearby

—chronic or acute illnesses in the family

—poor mental health of members of the family

—the circumstances under which the mother became pregnant (i.e., whether unwelcomed, or rape).

It is important to hear what is considered to be stress in a family and to evaluate its weight in the reality of the family and of the particular child. Sometimes it is possible to see enormous resilience or vulnerability in the responses to these different stresses. At times, in view of the social stresses that burden the family and negatively influence treatment, it may be necessary to involve Social Services to help and to work alongside the family even after treatment.

GROUP 4
MEDICAL: ILLNESS/DISABILITY

The importance of a sound developmental paediatric examination cannot be overemphasized, in view of the impact that medical problems can have on the life of an individual child and the family. It is essential to know about:

—the conditions of pregnancy

—any illness suffered, substance abuse, and so on

—birth history, birth weight, Apgar score (assessment by midwife)

—prematurity; any stay in a neonatal special-care baby unit, and the reasons for this

—presence of any congenital disability or anomaly, including syndromes such as Down's syndrome or Rhett syndrome

—presence of seizures or fits; explanations for these

—difficulties in breathing, sucking, calming down, moulding the body when held, keeping food in, looking, smelling, being in touch, reactibility (and to what)

—cerebral palsy, or other neurological diseases

—developmental delays, dissociation (e.g. lack of parity between fine motor development and sensory development), and disorders

—blind or deaf impairment

—lack of organs or limbs

—movement difficulties or stereotypes

—need of surgery immediately or soon after birth

—availability of information and support for parents, siblings, and patient.

It is also important to consider the consequences of a physical, cognitive, or emotional impairment on the baby individually and the mother individually, as well as on the rest of the family.

Research on narratives, feelings, and fantasies of parents of adults with disabilities (Bichard, Sinason, & Usiskin, 1996) has shown show how experiences around birth and/or disclosure of physical disability can become frozen and relate to disillusion about the desired/imaginary child and the phantasmatic child (see chapter two). The new reality might get enmeshed in past negative experiences, which are reactivated and knit new vicious cycles of unexpressed rage and guilt. These same narratives and experiences should be worked through as early as possible during infancy, to avoid secondary effects or symptoms that were not part of the original disability or impairment.

It is possible to divide disabilities into a number of categories:

—sensorimotor

—physical

—mental syndromes

—neurological damage

—vulnerability, if certain circumstances coincide

In our clinic we offer infant psychotherapy with the parents for any disability, clarifying with a specialist the characteristics of that specific disability. In studies done by Massie and Rosenthal (1984), 95% of babies born disabled or with physical vulnerabilities develop a psychosis as a secondary disability owing to: (1) the child's fragility and extra difficulty in integrating experiences within themselves, and (2) the parents' difficulties in dealing with damage, guilt, rage, and anger with regard to the disability. For this reason and from our experience with early interventions, as soon as special needs are diagnosed or suspected, it is recommended that at least three to five interviews are carried out with parents and baby to work through a humane relationship from the start.

CHAPTER SIX

Treating troubled babies:
infant–parent psychotherapy

From my exploration of the background of adult, adolescent, and child cases, I came to the realization that signs of being in trouble or of not coping with many difficult family situations became apparent early in life. The challenge that faced me as I worked year after year with cases of severe disturbance was whether these processes could be halted, and how. The more I saw different clientele with early difficulties in health centres, mother and baby units in prisons, neonatal intensive care units, and paediatric wards, the more I could see the wide range of normality, the different degrees of conflict, and the possibilities for help.

As I learned how to help, I needed to adjust my technical instruments and knowledge. Learning from this experience, and hand-in-hand with psychoanalysts, primary care givers, and paediatricians, the art and skill of early interactions evolved into the method of infant–parent psycho-therapy, with variations necessary for complex family dynamics. Of primary importance to this approach has been the discovery of the infant's personality, capacities, and communications, as well as the parent's. This is why I call it infant–parent psychotherapy, as it started by an infant in difficulties with his parents. One could say that the infant brings the parents to the consultation.

E fforts to give parents insight into the unconscious motives of their child's behaviour and emotions started as early as 1907, when Freud helped Little Hans's parents to understand his difficulties. In Berlin in the 1920s, Melanie Klein and other psychoanalysts began individual treatment of children as young as 18 months. In 1931, psychoanalytic consultations with parents and children together were initiated by the paediatrician D. W. Winnicott. He took into consideration the quality of anxiety underlying the behaviour demonstrated in the consultation, and he tried to understand the emotional causes of physical symptoms in children where no apparent physical cause had been found.

In 1947, René Spitz filmed and wrote about the devastating effects on the emotional and physical development of young infants if the mother has to leave the baby because she goes into prison, and the baby experiences grief in such a way that it stops growing and regresses to a pitiful state similar to marasmus. Spitz recommended that the remedy is for the baby to have the mother back. His revealing studies of infants in orphanages had a clear parallel with infants of depressed or unavailable mothers, demonstrated in the studies carried out by Lynne Murray in Cambridge aimed at helping such mothers to parent their babies through the provision of different kinds of therapies for the mothers (Cooper, Murray, Wilson, & Romaniuk, 2003; Murray, Cooper, Wilson, & Romaniuk, 2003). This approach seems to have led to improvement in the overall development of the babies.

In the United States, there have been variations on the treatment of mothers and infants. For example, Johnson, Dowling, and Wesner (1980) mounted a maternal infant programme at the Milwaukee Health Center where, for an hour a week, the distressed infant was encouraged to take the lead and the mother was asked to follow its behaviour as unobtrusively as possible. Johnson and colleagues used the mother as therapist, and the mother–baby interaction was supervised with the aid of videotaping. The psychotherapist was directed to sensorimotor patterns of response. Unfortunately, these investigators did not believe that psychic awareness could be functioning at this age, so subtle symbolic interactions were not examined.

Other workers have most frequently treated the distressed infant by working with the mother. Contributions in this area include the work, in the United States, of Brazelton, Young, and Bullowa (1971), Fraiberg (1980), and Cramer and Stern (Cramer, 1995; Cramer & Stern, 1986); in the United Kingdom, of Daws (1989) and Hopkins (1992); and in France, of Lebovici (1984, 1988).

Setting

The setting is similar to a psychoanalytic one, but a consulting-room is not necessarily used. The aim is to establish a suitable space and time where feelings and emotions can be explored with free-floating attention from the therapist. Factual information is being sought in order to assist in understanding the parents' concerns and the observations of the therapist, and links between the fragmented data are being made jointly by the parent(s) and therapist(s). It is therefore important for the setting to be as free as possible from distractions such as telephones, pagers, or other electronic devices often found in hospitals or ordinary homes.

Personal approach to interventions

At each interview the therapist attempts to analyse the situation as it is presented, taking time to consider which action or comment will be most helpful, according to the feelings transmitted. Whenever it is felt that the baby is showing signs of normal development and is just being used by the mother as an excuse to talk about her own concerns, this is discussed openly (Acquarone, 1986, 1987, 1992, 2002).

It is helpful to include a variety of cuddly toys and "test material" for babies, such as bells and a small container with rice in it. An in-depth knowledge of nursery rhymes also helps, as does getting down onto the floor with the baby early on in the interview to emphasize that understanding the baby is the focus of attention and interest.

Psychodynamic approach

Generally I ask the father to attend the meeting, and/or the health visitor if she and the mother wish, given the amount of time they have already invested together and the need for follow-up.

If the mother and the baby cannot come to me, because of mental or physical difficulties in either of the two, I may make one or more home visits. Sometimes after I establish a relationship in a home setting, the mother feels better able to come to a local consulting-room. External and/or internal barriers are thus removed.

Once with them, I inquire whether I can videotape part or all of the session, to enable me to think about the family afterwards and to keep a record of the treatment process. If they do not agree to this, the session continues; however, if they do ask to see some of the session with me, after thinking together about their reasons, we might view the videotape. Sometimes mothers are seeking approval or need support in seeing themselves with their child. I hear them, I observe them, I ask questions to clarify a point. I mention possible lost links in their narrative. Sometimes focusing on an earlier stage in a mother's life helps her own self-reflection, and she can go on to make links by herself.

I observe my reactions, and I tune in to the level I sense the family is at. My scale of evaluation has many points, ranging from mild to severe difficulties. For example, in severe cases of psychiatric forensic disorders and abusive or neglectful attitudes in the mother, the range might be:

- making known her difficulty to an appropriate professional;

- accepting referral, entertaining the idea in her head;

- discussing referral (or not) with her family, as this would already be indicative of further hope;

- missing a number of appointments, or whether and when she opens the door of her home to a professional.

Regarding the final point, Stanley Greenspan once remarked that, after arranging a home visit, in none of his severe cases had the mother refused to open the door more than twenty times (Greenspan & Wieder, 1984). Of course, this generous and patient attitude depends on resources and the professional's duties and training and commitment, but it is useful to know that even in severe cases the mother can be reached eventually. Much depends on how far we are prepared to go to call such attempts "success" or "failure". The reality is that it is important to know at what point *we* decide to withdraw our help, with the excuse that—in certain cases—"they" are unreachable.

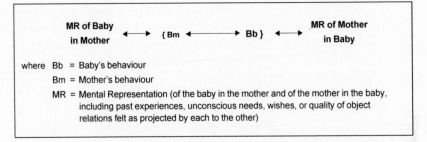

Figure 6.1.   Psychoanalytic intervention model (after Stern-Buschweiler & Stern, 1989).

Psychotherapeutic model

The first section of this chapter is based primarily on a particular model of mother–infant psychotherapy created by Stern (Stern-Buschweiler & Stern, 1989) (see Figure 6.1). He considered that a psychoanalytic intervention works on the mother's mental representations, as they are projected onto the infant. What is observable in interviews is the behaviour, body language, and expression of emotions—the mental representations themselves are inferred. Our focus in the following section is on working with these mental representations of the mother. Cases are considered in terms of specific disorders (see chapter five) and also of categories of interventions derived from analysis of work at a child and adolescent mental-health unit at a community hospital (previously a child guidance clinic), two sleep clinics for under-5s held at a health centre, and the Infant–Parent Clinic.

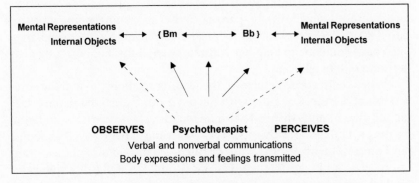

Figure 6.1.   Modified psychoanalytic intervention model.

However, when the consultation is about difficulties that lie within the infant, the above model of working only with the mother's representations is inadequate, and I consider it to be a resistance on the part of the psychotherapist not to confront the baby's primitive transference and the countertransference (Acquarone, 1992). My proposal is that modifications need to be made to the model, as shown in Figure 6.2. The psychotherapist observes and perceives the verbal and nonverbal communications, and the body expressions and feelings transmitted, and from these forms an internal picture containing all this information and institutes treatment primarily through:

- verbal communication to the mother of her unconscious feelings, phantasies, wishes, and repetition in the transference of her past experiences
- verbal communications to the mother of feelings in the baby demonstrable at the time—both on its own and with the mother—that the mother has not perceived.

It is this model that forms the basis for the second half of the chapter. This looks at work focusing on the infant involving developmental crisis, reactive crisis, psychosomatic disturbance, difficulty in integrating experience, and physical damage at birth or in the first year.

WORKING WITH THE MOTHER'S REPRESENTATIONS

Mothers themselves need to have had an experience of being nurtured that they can recall and identify with internally. Different cultures have what seems to be a universal attitude towards birth: mothers' mothers are around. Nowadays, the partner/father is around more, and usually—if neither grandmother nor partner is available—the mother may also have someone to help her with the baby at the beginning, such as a friend or a neighbour.

When there are difficulties in the feeding relationship and the clinical infant is in consultation with the psychotherapist, the parents talk about their infant's difficulty and unconsciously reproduce in relation to the psychotherapist their own early feeding experiences (behaviour and attitude) with their mother or carer. The infant also shows, communicates, and transfers what is not fitting. Symbolically, this early and important experience is revisited by the therapist with acceptance of the family's state of vulnerability and fear of what might happen. A model to consider would be literally of holding the mother in our arms and starting again with the mind and the body in psychotherapeutic reverie and allowing a new or a past experience to present itself. Talking—if possible—is helpful in talkative cultures, but the nurturing experience is the key to psychic change. Helping the parents to stay with the baby's experience, to tolerate anxieties that the mother and the baby are feeling, and supporting them with love, understanding, and endurance are as important as technical skills. The therapist's commitment to helping the baby and confidence that the family will succeed are equally important. The therapist needs to proceed with care and respect, with tips or suggestions that allow experimentation and reflection. The triangle of therapist–mother–baby allows perspective, space, and safe movement. The father also needs the experience of thinking, acting, and modulating communications without persecution, but with care.

In this way we reach awareness of inner states, feelings, reactions, and memories that are painful or rejected.

CASE 43: SEBASTIAN, AGE 18 MONTHS

Sebastian's mother was in a panic, filled with doubt and confusion about her son starting nursery school so young.

Both parents came to the first interview and talked about schooling for their child. Sebastian's anxiety was lost sight of under the concern being expressed as to what was best for Sebastian academically. The parents, mainly the mother, talked in a very worried but detached way about Sebastian, going over and over the pros and cons of his starting nursery. The father appeared to be a very quiet and supportive person. Sebastian was playing by himself, isolated. I felt more as though the mother was ruminating about her past, although when she was questioned about her childhood she said very quickly that she had been brought up by her mother on her own and that she had dedicated her life to her mother to such an extent that it was only now that she was allowing herself to work for a university degree. Further exploration along these lines was curtailed, as the mother kept returning to the matter of Sebastian's immediate future—that is, about school or nursery. Both parents answered questions about their family background reluctantly and quickly, and somehow the child's individuality was overlooked entirely. The mother, an architect, was desperate to go back to work, and the father, a musician, seemed puzzled by the family's situation.

Twelve sessions took place, including two jointly with the grandmother and mother. The child was taken to the nursery for two weeks but did not settle. He would scratch and bite people, which was behaviour that he had not shown prior to attending there.

The mother gradually regressed into feelings that had been awakened by her child. First, she began to realize that the relationship she had with her son was almost symbiotic, just as hers had been with her own mother. Her father had left suddenly when she was 18 months old (the same age as Sebastian was now), and in the sessions she re-experienced the anguish of separation by cutting her husband off and clinging to her baby, even though she wanted to resolve the situation. Anxiety prevailed, with grandmother and mother competing over the mothering of the child, now overshadowed by the ghost of the abandoning husband and father. During the seventh session, mother asked for a session with only herself and her mother. They shouted at each other for the first time about who possessed the males; Sebastian's mother talked about the suffocating love she felt from her own mother and the fear of hurting her if she put any distance between them, and she expressed her longing for the return of her father and how impossible it was to talk about feelings relating to her father. The grandmother shouted back, surprised at her daughter's first temper tantrum but demonstrating her profound hatred and pernicious jealousy of her daughter who had managed to keep a partner for fifteen years. The therapist needed to verbalize very little, since the two women were realizing and acting out, there and then, the baggage of emotions they had been carrying.

The tenth session was attended by mother, father, and Sebastian. The parents had got married privately, decided to try for a second child, and, for the first time in their relationship, they began to disclose their secrets—for example, the mother's fear of getting married and then being abandoned by the father of the baby, or the happiness that would disappear, as had occurred for the mother as a child.

The father had always felt rather redundant, since his partner had kept her money and accounts secure and secret and had made decisions about the child without ever consulting him. Also, she

would be the one who spoke all the time. The mother was horrified to see her own mother reflected in herself, talking as though
she were possessed by her—acting out the intergenerational conflict of revenge. The boy was scratching at eyes that were too close
to him, and he was pushing and hitting children out of the sadness he felt because of not being allowed to develop his own self
more freely.

The parents began to look at their child with new-found respect,
seeing him as an individual, separate from the conflict that belonged to them and not to him.

Discussion.   In a summary such as this, it is impossible to convey
the full richness of this case vignette. However, it does show how a
current conflict with a child can reactivate in the parents unresolved
past conflicts (as well as good experiences) that can interfere in their
relationships with each other and the normal development of the child.
In this case, the difficulty arose fifteen years after the parents began
living together as a young couple, while continuing to study and travel
before having a child.

Sebastian was showing very withdrawn and sad behaviour, as well
as scratching and annoyance. It seemed almost as if he were building a
crust around himself, fed up with his individuality being ignored. The
sessions revealed an amazing amount of intergenerational maternal
psychic material, including the passive role the mother had taken in
her infancy, and how it had taken her thirty-five years to be able to talk
about such things as her anguish at her father's sudden disappearance.

Her anxiety focused on her son's behaviour at the nursery. Sebastian was actively withdrawing or hitting, showing anger and worry,
reacting intensely. The psychotherapy focused on these symptoms of
the child, the interactions of the family, and the links between the
mother's memories/infantile neurosis and the effects these had on the
child and on their family relationships.

Post-traumatic feeding disorders

Post-traumatic feeding disorders are often overlooked since, in many
cases, the life of the infant is at imminent risk from other causes.
However, several feeding disorders—not being able to move on in
habits, keeping pieces of food in the cheek, overeating, rumination,
and many other anomalies—are a consequence of trauma experienced

by the baby. Post-traumatic feeding disorder can be a consequence of having choked on a piece of food or something introduced into the mouth by accident, but more often it is a result of hospitalization (Acquarone, 2003).

CASE 44: ANGELICA, AGE 20 MONTHS

Angelica was expected and planned, after ten years of living together, by an older couple, the woman aged 40, the man 50. The pregnancy had been going well, but in the eighth month a radiologist told the parents that the baby had a malformation and that an immediate operation was needed. The Caesarean was performed the following day, but the baby turned out to be normal; however, she was too small to survive outside an incubator. She was intubated, and the parents were distraught. She remained in special care for two months and was never a good eater. At the time of the consultation, Angelica was 20 months old and did not eat solids at all. She only fed from the bottle, and then very little. She was extremely small for her age, and the parents were worried.

It was later that I learned that Angelica did not sleep much either. The behaviour that the parents and child showed in the consulting-room indicated complete equality between adults and child. Angelica had no rules or boundaries, and they were all rolling around, aimless and seemingly frightened.

I began by inquiring about their imaginary child and family, the one they had constructed in pregnancy, the one they were expecting. There was before the event a life I wanted to recover: how and whom they thought they were having, what the mother preferred eating, what the father thought that he would do with a baby— after all, he had not had a child before he was 50. So they went back to that stage, of knowing about pregnancy, of feeling, seeing changes, and now smiles and jokes began to be exchanged and the excitement, the pleasure, came back to them.

During the pregnancy, everything had been going so perfectly, and they had all these thoughts and wonderful ideas about their new family-to-be and the baby. Then all of a sudden there was very bad news. They went on to explain that their little baby was taken and made to be born prematurely and how poorly she looked in the incubator. I asked them to tell me exactly what they thought that evening and night of the news from the radiologist. They said that they were so shocked, they cried, they despaired, they phoned the wife's mother who was ready to come from Denmark, but how, of course, she arrived afterwards. They could not believe what was happening, how the baby might look, a monster, plus the Caesarean and the confusion. And afterwards, when they saw the baby in the incubator, she was so tiny and full of tubes.

My opinion was that they had not yet recovered from their first shock of being told the child was abnormal and from their upset at being in the hands of an inept radiologist. In the session, they were now annoyed. Anger came up for the first time, and they cried. This child was being damaged by the vision their parents formed of her on their night of panic and disillusion before having her. Angelica, on the other hand, did not have contact with the parents in the incubator and so had to struggle by herself, probably with a great resentment about been taken out of her mother's womb. The reality was that she suffered physical and emotional upheaval. It seemed as if she grew into the world of pain and feelings too quickly and managed to play into her parents' guilt and phantasies.

We improvised in the sessions with a play about the hospital situation, using cuddly toys; one was the baby, others the mother and father and nurses and doctors. The parents felt released of things they felt and wanted to happen, and Angelica talked about her fantasies then and at the time of the interview. In her mind, the parents were little and weak, and she was the powerful person that could battle with knives and villains.

About three sessions were dedicated to this theme, and soon the night battles surfaced. The parents had by then bought cuddly toys that represented the family "changing", and they played with these at home as well. The "newcomers" were seated at the table and "ate" with the parents, who had to organize family meals. Until then, food had not been organized around the table, as the parents could not face food and relationships. The tubes attached to the baby had been a constant reminder of what they did wrong and of damage to their baby. Another four sessions helped the integration of all the issues, and Angelica began to eat at the table with her parents, who felt really happy again.

A year later, the parents asked to speak with me as Angelica had resumed her sleeping difficulties: a dance of getting into their bed and then going back to her own bed, up to five times a night. And mother was pregnant again. Both parents were only children, and, with the morning sickness, the mother regressed to a weaker stance with Angelica, who was again feeling abandoned and needing to take charge of the household. We discussed the parents' anxieties, relating to their fear of what might happen again in the pregnancy. They resolved that they were not going to have scans as long as the pregnancy was going well. In view of the mother's age, there was a risk of Down's syndrome, but she wanted to love whatever baby arrived. Angelica needed to be given explanations and elaboration of the meaning of the sickness and of the baby growing inside the body, though not in the tummy, in order not to confuse food and pregnancy, which is a common primitive fantasy used to deny sexual and creative capacity in the parents.

Angelica began to eat everything, and I saw the parents twice more. Follow-ups showed increased acceptance by the parents of Angelica's individuality and proper mourning of their pre- and postnatal traumatic experience.

Discussion.   In post-traumatic cases, we discuss with parents what they had experienced while their child had been undergoing traumatic feeding. It is important to get details of where they were at before and after the traumatic events occurred—for example, what fantasies or illusions the parents had about the baby and their new lives; what thoughts were around about them as individuals and as a couple; when difficulties with the child occurred, what were they reminded of, what were their anxieties and fears.

It is important to tell the parents to let the child choose the toys to bring to the consulting-room. The therapist should then observe the child playing, in order to watch its freedom of expression and attachment to what it has brought, what it does with them, and how it expresses feelings or moods. Then, through play or through drawings, exactly what happened at the time of the trauma is reproduced. This is preferably done with the aid of cuddly toys, which need to be dressed up in a such a way that the child's internal material gets activated or triggered. Medical or other originally distressing settings are best reproduced only after the child is out of danger.

Patience and firmness are needed for the trauma to be fully mastered by the child and the parents. They need a few session to go over the situation again and again and slowly start to find solutions to their difficulty.

Feeding disorders of homoeostasis

CASE 45: SYLVIA, AGE 10 DAYS

Sylvia was born by Caesarean section and weighed 2 pounds. Extremely irritable, she cried very often and fed very little but very often, and she seemed to like to be held all the time. The mother had an infection from the stitches in the womb and felt very weepy. Her husband was working and, when consulted, suggested that his wife's mother, or a friend, be asked to come and help. The Caesarean had been not planned or expected, and the mother was in shock and annoyed about it. The baby, small, irritable, and distrustful, was not a good match for an annoyed mother who was still in pain. Acknowledgement of her feelings and reliving the difficult birth, with recognition of the baby's individuality, allowed this mother to ask for and accept help from her own mother. As a result, the baby grew fat in her mother's arms, feeding at her own pace. The baby's grandmother patiently talked to her own daughter, letting her become stronger and more knowledgeable about life, events, and babies. By the fifth month, Sylvia had established a pattern of feeding and was sleeping well.

Discussion.   This treatment has a quality of paediatric intervention in the sense that there is an understanding of feelings that are behind the mother–baby relationship, together with a focus on the specific characteristics of the baby, thus providing information and hints about how and why the situation is happening.

Problems with feeding a newborn may arise from the mother or from the baby. This creates a difficult start for the new relationship and for inner development in the baby and in the mother (and father). Infants who from the start present an irregular pattern of behaviour and responses to the new sensations experienced will be better off once this is clearly recognized. The mother can then be helped to understand and become able to assist the baby to regulate its rhythms. Otherwise, a vicious circle may begin, in which the mother experiences a sense of failure, reinforced by any previous negative experience, leading to further problems with the baby. It is important to differentiate whether the behaviour of the mother is a *cause* or a *consequence* of the innate sensibilities or difficulties in the temperament of the infant.

These difficulties in the infant can be related to sensorimotor hypersensitivity or difficulties in tolerating frustration, or pain, or discomfort, or silence, or other normal experiences for babies. Mothers may be first-time mothers, or busy with other children, or easily frustrated, and the baby's difficult pattern may not get regulated. The time for a meal arrives but the meal does not appear, nor is there awareness in the mother of the baby's sensation of hunger; learning to wait, a sense of order, and routines are not attained. The outcome is that the mother feels upset and battles develop over food. A feeding disorder of regulation occurs where it is clear that the mother finds it difficult to create a pattern, no matter how much she tries.

Cases such as these will benefit from making a feeding chart for a week, to note what feeding is taking place and when, and to help the mother to look for a pattern that can eventually suit both her and the baby. Support and understanding of the feelings evoked by the feeding difficulties are needed for the mother to find inner resources that can help her to build up confidence, patience, and awareness of changes in behaviour her child and an understanding of its specific difficulty.

CASE 46: BEVERLY, AGE 15 DAYS

This consultation was set up because the mother felt in great conflict about feeding Beverly. The baby recognized her father's music so well that she would stop crying even when his playing was on the radio. Other than at these times, the mother could not console her easily. After a few interviews, it became clear from her obsessiveness that, though the mother herself had not been breastfed, she was determined to breastfeed her daughter.

With idealized and envied images of her siblings having been breastfed, she felt left out and unaware of other elements that were interfering with her relationship with her baby. I then learned that Beverly had had an amniocentesis diagnosis of a chromosome abnormality that was not going to be visible physically but could manifest itself in the future in mild mental retardation and infertility. The mother herself was 45 years old and knew that her chances of having another child were extremely low or non-existent. Both parents nevertheless decided to continue with the pregnancy, but they were offered no counselling to deal with their emotional turmoil about the diagnosis and their decision. The mother subsequently realized how much she needed to talk about that traumatic period.

Discussion. From age 3 months onwards, there may be difficulty in the baby forming an attachment to the mother. From age 6 months onwards, when the baby begins to separate or become individualized, there might be lack of acceptance of the baby's difference and separateness by the mother, especially for young, insecure teenage mothers who find separation difficult and/or for fragile infants. Conflicts between mother and infant at this time may also generate feeding difficulties, with resulting failure to thrive. Therefore, difficulties need to be addressed as soon as they are discovered or help is requested.

The difficulty may be a cause or a consequence of other more subtle and intricate difficulties, problems in the couple, or intergenerational transmission of conflicts, for instance. It might be the peculiar sensitivities of the child, or degree of tolerance of frustration, incapacity for waiting, slowness or being easily distracted when feeding, or another individual trait of the infant.

Feeding disorder of culture

I work with mothers from a whole variety of cultural backgrounds and linguistic abilities. Some women might be in a monogamous relationship with their husband, but others might be in a polygamous situation. Accordingly, my methods of working also vary. If we have no common language, I might use interpreters or rely on nonverbal communication, video replay, or modelling techniques.

Freedman (1974) considers that "cultural anthropology" has changed popular thinking by showing that behaviour unique to a nation or tribe is due largely to a lifetime of learning and social interaction within that given milieu. He goes on to study the so-called universal characteristics of infancy in different groups, showing how biological and psychological capabilities and potential appear, adapt, and interrelate with the realities of life in any given environment.

However, whatever the cultural variations, it is agreed by most psychologists and psychoanalysts that the child is born with the capacity to grow, adapt, and develop and to relate to its mother and/or carer in response to signs and expressions that are universally necessary for the survival of the species (Darwin, 1872; Fraiberg, 1980).

A mother who has difficulties adjusting to life in a new country and experiencing the anxieties of loss, identity confusion, and fear of damage may come to identify the new culture as the aggressor. This paranoid anxiety, acting as a defence against her feelings of isolation, of being cut off from her own traditional customs and beliefs, adversely affects her capacity to form a healthy attachment to her infant, whose capacity to thrive is thereby stunted.

Where a foreign mother comes to consult regarding her infant's difficulty, she may feel handicapped by her need to adapt to an alien environment, unaware of what resources and support may be available to her family.

When the consultations first starts, I find it useful to clarify the negative transference. This includes acknowledging that I do not belong to the parents' culture. While closely observing what is going on, I show an interest in and listen attentively and sensitively to the mother's account of her culture and family customs. My purpose is to reinforce natural competence, and I, too, learn to value it and to feel connected to the family's immediate and more distant family history. I pay close attention as well to what is going on inside me. I allow my countertransference to guide my inquires and comments, and I also allow my maternal responses to be aroused, which enables me to empathize with the mother's mothering and to understand the symbolism that permeates the whole feeding process/ritual. I allow myself to be immersed in the primitiveness of the difficulties being expressed.

CASE 47: JANET, AGE 5 DAYS

The mother was Turkish. The baby was refusing to feed and was in a constant state of lethargy. As a therapist, I suddenly sensed from both mother and baby that there was a sexual component to the difficulty. The mother had come to London for an arranged marriage, became pregnant, and gave birth to the baby. The breast-feeding was producing hormones to contract the uterus, which caused a kind of sexual excitement that appeared to disturb the mother, reactivating infantile needs, anxieties, and fears. The hospital setting, lack of family to support her, and the physical changes in her body were all paralysing her capacity to bond with her baby. My sharing an understanding of her physical sensations and her emotional loss enabled the mother to also understand and thus separate her own feelings from those of her baby: she learned to see the baby as an individual in her own right.

CASE 48: KIP, AGE 6 WEEKS

The mother was Ghanaian. Kip was 6 weeks old. This was the fourth child, after three daughters. The infant was lethargic and not feeding, and he presented a regulatory disorder. The mother had come from Africa, pregnant with Kip, to join her husband. This meant leaving the extended family who had helped her to bring up the older children.

During the assessment, Kip was extremely difficult to reach, and the mother found it difficult to persevere. She was grieving the loss of her homeland, her culture, and the support of her extended family, and she was suddenly faced with having to cope on her own with four children. When all these aspects of her grief were considered and fully talked through, the mother was open to consider how she was projecting her paranoid anxieties onto the English community and neighbourhood and how, in this strange new setting, she needed her own confused, angry, primitive baby-self to be held.

CASE 49: RAMISH, AGE 8 MONTHS

An Indian mother had an 8-month-old girl who was failing to thrive. Ramish was refusing solids. The mother spoke very little English and had brought apple purée with her. She had been given to understand that the only kind of food she was supposed to give her child were English baby foods (e.g. cereals and baby purées). The mother herself ate spicy food but had been advised against feeding her child with such food. Her confusion about what was right for her child, and feelings of inadequacy in this alien culture, needed to be validated so that she could then make an informed choice herself.

CASE 50: ALEK, AGE 13 MONTHS

A Russian mother had a 13-month-old son who was failing to thrive and had feeding difficulties. The videotape showed an angry and oppressive mother holding and feeding her baby. She would sit, at home and in the consulting-room, with the baby on her lap leaning on her left arm, as if he were only 3 months old. She held the left arm of the baby with her left hand, the baby's right arm placed behind his back. The mother's right arm was busy spooning apple purée into the baby's mouth, as fast as the baby spat it out. No allowances were made for the child to explore, initiate, converse, or negotiate over the meal. I saw the "baby within the mother", feeling similarly tied by lack of language, stifled by unexpressed anger and frustration, and feeling trapped and powerless.

The actual baby had been hospitalized many times for various tests, which must have increased the mother's anxieties of being torn between looking after her other two children at home and her duty to her English-born baby. My use of various techniques, including video replay (as we had little shared language), enabled the mother better to understand and express her feelings about herself and to understand her mental representations of her English baby. Encouraging her in the consulting-room to allow her baby more freedom of movement also gave the mother more freedom to explore alternative feeding methods.

CASE 51: *JERAN, AGE 3 YEARS*

This was a Moroccan Arab mother with her 3-year-old son, who was only feeding from the bottle, refusing any other feeding methods, and so causing great concern to the GP and health visitor. During my first and subsequent interviews, the mother would constantly make up stories by way of explaining away the problem and would later admit to having told lies. I learned to understand that this so-called lying was her culturally acceptable way of defending herself. It was clear to me that this mother was expressing a great deal of anger towards her child. Then I learned that her own father had abandoned the family when she was 7 years old. She was then obliged, instead of going to school, to stay at home and look after her five brothers and sisters. At the age of 20, her marriage was arranged to a man who already had nine children. It was clear in my mind that this mother might, by projecting her anger onto her small, helpless male child, be taking revenge against the men in her life who, in her terms, had mistreated her. However, as time went by, I felt I could not progress, being faced as I was with the mother's lying responses, and I felt completely defeated. The turning point came when I expressed my own sense of failure to the mother. It became evident that she had been transferring her sense of powerlessness onto me. Hence I was feeling defeated in the countertransference. Once this became clear, the relationship between the mother and her son improved, and he began to feed normally. The mother went into long-term individual psychotherapy.

Discussion.   Being subject to the swings of fashion in the Western world regarding what constitutes a healthy baby, and being told or having interpreted that spicy food was not good for breastfeeding mothers and their babies, the mothers in some of these cases seemed to be in a state of acute conflict, which connected with their own primitive states of mind relating to food: hunger, early experiences of delayed gratification with concomitant fears, being held, their mother country, familiar cultural patterns, and weaning.

In normal development, the baby arouses in the mother mainly positive past experiences. But in these cases it seemed as if the paranoid anxieties aroused negative ones—such as fear of invasion and disintegration—that interfered with the feeding process and created serious difficulties. Feelings of being abandoned by their own families, even though they had left them voluntarily, seemed to be a recurring theme, and spicy food represented a tangible link with their own mothers and their native countries. But the anger and resentment at having left their homes in order to follow their husbands (supposedly to serve their own interests, at least initially) tended to make them split and project their negative feelings onto the English-born baby, who is seen to be something alien that has to be fed alien food. The babies, however, seemed to resist this approach. Sometimes they would be breastfed by mothers who had eaten spices; sometimes they would only be able to smell spices in the home; but in those cases where a baby might be allowed to taste the traditional spicy food, they seemed to enjoy the experience. It was as if, in this way, they felt a sense of belonging in the family, just as traditional food reminded their parents of their families back home.

With non-English-speaking mothers and using the methods I have described, the feeding process seemed to improve and to become freer by the third interview. Even when I could not verbally transmit my understanding of the situation, I would patiently allow myself to experience their spontaneous behaviour, comments, and expression of feelings, allowing my countertransference to guide me. This suggests to me how useful such nonverbal methods of communication can be for transmitting containments, acceptance, respect of customs, love, and the encouragement of individuality.

I have, in fact, found this sort of early intervention to be more effective without an interpreter. Encouraging a mother to feel strongly and positively connected to her culture and her own experience of being mothered helps the grieving process. She is then better able to move forward from projective identification of the new surroundings as critical, unfamiliar, different, nasty, faulty, frightening, or persecutory to a more positive, self-confident position.

Winnicott (1960) pointed out that there is no such thing as an infant. What he meant by this is that the mother–infant dyad is an inseparable unit and that the attentive care of the mother is essential for the survival of the infant. In this attentive care, the respect for and involvement and link with her cultural background seems crucial. Raphael-Leff (1991) advises that professionals working with ethnic minorities (and, I would add, with any foreign mother) should concentrate on increasing their client's natural competence rather than imposing foreign practices. This would be a better way of ensuring the baby's healthy growth.

Categorized interventions

Crisis interventions

Some mothers expressed feelings of being caught up in a temporary crisis/panic situation, which at times seemed insoluble and sometimes led to extreme reacting in the infant. Intervention in these cases comprised one or two meetings. They were mostly seen once, the mother specifically saying that she wanted help for the problem the baby was presenting. The mother (or parents) did not show any inclination to explore further aspects of her life. I have frequently questioned whether an intervention comprising only one meeting has, in the long term, any value or justification.

CASE 52: JANET, AGE 5 DAYS

Janet refused to breastfeed or to feed in any other way. The doctor had checked but found that nothing was physically wrong, and the mother had become very frightened.

The interview took place in a room in the maternity ward. Baby Janet was sleeping while mother described a good pregnancy and delivery and the breastfeeding situation. Looking at the baby, the spontaneous thought that the baby had sexy lips occurred to me, and remembering Racker's (1951) concept of considering spontaneous thoughts with a patient as part of a countertransference reaction, I verbalized the thought and watched the reactions.

The mother asked me how I knew how she felt, and, when asked to elaborate further, she commented that from the moment the baby started sucking from her breast she felt terribly aroused sexually, that she had never felt like this before, that it was unbearable, and that she feared she had damaged her daughter by her panic and despair. Once she started talking about this situation, she began to speak in her native language, confusing me with a person from another country of origin. She could now admit her confusion since she was experiencing so many new sensations: in her body, in her hearing, and in her head. I made a link with the newborn in the mother reactivating memories and also suggested that there might be conflict about her sexuality. The mother said that sex was not spoken about in her culture, that her marriage had been arranged—she had not previously known her husband—and that she did not like him. She never felt excited by him in the way she was when breastfeeding. I said that we could talk about her sexuality and changes in the baby and in her feelings. I wondered whether the new-born baby in herself was puzzled and trying to make sense of both her body and baby. On the other hand, the real newborn might also be experiencing difficulties; she might feel as puzzled as her mother was in accepting all the body sensations and the sensual stimulation.

By this time the baby had woken up, and the mother mentioned her fear of damaging the baby. On being asked whether she thought the baby felt the damage, she replied that she did. Encouraged to feed her baby and share her feelings she did so, in spite of her doubts as to whether she was liked and wanted by the baby. I put into words what the baby might possibly be thinking, such as "Mummy, I feel strange sensations in my body, heart, and mind; what about you, Mummy? We are partners, we both have new things to tell each other." The mother said this was so nice that she would try to bring her up to talk and share.

The intervention took an hour and a half, and I had follow-up from the maternity department and the health visitor, who reported that mother and baby had a good developing relationship.

Discussion.   In this case, a quick, short intervention fulfilled the mother's immediate need to connect with an understanding adult and overcome what seemed to be an insurmountable obstacle. The therapist's work in such cases usually ends after a deeply entrenched feeling is modified and ensuing difficulties are overcome. The possibility of change is directly related to the parent's feeling in crisis. Some mothers return for consultations at a later date.

Brief insightful work

Mothers in this group showed concern about ongoing difficulties they had with their infant, without necessarily panicking. The work usually took place over three to eight sessions and involved identifying and exploring the mother's own infantile emotions connected with ghosts in her past that were interfering with the mothering of her infant in the here-and-now. On gaining insight, these mothers worked cooperatively with the therapist towards some kind of resolution of the presenting problem. (Such interventions are described as mother–infant psychotherapy by: Cramer, 1995; Daws, 1989; Fraiberg, 1980; Lebovici & Stoleru, 1983; Palacio Espasa & Manzano, 1988; Stern-Buschweiler & Stern, 1989.)

CASE 53: EURICKA, AGE 14 MONTHS

Euricka kept waking during the night and would only go back to sleep if held. The mother had undergone IVF treatment for ten years before giving birth to a son, and Euricka was born ten months later. The nanny left while the mother was in hospital. Breast-feeding was difficult, and the baby had continuous urinary infections. In therapy, the baby played well with the mother and therapist but found it difficult to separate from her mother's body.

The mother felt bewildered by the changes in her life and the lack of support. Her wish to have a baby turned to shock at being overwhelmed by two children born so soon after each other and regret at not being able to attend to their individual needs, or regaining space for her and her husband to think about them.

Euricka sought closeness at night because the brother was jealous and demanding during the day.

Both parents were only children, and when the mother was 6 years old her own mother had died of a heart attack. The therapist helped the parents to start talking about their feelings and about the pressure of each child demanding individual attention. The children had been acting out their distress of feeling unheld emotionally by disturbed/damaged parents, whom they felt as not strong enough to deal with their fears and anxieties.

Play with soft toys helped the children to start putting their feelings and dreams into words that were shared with the therapist. The parents could re-enact their anxieties about unborn siblings and understand better other feelings linked to the experience of parent-hood. Limits had to be understood and developed, as well as other ways to hold young children: through songs, words, joint activities, and games. Once the attachment was felt as secure and understood, separation—as distinct from loss—was integrated in mother's mind and could be played and explained to Euricka about com-plete and safe withdrawal of attention at night and been easy to endorse and for the child to do it successfully.

Paediatric supportive work with aggressive or very disturbed mothers

The mothers in this group showed great anger towards the thera-pist and evoked concern in all professionals involved with them. These cases presented the most problems in early intervention and the thera-pist felt least able to help, and there was the risk of serious difficulties arising in the future.

Some of the mothers failed to attend even their first appointment after reluctantly agreeing to be referred. In other cases, the mothers presented a very high level of anxiety, or felt persecuted. A different approach was needed that avoided over-involvement with the moth-er's psychopathology.

Surprisingly, although some very disturbed mothers were not in-terested in gaining insight about themselves, they did seem willing to develop insight into their baby's feelings. The focus was therefore on shared infant–parent observations and interpreting the infant's indi-viduality.

CASE 54: SABINA, AGE 15 MONTHS

The mother and father, aged 46 and 50 years, respectively, both suffered from multiple sclerosis. The father had had the condition for ten years and the mother for four. They had another daughter, aged 4 years.

The mother looked old, tired, dispirited, and mistrustful, whereas the baby was bouncy and lively, demanding attention all the time. The mother complained of the child's exhausting behaviour, saying it should be the reverse. On being asked what she meant by that, she explained that the child should be happy just to have two parents alive. This made the therapist inwardly uneasy: were the children born just to look after the parents? Or were the parents aware of the children's needs apart from having parents alive? It did not seem as though they were. The father had periods of feeling exhausted when he stayed at home. The mother seemed easily annoyed and did not want to volunteer information about her childhood or family set-up: everything had been all right. "Just do your job" seemed to be the attitude. She began by saying she was beginning to feel murderous towards the therapist, and wishing to run away from the consultation. The therapist realized that it might help to focus on enhancing the mother's knowledge about the child. So she began to describe the child's actions and possible thinking and feelings as though she were the voice of the child— "Mummy, I am lively and you want me to be quiet; I am trying to get as much as possible from you; I am frightened about your health and Daddy's." Mother laughed at this and said that babies don't think. Sabina stopped demanding and handed a teddy-bear to her mother. The mother said: "That's a good girl, I want you to be a good girl." The baby screamed and wanted to be picked up, and the mother did so. The therapist suggested that the baby actually meant "No, no, I want you to play nicely" and was looking upset and also that the girl might have felt annoyed about having to be only what the mother wanted.

The girl moved uncontrollably, fighting the mother's tense grip, and the mother said she could not stand it. The therapist mentioned the little girl's fear of not being liked and her wish to be able to communicate her unease, distress, discomfort, as well as good feelings. It seemed obvious that the girl was lively and full of frustrations with an internal persecutory mother who was not acknowledging her limitations and expectations.

The therapist continued by saying that she would sit on the floor and play. The mother did not. The therapist said, "Come on, Mummy, I like playing with you, take the telephone, ring a friend for tea." The baby was playing delightedly with some plastic rings, a little pole, and a doll nearby, and then everything began to get confused and her game became unclear. The psychotherapist held the baby doll, gave it a cuddle, and sat it up, observing the girl's play. The mother then expressed confusion and exhaustion, and it looked as though Sabina's game had become more frenzied than it ever was with any other child and that the child was enacting the mother's confusion.

The therapist said that probably Sabina was feeling confused about herself and her parents, and a few sessions could help to contain this and clarify feelings. The mother accepted this, provided that the work was linked to understanding the baby; she did not want to be told anything about herself. The mother was able to hear and understand about her daughter's individuality and needs. Indeed, she did eventually change her attitude to her baby, the process taking seven sessions.

Discussion.   The mother developed in her mothering of Sabina and probably also of her own confused, frightened, and debilitated baby within herself.

The mother's constraints did not allow insight into her own past, but the work may have permitted some of that past to be relived, perhaps through learning tolerance and skill in reaching her baby. I think it demanded tolerance on the part of the psychotherapist towards aspects of the parents' relationships with their own parents that could not be changed, either because of the parents' own attitude or because of their relationship with the grandparents.

Network support or psychodynamic network assessment

This group consisted of mothers who were unable to cope with motherhood but nevertheless wanted help because their babies were failing to thrive or develop appropriately. Some of the mothers had a psychiatric history. The therapist had to hold several interviews in order to ascertain what would be the most appropriate referral and to set up a referral network.

CASE 55: RIO, AGE 7 MONTHS

Rio, a baby boy, was displaying gaze and social avoidance; he was also hyperactive, crawling non-stop and trying to stand up. Mother and father were professionals in their thirties and of Turkish origin. Rio was the second child.

The mother—an undiagnosed chronic manic depressive—wept during the consultation, feeling rejected by her son and too exhausted and unwilling to do any housework. She had been in this state of extreme depression for the previous four months, according to her husband, who accompanied her to the first interview.

Mother was also drinking heavily. Though concerned, the father was avoiding coming home early.

Rio's brother, five years older, was refusing to go to school. Mother showed that she had the desire and the ability to try to get to know her baby's individuality, but she failed to understand it, no matter how hard she tried to be more alert to the baby's likes and dislikes. Clearly, she was finding it difficult to link thoughts, to identify with the baby and his needs, and to satisfy them accordingly. Her excessive crying and her inability to verbalize her feelings or to examine her past alarmed the therapist. Mother could only talk about her inability to do things and how she could not understand people's feelings or what went on in their minds. This included her baby.

Home videos of the baby from birth to 2 months showed a very quiet infant who, right from the start, did not engage or seek attention, already suggesting gaze and social avoidance. It seemed that a vicious circle had been clearly established: a chronic manic-depressive mother with a fragile infant who was not very interested in people or found them frightening or overwhelming.

Mother attended the third interview, quite drunk, and had driven for half an hour to get to the consultation. The therapist felt that the mother should be helped to see an adult psychiatrist to take care of her own mental health needs and physical safety. She was totally resistant to the idea. They also discussed the prospect of her mother, who was concerned about the situation, coming to stay with the family in London if needed. In the meantime, Rio was relating to and playing with the therapist and the mother, which gave reassurance to the mother about the baby's ready acceptance of her, but she herself couldn't help crying and being miserable. Since I felt that the baby and she were in danger, I firmly requested a psychiatric consultation.

The mother was diagnosed as manic depressive, was prescribed medication, which she took, and both mother and father were seen for four weeks, once weekly, by the psychiatrist, in order to monitor the effects of the medication. Thereafter, individual psychodynamic support work with the mother took place in her meetings with the psychiatrist, whereas I, the psychotherapist, had meetings with the mother and baby in order to help both the baby and the mother–infant relationship to develop healthily. Twelve fortnightly sessions took place.

The mother's mother came to London for two months to stay with the family, and soon after she first arrived in the country she attended one session, in order to gain some insight into the family situation. She played with the baby during the interview. The therapist explained to the grandmother that the mother should be included and should be encouraged to participate more and more, if not to model herself on her. Feelings of acceptance and understanding rather than criticism were discussed. The mother–baby relationship had improved by the time Rio was 13 months old, and different feelings developed. The mother was able to start feeling strong, loving and loved, and interested in knowing what she felt and what her children, mother, and husband felt. The child behaved in a calm way. He played, made eye contact, and showed determination in getting his message across. He built a secure attachment to the mother and enjoyed socializing with her.

Discussion.   When a symptom in the child is present in the consultation and the mother is showing signs of unsafe and/or psychotic behaviour, it is necessary to monitor the deterioration and/or degree of risk to the child within that situation. It is also important to think with both the family and the psychiatrist about ways of measuring the seriousness of the mother's mental state and what kind of help is needed, rather than collude with it or escape from it as a result of internal objects in the patient being projected into the psychotherapist, and the patient not being able to think them through. It was necessary in Rio's case to allow the psychotic state of the mother's fragmentation to be contained, to acknowledge the underlying anxieties, and for help to be given, received, and integrated. In such cases, it is important to form a network that includes the father, any other willing members of the family, professionals from a mother-and-baby unit or in the community, Social Services, or other health agencies. The role of this network is to plan together effective support for an extremely disturbed mother–infant relationship and enable the therapeutic work to take place, allowing the child to grow and develop emotionally in a good-enough environment.

Parent–infant personality mismatch

Within this group there were parents who shared a common interest and had an infant with quite a different preference or aptitude. The parents within this category whom I have seen have brought their children for consultation at around 2 years of age, with severe symptoms such as pulling out their own hair, making themselves bleed, head-banging, or being socially withdrawn. It seemed as though the symptoms had to become severe before the parents could become at all aware of any need for help.

After an initial meeting with parents and child, I would hold two meetings to assess the child's need for individual psychotherapy. I would then discuss my recommendations with the parents and see if they were willing to accept the individuality of the child and to make changes within the family in order to accommodate the child who had been effectively left out. "Working with interaction" meant that, apart from just working with the behavioural interactions, we also had to think, understand, and work on the psychodynamic transactions that had to take place in order to incorporate the new member of the family, with different characteristics from their own.

CASE 56: ANDREW, AGE 2 YEARS

This little boy was brought for consultation due to his withdrawn behaviour and hair-pulling. Both parents were gym teachers and members of a sports club, and they would spend all weekend playing sports and socializing. Andrew's 5-year-old sibling had flourished. In the interview, the elder child and parents played, laughed, and communicated with each other, while Andrew remained quiet and had to be drawn into the situation. He seemed bothered by the noise and preferred to go to one side and play on his own with a toy car.

The psychotherapist saw Andrew twice on his own; he had a calm attitude, was willing to engage, and smiled when acknowledged or when he changed from one game to another. From time to time, he would lie on the couch and hum nursery rhymes to himself, sometimes stopping so that the therapist could continue the tune; when she stopped, Andrew would take over the tune, and so on. In the second session, his eye contact, confidence, and capacity to develop his games had all improved, with no signs of anger or frustration.

In an interview with the parents on their own, the psychotherapist spoke about these two sessions with Andrew. They showed interest and a willingness to discover more about his individuality. They realized they had been unable to imagine that a child of theirs could be so different—averse to rushing in the mornings and to sporty weekends. They thought about ways of incorporating his needs into their routine and how to "discover" him.

The psychotherapist raised the possibility that their original "blindness" towards their son might have been because they were basically intolerant of difference, and what that meant and why. The parents talked a great deal about how important for their happiness had been their choice of a partner who shared the same interests and their wish for their children to have the same interests—a "cosy" family plan. One month later, the family interview was quite different. There had been incidents because of the compromises that had to be made to accommodate the second child being slow, dreamy, and musical—the 5-year-old had become jealous and resentful of the attention now being paid to his younger brother, who was no longer showing any obvious signs of disturbance.

Discussion. The parents' narcissistic choice of partner indicated that there might be a low tolerance to difference. However, once this was pointed out, they were prepared to accept it as a possibility and were willing to try different ways of communicating with their child. Such cases surprise me, because of the degree of disturbance that the children have to reach in order to be taken to a consultation, and the speed with which change occurs when this is described. I wondered whether, while they are newborns and early infants, the children do manage to have a good-enough relationship to form stable object relations that help the child to protest violently when he reaches toddlerhood and is requested to perform differently. He can then transmit clearly his message to parents who are able to adapt at once.

WORK FOCUSING ON THE INFANT

This section considers work that involves looking at the child from the point of view of its transient psychic organization at a given developmental stage.

Developmental crisis

A developmental crisis may be a healthy, transient response, and the mother needs to be reassured that the child is changing internally and is letting her know this.

CASE 57: TOBIAS, AGE 8½ MONTHS

Tobias screamed whenever he woke up in a different room in a family friend's house, or whenever he was held by a stranger. He had not reacted like this previously.

In the interview, the child's play and interactions with his mother seemed rich, varied, and relaxed, but with the therapist the child showed caution, scrutinizing her face and showing age-appropriate anxiety. He examined toys and handled keys. His behaviour was explained to his mother, and we discussed how to help him with transitions throughout this stage of development by planning and preparing the child for overnight stays with family friends or other unfamiliar events. Though mother felt that the child was too young to understand, it did make sense to her and she was prepared to do this preparation work. She was given an appointment for a month later, though she could contact the clinic before this if she became worried, but it did seem that their attachment was secure. In general, such cases are dealt with by the primary health caregivers.

Reactive crisis

In reactive crises, the infants seem to be reacting to a traumatic family event, such as when mother goes back to work or a grandmother dies.

CASE 58: SUZANNE, AGE 6 MONTHS

Suzanne had been a planned baby, the pregnancy and delivery had been good, and the breastfeeding had been wonderful for four or five months, at which time the baby readily accepted the withdrawal of the breast and mother's return to work. This had been the plan, and great pains had been taken to find a suitable nanny. Suddenly the baby began screaming at night, wanting only mother and breast.

Mother was exhausted in the consultation, since she was working all day and attending to the child all night. The psychotherapist asked the mother about her feelings with regard to going back to work, and she quickly answered that she was very satisfied with the domestic arrangements, including the baby-care.

The baby, meanwhile, seemed very content playing with keys and rattles. There was a sense of not being allowed to talk of sadness and loss. The fact that perhaps the baby was sad, could not so easily accept the change, and was missing her mother seemed unthinkable. The mother said, very rationally: "So what can I do? She doesn't understand the economic reasons for my having to go back to work." The abrupt answer, avoidance, and the countertransference indicated an unplanned, unresolved attachment to the baby, for which there had been no space. The work had to focus carefully at the level of acknowledging new feelings and experiences by indicating that perhaps there was a part of her that needed and wanted to be with her adorable, cosy baby and whom it was unbearable to leave behind.

The baby sought to be cuddled, and mother did so. The mother said that she had to work, and would the psychotherapist please help the baby to sleep at night. The baby stiffened and began to whine. I mentioned that the baby was comfortable to be with her mother when she was trying to understand the situation, but that she became tense when the mother vocalized the situation so stiffly.

I raised the question as to whether sadness was allowed from either of the parents, and whether Suzanne would be allowed to cry while mother was preparing to leave for work. The mother said she would not be able to leave the house if the baby were to cry. I suggested that Suzanne might be reacting at night because she could not show her feelings during the day, and that it was a healthy reaction for both of them to be sad when separating; this sadness could be kept in mind and shared, even if it did hurt. The mother said she would be unable to keep this in mind. She would not be able to work. We explored the theme further.

In the second session, both mother and baby were quite depressed. I felt that this was a healthy change. Suzanne was behaving like a new-born baby, and the mother was angry with the psychotherapist.

What seemed to have been transferred to the psychotherapist was a need for the mother to take in and contain sadness, depression, anger, and frustration, as well as smiles and contentment. There was also a need to help integrate the stage Suzanne was going through by understanding her internal state and sharing it with her mother, emotionally and verbally. The timing of the event, the actual leaving for work, with the previous detachment and denial of feelings, seemed to prevent Suzanne from reaching the "depressive position", where positive and negative aspects of mother are integrated in one person. This could be reassuring in the sense that the mother was felt to be always there, that she could be both unreliable and persecutory at times and very much loved and wanted at other times.

The mother's more open expression of anger aroused in her the fear of damage to her daughter. The mother experienced this as persecutory, as well as fearing losing control of her new emotions and other new experiences in the world. She realized that she could be annoyed with the psychotherapist for opening up painful areas, that some old feelings had been reactivated in this new state of motherhood. She was invited to explore this further.

I felt that there were two babies—the real one struggling to integrate and to feel at ease internally, and the one in the mother who was feeling persecuted with the fear of losing control of the perceived stability of her plans. The adult part of the mother was available, however, to listen and to accept both babies and to continue the thinking at home.

We then explored Suzanne's message of experiencing the mother as capable of taking in her true feelings, her weaknesses as well as her strengths. She might well have experienced her mother as feeling too persecuted before, too preoccupied with the idea of having to go back to work, not feeling attached, and having to build a false image of Suzanne that could put up with everything, until it became insupportable. I suggested to the mother that she allow herself to think about and tolerate the experience. She cried and thought more about Suzanne's feelings in what seemed like a state of reverie, during which time the infant became relaxed, patting her.

From the third session, the infant slept through the night, and the mother continued to think about the changing experiences with her baby and about motherhood as a dynamic process rather than a plan to be rigidly followed. In the interview, Suzanne displayed different behaviours towards the psychotherapist and the mother; these were then taken up and enjoyed by the mother, and she talked about the new feelings she had for Suzanne and the richness of the baby's personality.

Discussion.   The baby complained at night only; she showed perfect adaptive behaviour during the day and in the interview. This is a common pattern among certain babies. It seems they cannot fall asleep, or stay sleeping, because they have undigested experiences that prevent the process of wish-fulfilment through dreams and feelings of connectedness with an internal safe, positive experience. It is important, therefore, for the psychotherapist to find out this process by accepting it in the consultation and by observing the infant's behaviour and transmitted emotions, to be able to explore with tolerance, to share and understand the infant, and to create a space in which the mother can enter, even when her negative transference is being worked out. This is, in fact, an opportunity for emotional development to resume its healthy course. It must be stressed that it is healthy for a baby to complain, since, if it is persistent enough, this forces the parents to seek a solution.

Psychosomatic disturbance

In cases involving psychosomatic disturbance, babies may hold their breath, generally fail to thrive, have eczema, or display vomit symptoms that seem to have no physical cause. It would appear that the babies are seeking their mother's attention. This may be due to depression or to excessive anxiety from the unconscious mind transmitted to the body. Parents may panic, and it is necessary to find out what the message is that is being transmitted by the baby to them.

CASE 59: MATIAS, AGE 15 MONTHS

Matias was the fourth of five children, all under 6 years old. He would hold his breath and turn blue, and his mother was afraid he would die. A fifth child had just been born.

The mother had also come from a large family, of nine, and had been used to children, but Matias, with his breath-holding, was very worrying and could not be ignored.

During the home interview, the four children were scrambling about and playing all over the place, even Matias; but when the baby cried and was breastfed, he stopped what he was doing and observed, looking sad, as though he had irretrievably lost something wonderful. The father talked to me or looked at the children, but not at Matias. I said that Matias wished he could be the baby; he wanted to have and keep Mummy all to himself; how sad he was. He went to the teddies and threw one around. I continued, saying that Matias might want to do things to the baby, swing him around and get rid of him. Matias continued to knock the teddy around. When mother asked if this was really so, I drew her attention to the immense sadness and look of longing on his face. Mother explained that they were going on holiday to grandmother's, and she would try to give him some more time. On their return, mother reported no further incidents of breath-holding until two days before coming to the interview. Again, we used the session to try to understand Matias's communication of his needs. We also thought about whether it was a good idea for me to come their home a few more times without Matias having to display breath-holding in order for mother to understand the child's individual needs—she was not used to an approach of this kind.

Discussion.   Physical symptoms without actual physical cause require thorough paediatric investigation. It is interesting to discover and translate the message to the mother, when the message contains boredom or fear of the mother's mental state; it is important to reflect back to the mother how difficult it is for her to tolerate this nonverbal communication and to help her to examine the nature of the difficulty.

Eczema can be due to a food allergy, but it can be a condition signalling a growing state of depression in the mother that causes the child to feel unheld in her mind, thus producing an irritation in the baby that is equivalent to the irritation being experienced in the mother.

In babies who fail to thrive, a similar internal process occurs, whereby there is a difficulty in integrating experiences owing to faulty or no attachment with the mother: she is mentally and emotionally unavailable. The infant feels dropped, unheld, and uncontained, and the feelings are somatized, with varying degrees of severity (Selwyn, 1993).

My approach is to draw mother's attention *concretely* to the child by observing the child, both visually and emotionally, thereby gradually promoting the kind of specific attachment needed by that particular child.

Difficulty in integrating experiences

Some infants display difficulties in organizing behaviour, either by being too organized or, showing early signs of obsessive, ritualistic, or phobic behaviour, or they may display disintegration and chaos. In any case, the element of panic in their behaviour can appear very easily either through breaking the ritual or by trying to pull them out of their withdrawn state.

In order to "hear" their message, their vulnerable or frightened self has to be shown and time allowed for minute details or signs to be picked up and understood. Any sensory activity can be a source of information. These infants fall into two main groups:

1.   *Crying excessively and not smiling*, showing panic very quickly after reaching 3 months of age:

CASE 60: TOMMY, AGE 4 MONTHS

Tommy cried continually and did not smile. His parents were mature in age and artistic. He demanded to be constantly held in mother's arms in such a way that he could look around. At the slightest noise he would appear startled, turn red in the face, cry, and scream, and this caused the mother to feel increasingly frightened. He seemed to feel persecuted when he could not see where a noise came from. He did not mind whose arms he was in, provided he was upright and had a good view of his surroundings. Paediatric examination failed to find anything physically wrong or anything wrong with his nervous system.

The mother and father came from families of three children each. There appeared to be no factors in their past history which seemed to link up with the presenting problem. The mother, Mrs P., had started to sit the baby in front of the TV as he was getting heavy, but he cried. After careful and detailed observation of the child's behaviour and reactions in the room with mother and me, as psychotherapist, it became clear that the focus needed to be on helping the child to overcome his hearing sensitivity.

The baby seemed to be trying to control the environment visually and would become startled at the slightest noise. His hearing seemed over-sensitive, and his body was tense and watchful. I asked mother to lower her tone, until, by whispering or singing softly to him, it had a soothing rather than excitable effect on her baby, whose tension then seemed to ease.

Since sound seems very loud *in utero*, I inferred from my observation in the consulting-room that the child might have had to overcome a great deal of discomfort in the womb and that he continued to experience this in a normal environment with normal tones of voice.

The richness of the mother–infant experience appeared to have got lost because of the mother's lack of attunement, reciprocity, mirroring, and rhythmical sharing. Her inability to translate for her infant the experience of an unsafe, noisy world reinforced his feelings of persecution.

The mother herself suggested that she pursue this issue at home. She would go through the house, checking out all the possible noises her son was exposed to, and their source. The point of the exercise was for her to enter her son's world, stay with his fears, and thus help him find a "container" for them. He could then gradually form a more secure base for his experiences, according to his own pace and rhythm.

Discussion.   In this family, a greater value was put on visual than on auditory experience. In the interview, the baby needed the experience of showing his fears by communicating them to the psychotherapist who, in turn, shared the information with his mother, thus helping the baby to overcome the difficulty. The process of developing a more secure attachment between mother and child was also initiated.

2.   *Visual, social, or total withdrawal.*   These infants, after the age of 1 month, usually display placid, lethargic behaviour most of the day.

CASE 61: JOHN, AGE 4 WEEKS

After a fortnight of wide-awake behaviour, John rejected the breast and tended to sleep most of the time. This was the parents' third child, and as they had not experienced this kind of behaviour with their other two children, they were very worried. His muscle tone seemed to be very weak. The health visitor had given all sorts of advice, but the family situation seemed to worsen.

The extended family seemed supportive, even though the mother had moved from her country of origin with the birth of her third child. It had been difficult at the beginning, but she was happy in England. The baby did not respond to his mother or siblings talking to or caressing him. I suggested that it might be useful to hold him and to try different tones of voice, touches, and smells. Finally, after forty-five minutes, he opened his eyes, and it was necessary to keep him interested. This child took longer than usual to react, and in order to hold his interest, he needed more stimulation than other infants of his age. He also displayed a reluctance to share with his siblings, as if, even at this tender age, he were jealous.

On learning all this, the mother decided she had to make more time and space in her busy household schedule to provide this infant with whatever it was he needed. The father understood how he could help him as well, and the child gradually recovered muscle tone, became more alert, and could begin to enjoy the richness of family life, which would enhance his development.

Discussion.   John's withdrawn state had to be understood in terms of his need for attention; he was passively demanding touching, holding, and talking more than other children. The mother, who was used to carrying the baby on a sling on her back, began to hold him in her arms, to touch him, look at him, and mirror his identity for him. Unlike his siblings, John showed an apparently innate weakness in integrating experiences and persevering with communication.

Physical damage at birth or in the first year

A double process comes into play with physically damaged babies (see also Fraiberg, 1980; Massie & Rosenthal, 1984):

a. the parents mourning the infant imagined before birth as compared to the reality of the imperfect newborn;
b. the parents suffering shock and trauma after discovering this reality, or from living in a state of uncertainty for what may be months after the birth.

CASE 62: MARTIN, AGE 2 MONTHS (DOWN'S SYNDROME)

Martin cried incessantly. The mother was confused by the anxiety being expressed about the baby by professionals and by the baby being too soft to hold. The mother, Mrs G., came to the interview, wanting to have classes on how to hold this kind of baby and how to tell when his heart was malfunctioning.

Mrs G. already had a 5-year-old child and a good, secure marriage, but this baby's crying was different and it disturbed and frightened her. She claimed that she didn't mind having a child with a disability, but she did mind feeling anxious and not being able to understand the baby, since she, herself, was not Down's syndrome.

As none of us shared the baby's disability, we agreed that we should be careful in interpreting the baby's communications, but how would we know whether or not our understanding was correct? It is generally thought that, in humans, crying is a sign of distress. The question in the parents' minds seemed to be whether this child was, indeed, human, or whether he was an animal, a monster, or even a vegetable. His gestures, body posture, responses, and reactions were then carefully observed, and the mother was encouraged to hold the infant while we discussed how she might explore her baby's personality in spite of her fears of having damaged him, and of continuing to damage him.

Similar work continued over the next four sessions, helping their relationship to grow and develop, gradually getting to know the baby, while staying with the reality of the ambivalence and guilty feelings of the mother. The mother could then talk about what she expected and her horror when she heard that her newborn was not normal. She had thought that it might have been a punishment from God.

Discussion. It was important not to get into the mother's unconscious needs and wishes before facilitating the relationship and the attachment, since it felt more beneficial to reduce the guilt first and then facilitate the process of real separation; otherwise, there would be no distinction between the real and the imaginary damage. There were issues of extreme confusion arising from lack of both information and emotional support—the exploratory work on her feelings and the baby's feelings developed rapidly once a mental and emotional holding of the dyad took place.

SUMMARY

In difficult infant–mother/parent relationships, the description of different early psychoanalytic consultations and psychotherapy can provide a rich framework for preventative work. It may well be that psychotherapeutic work is done on a daily basis by health workers, teachers, nurses, paediatricians, paediatric physiotherapists, play therapists, and the like. However, what distinguishes our kind of work at the Infant–Parent Clinic is that we are thinking psychoanalytically—we observe closely, we try to understand how the parents and children think and the processes that go on between them; we make hypotheses about the unconscious dynamics and the structure of their emotional growth, based on the behaviour observed and how it is experienced by us as psychotherapists in the room (the countertransference). The materials we work with are the unconscious needs, wishes, defences, fears, and anxieties. By understanding these, we help mother and infant to attach securely, in order then to be able to separate appropriately, to form object relations that can mature. During assessment, we try in the first interview to elucidate where the pain is, what expectations there had been, whose these were and how they are not being met, and when and where development became difficult, lonely, or impossible.

The model presented, at the beginning of this chapter, for psychoanalytic mother–infant psychotherapy (Figure 6.1) represents the work done with mothers/parents who are able verbally to express their concern and whose mental functioning and personality structure allow the positive use of the links made by the therapist of their unconscious causes of actual projections or impeded real perception of the individuality of their infant. However, it does not include mother–infant psychotherapy where there is a mother with a mental disability or borderline psychotic personality; nor can the model be used where there is a psychiatric condition. In such cases the technique has to change, as is explained in chapter seven: the transference and countertransference are used as indicators of the state of mind; help may be given to support the family or network to create a system for caring safely for the mother and infant; and the mother may be assisted to develop skills to compensate for a given vulnerability in the baby. It also shows how to work with the infant in difficulties and get across to the parents the infant's specific sensibilities, likes, dislikes, and deficiencies, explaining the delicate and skilful way of exploring these with the parents.

PART III

FRAGILE INFANTS AND MOTHERS

CHAPTER SEVEN

Special-needs babies:
helping to secure attachment

Arriving in this country as a young professional, speaking a different language, produced a certain ambivalence in me. Lack of knowledge of the cultural ground rules, looked down on as foreign, not being understood properly, and appearing mentally slow because of difficulties in following conversations produced a feeling of being disabled. On the positive side, the parallel thinking I developed led to a better understanding of autism and special-needs infants. How much more difficult it must be for a fragile or special-care or special-needs child, who has to face the parents' failed expectations and is misunderstood, mistreated, and undervalued. I explored the possibility of becoming a last resource, when all other professionals had given up or could not work with a family, to try to find the unique challenges facing the infant and the family.

It is terribly painful for parents who have produced a deformed child, or a child with severe, possibly life-threatening difficulties, to admit their love. But it is that possibility for love and good attachment that will make life worthwhile and fuller for family and professionals. The problem is how the professionals can contain the parents without themselves adopting the same devastating defensive mechanisms employed by the parents, leaving the child with a double deficiency: the syndrome, and an outside world that has difficulty accepting them.

In order to treat infants with a physical or mental disability, it is necessary to expand the scope of psychoanalytic psychotherapy by utilizing communications at all levels, including the sensory/tactile, to help the first stage of object relations to take place. The perception I have of my job as an infant–parent psychotherapist is to tune in to the basic sensorimotor experiences and mental representations of the baby and then to describe these to the mother and empathize with her difficulties in reaching her infant. It is also necessary for mother and infant to acknowledge each other's individuality in order for them to attach properly. Whatever the disability, an extra burden is placed on emotions and thinking, and it is important to identify emotional difficulties at an early stage in such children.

Before I discuss any cases, I would like briefly to point to a few of the areas that have been explored in the psychoanalytic psychotherapy of children with disabilities since Sándor Ferenczi (1929) wrote about the vulnerability of the unwelcome child to repeated childhood illness and low self-esteem. First, parents of a child with a physical or mental disability have difficulty in speaking about their child as a separate person, as if they have never mourned the expected healthy one (Sinason, 1986). Second, parents fear their murderous wishes, which sometimes go back to prenatal experience (Clar, 1933; Mannoni, 1973; Sinason, 1988). Third, it may be questioned whether from birth there has been a bonding attachment (Blacher & Meyers, 1983). Fourth, the disabled child defending itself against trauma is also defending itself against psychosis (Sinason, 1986; Spensley, 1985). Finally, a high proportion of psychosis before 4 years of age in has been found in children born with or developing an early physical disability (Massie & Rosenthal, 1984).

It is important, too, to consider the capacity of the mother to accommodate to the child's special needs and of the professionals to provide effective support. We have to offer parents guidelines for thinking from the time of the birth about a disabled or malformed baby. Emotional and psychodynamic assistance in the form of a number of interviews, or support groups for parents with similar needs, should be available, as these parents are shocked and hurt. Such feelings, with all the other feelings reactivated by the traumatic birth, should be contained, thoroughly explored, and talked about.

It is important that professionals dealing with trauma prepare themselves to be emotionally available. Briefly, professionals in special-care units, children's wards, and maternity wards have unconscious needs and anxieties that significantly influence the quality of services offered to parents and babies. These unconscious needs are linked with mental self-preservation. Dealing with pain, damage, and death makes the professional invest more energy than usual in the continuous reactivation of feelings related to these issues (e.g. guilt and reparation), to previous sad experiences, and to impotence and discomfort. The anxieties related to fear of death and dying in grieving relatives and angry colleagues needs containment and discussion rather than avoidance, denial, and manic reparatory behaviour in bureaucratic rituals and obsessive rhythms of unnecessary activities. Discussion groups in which cases are examined individually, and in which professionals can be helped to put into words their reactions and behaviours, allow individual professionals more emotional availability and creativity.

It is possible for a hospital unit or ward to be a wonderful opportunity for preventing early relationship and emotional disorders. It could become a *place for patients*, a patient-centred place of treatment where the hospital experience is made more bearable by a relaxed, holding, trusting, safe atmosphere. It could also be *a place for parents,* where their personal and psychic pain are acknowledged and contained and their feelings of anger, resentment, exhaustion, and guilt as well as love and care can be helped to be put into words. Finally, it could be *a place for the family*—for siblings or grandparents—since they, too, suffer. They are often the satellites who carry the anxieties and projections of their parents or the disabled child and so can either diminish the strength of the family or increase it through better understanding. This can be achieved by providing support groups for siblings or grandparents. A maternity ward in Buenos Aires, Argentina, hosts a grandparent's group in the special-care baby unit, and this has produced very good results.

* * *

The idea of helping babies with a physical or mental disability, whatever the cause, is to prevent a secondary cognitive or emotional derailment and to foster attachment between mother and baby. Before going on to discuss the psychotherapeutic method in greater detail, the following two brief case descriptions are presented to outline the topic.

CASE 63: LISA, AGE 5 WEEKS (DOWN'S SYNDROME)

The mother was Chinese, and she had had a Down's syndrome baby. She was extremely angry, didn't want to collect her baby from the special-care baby unit, and was abusive to the staff and to her husband. The baby was normal weight at birth and had no other particular problems. I observed that he had very good muscle tone and that he was good at communicating his affection and states of mind. This enabled him to have good stable relationships with two nurses during his five-week stay in the unit.

In the first interview I found it difficult to bear the mother's level of anger, and I transmitted this to her. I then discovered that her father had recently died, as had her mother-in-law. According to Chinese custom, my client was obliged to give first priority to her newly widowed father-in-law and to house him rather than protect her own mother. The house was too small for her two older children, the Down's syndrome baby, and the father-in-law, and she felt depleted of maternal support and mental energy. It took several interviews to separate out the mother's anger, her mixed feelings of confusion and divided loyalty, and the individuality of her newborn, who was taken home three weeks later. Ten fortnightly home visits were needed in order to help mother and infant to form a healthy attachment that would enable the baby to grow emotionally. This was done by describing his physical and mental boundaries, images, communication of signals and needs, and the ways he related to himself. The mother was able to create a space in her own mind for this child, who needed—more than anything else—her care and attention in order to thrive.

CASE 64: ABIGAIL, AGE 9 MONTHS (CEREBRAL PALSY)

This case involved a mother with a professional career whose 9-month-old daughter had recently been diagnosed as suffering from cerebral palsy. The referral was due to the baby's continuous screaming. The baby screamed unless she was held in her mother's left arm. Although in this position the mother and the infant could not look at each other, and the mother transmitted unspoken anger and frustration to the baby, the baby's reaction to separation from the arm was one of complete panic, screaming as though she would die. I based my approach on Bick's (1968) concept of the skin and its function in object relations, Spitz's (1948) studies on the somatic consequences of emotional starvation in connection with mother's grief, Ferenczi's (1929) idea of an unwelcomed baby's wish to die, and Adamson-Macedo's (1984) technique of tactile stimulation for premature and low-birth-weight babies. I devised a way of opening up a dialogue between the infant and the mother by thinking about the infant's needs communicated via the transference from the baby and the countertransference in the therapist (myself) of his states of mind, and I encouraged the mother to establish positive, basic skin communication by stroking the infant while maintaining a secure empathetic relationship with me. By continuing to interpret and translate the infant's reactions to new needs over eighteen fort-nightly sessions, the baby's inner world was seen to develop. It took another eighteen fortnightly sessions to then work through the changes of mental representations that the baby and the mother had formed of each other. Positive interaction with the mother became established, which facilitated further cooperative work with other professionals who could help to rehabilitate the infant. The mother could now be in touch with her child's and her own feelings, and she cultivated a secure attachment with the child, who was able to continue developing in an emotionally stable manner.

In the case of Lisa, the baby with Down's syndrome, once the mother was able to create the mental space necessary for therapy to begin, she needed help in discovering her baby's individuality and also in becoming aware of her baby's potential. For Abigail, the baby with cerebral palsy, it became apparent that she needed interpersonal com-munication through more skin contact and development of her body boundaries by touch and the verbal expression of concomitant pleasur-able positive experiences. Regular sessions over a substantial period of time were required for the mother to gain insight into her own per-sonal difficulties and those of the child. Though such interventions took a long time, follow-up has shown healthy development of the child at home and school. (Abigail is discussed in greater detail in the next section; for a full discussion of this interesting case, see Acquarone, 1995).

DISABILITY AND EMOTIONAL PROBLEMS

Children with single and multiple special needs referred to child and adolescent mental-health departments or clinics will often show that, aside from their specific difficulty, there are other underlying factors that seem to have attacked and partially disabled the thinking process. With children who have a low IQ, the possible causes may be:

1. brain damage or deficiency, either congenital or acquired;
2. a physical disability, which can:
   (a) restrict the lifestyle (e.g. polio or arthritis)
   (b) produce a lowering of expectations (e.g. cleft palate or malformation);
3. an emotional disability, which can derive from difficulty in the integration of experiences on the part of either the mother or the infant.

The hypothesis is that with all three causes an emotional component accessible to psychotherapy may be contributing to the cognitive development.

We examine in this section the treatment of an 11-year-old with facial malformation, and two babies, one a 2-month-old with Down's syndrome, the other a 9-month-old with cerebral palsy. Through thinking about the treatment in cases such as these, I have become aware of the feelings of immense pain and fear experienced in the re-enactment of the traumatic scenes while the treatment was in progress. This has allowed me to understand why children, parents, and professionals build such strong defences against having insight into these feelings, and why sometimes the "sick role" is used so much.

Each of the three cases required a different type of treatment:

1. the 11-year-old with facial malformation was in intensive psychoanalytic psychotherapy three times a week;
2. the baby with Down's syndrome was seen in a brief mother–infant psychotherapy intervention at a time of crisis when the mother asked for a consultation;
3. the baby with cerebral palsy was treated in a long-term mother–infant psychotherapy intervention in which mother and infant were seen separately by an adult psychotherapist and a child psychotherapist.

Case 65: Alex, age 11 years (facial malformation)

Alex was referred to his local child-guidance clinic from a teaching hospital because they considered that the child would benefit from having psychotherapy. Alex looked like a scarecrow—just skin and bones, with long limbs and a large deformed head with different-sized eyes. His nose and ears were very long and protruding. His teeth were very big, and his mouth was expressionless. His skin was very pale. He wore glasses with different prescriptions for each eye. His clothes were old-fashioned and too big, and although he never dressed warmly, even in winter, he didn't seem to feel the cold. He had a habit of whistling constantly, flapping his hands about, and clowning around.

Alex had a sad history. He had been left by his mother at the age of 2 years, and he had been fostered on two occasions previously after having been found several times by the police, following neighbours' reports, in his cot with an empty bottle, banging his head against the bars.

His current foster-mother's account of Alex as lovable in spite of his appearance and lack of social skills was very moving. Until he was 2 years old, he had never eaten with a spoon or taken solids. He did not speak a word, and he did not cry at all. The foster-mother wished to put right in Alex what seemed very wrong. She realized that she had to begin very slowly towards helping him to develop human skills—for example, his capacity to accept human beings, a spoon, food. Very slowly he learned domestic and social skills, but his way of speaking, moving, and behaving remained very primitive and sad. For this reason, his foster-mother took Alex to different teaching hospitals to try to identify his disability. The need to find the appropriate secondary school was a major factor in her taking him to a psychiatric hospital, which then referred him to the child guidance clinic.

At home, Alex was very destructive with his toys—they would last for two hours at the most. His movements were all over the place. He had two other foster-siblings and two sisters born from the couple: a 17-year-old and a 2-year-old. Alex had no sleeping problems and had never been physically ill, not even with a common cold.

Alex appeared startled and paralysed when I went to the waiting-room to collect him for his first interview. His foster-mother had to accompany him into the consulting-room, where he looked vacant and moved aimlessly about, allowing her then to leave without complaint. He transmitted to me clearly overwhelming feelings of panic, distress, fragmentation, and despair.

In the first session he made the word "TIT" out of red toy cubes, but in a very pitiful way. He seemed not to know what he had written, except that he had used two Ts. When I explained to him that he had written "TIT", as in breast, and that he was perhaps showing his need to start again from the beginning as a new-born baby in a confusing world in which he needed nourishment to survive, Alex seemed not to understand.

Summary of the first six months of treatment

My interpretation of Alex's needs, wishes, anxieties, and defences as they were felt, thought, and spoken did not seem to affect Alex's behaviour. He would interrupt me with all sorts of noises and get carried away by what appeared to be a desperate attempt to continue with his inhibition to communicate with me through play or work. Alex's great capacity to exclude me and waste the session, and his feeling of power in relation to me, seemed to be constant. He had a habit, session after session, of looking at his hands, gluing them to paper, then peeling them off. It appeared as though he dived into this security, regardless of outside occurrences. At times this gave me the impression of a baby holding on to what was very familiar, like his mother.

In Session 78, after having been away on a school holiday for one week, he came into the room indifferently, whistling as usual in different tonalities, deafening me. He went straight to his paper and pencil and began drawing a coach in great detail. I said it seemed as though Alex had forgotten me, and I asked, "Is Alex showing me how empty and lonely he found the bus, the school holiday, the break?" He gave no answer. He gazed into the air and concentrated on his drawing of the big, empty bus. I quickly carried on speaking about his drawing, his not listening to me, and his safe retreat into himself. He asked for a circular object to enable him to draw the wheel on the bus. I said that he wanted to make it perfect. He began to whistle again, as usual, as if to shut me up. I said this to him. He carried on and on whistling. It was painful to my ears, desperately shrill, and I said that Alex wanted to tell me something very painful and he was acting it out. He could not hear me, and he carried on and on. I had the impression that something terrible was going on, and I said so. He would not respond and continued whistling.

I then started copying his whistling a little, in order to see his reaction. Alex looked at me and said, "Not like that, like this: higher, higher!" For the first time he was actually looking at me, taking an interest in something I was doing. His facial expression and attitude was of extreme concentration, watching me, unlike his usual distorted expression. Once again he said, "Higher, like this— like a kettle." I asked him, "What about the kettle?" He commented, matter-of-factly, in clear English, that when he was 2 years old he had been burnt by a kettle. He did not show pain. Alex said that he remembered the kettle whistling non-stop; he had gone nearer and nearer to it and pulled the electric lead; the kettle fell onto his head and shoulder, and he was taken to hospital.

It was now near the end of the session, and I was struck by the horror of his story. I mentioned that he must have been shocked by the pain and the surprise. He showed me the bald patches on his head and the scars on his shoulder. I expressed his wish to let me know for sure about his past experiences.

His foster-mother was asked about Alex's disclosure. The accident had indeed taken place: he had spent six weeks in hospital, and his mother had not visit him once. When discharged from the hospital, he had been transferred to another temporary foster-mother.

I discovered moments in Alex's behaviour and movements when I could reach and synchronize with him through imitation. This started to help me to gain entry to his inner world.

Later development

In the following sessions, Alex asked for cuddly toys. He kept bringing two magnets with which he played continually, one exerting control over the other and attracting or repelling it at will. In this way he expressed his new capacity to initiate and to experience feelings of power.

Alex spent the next 120 sessions sticking glue to his hands and peeling them from the paper very slowly, crying every now and again. This re-enacted his experience associated with the kettle and the burns. After these 120 sessions, Alex compared the size of the handprints made with glue and realized that he was growing up. In Session 198, he lay down on the floor near the radiator, covered himself with a blanket, and said, "You know something? I can feel my heart. Last night and now, if I put my hand on my chest I can feel it. Did you ever feel your heart? Do you do it very often? It's nice."

From then on, it seemed every now and again that there was an integration in his personality of his body image and his self-image. I had to look constantly for ways to claim his attention and tune into the state of mind that he was in. I had to watch carefully his reaction to any interpretation, and I would keep giving alternative interpretations until I felt that he had grasped one and that that interpretation made sense to him.

In the sessions, he re-enacted being left cold and hungry by his mother, by going to the couch and lying there shivering and crying or looking at me stupidly. At times when he seemed very withdrawn and not wanting to make any contact with me, I recorded his positions on a sketch-pad and talked to him about what he was feeling then. I had heard that at home he had begun to feel the cold and had started to ask for jumpers. He also used the heater a lot, and at times he would even embrace the heater. Separations became very painful, and his manic defence of whistling would return in all its strength, alternating with severely withdrawn behaviour.

Alex's rational thinking finally appeared in Session 422. He came in extremely hyperactive and seemed to be all over the place again, thus satisfying his need for showing great distress in his own clownish way. It appeared that his foster-mother had gone away for a week, because of an emergency with her mother, who was in Jersey. Alex could not speak about this, but he acted. At the end of the session, he linked the unspoken comments he had made with my interpretations of his distress, and he began to calm himself down. He made links between my interpretations then and his awful past experience. He said he was in a panic that he would lose his foster-mother for ever. Then he asked me why he could think now, when he could not think years ago. I mentioned how unbearable this feeling of panic was in his mind. He admitted that he did not trust me either, because I was always leaving him. From this session on it was possible for him to listen, think with me, and draw conclusions. He started progressing at school.

Discussion.   In Alex's case, the traumas of the first two years of life were evident; what we did not know was whether the rejection and neglect by his mother was due to his physical deformity. The work with Alex was aimed at trying to find the level he was at. In Session 78, the imitation of whistling seemed to give him back his ability to ask for help, and he was able to express one of his traumas. By my physical and emotional reaction, he tested my capacity for sympathy and forbearance, and he talked about neglect that was previously unthinkable.

His foster-parents knew about some of his past neglect and traumas, but Alex kept himself very busy not knowing. He seemed to prefer being the stupid scarecrow, the focus of the clowning in the classroom. Towards the end of the treatment, he became aware that his behaviour was mindless or "silly" because to know would have been too painful for him and he might not have wanted to live. When he finished his treatment, he talked to me about going with friends to a fancy-dress party where they chose what to wear. He chose a mediaeval knight in armour—a tough exterior for his now vulnerable self!

It was cases such as this that made me decide to offer, as soon as there was cause for concern, psychotherapy to mothers and infants who were experiencing difficulties in their relationship. I offered my services to health clinics and other primary-care-givers in hospitals, with the specific request that they refer for treatment infants under the age of 1 year. The following two cases are taken from 450 referrals over a nine-year period.

CASE 66: MARK, AGE 2 MONTHS (DOWN'S SYNDROME)

Mark cried non-stop. He was referred from casualty, as his mother was asking for a sedative for him. She had followed all the advice given to her and had sought help, but she was just told he would grow out of it.

The mother came to consultation with me in despair because her baby would not stop crying. She seemed very confused. She told me that she had accepted this baby very well, that she had had a normal child before Mark, and that she was still young (26 years old). Her marriage was well established, and she had sufficient material comforts. However, I noticed that there was something missing from her talk with me, and I realized that the missing part seemed to be a complete lack of negative feelings. She spoke about the baby as if he were an object, not a person.

With regard to Mark's physical disability, it seemed that she did not have a very clear understanding of Down's syndrome, even though she had been given many pamphlets about it on leaving the maternity ward. She said that she did not mind having a child with Down's syndrome, but she had not looked at her baby and found anything different.

After listening to her reasons as to how well the whole situation had been accepted, I noticed that the baby was already moving his mouth and trying to imitate his mother's mouth movements and that he was, in fact, nice-looking. I commented on her urgency in bringing to me her confusion about her feelings and about her baby. The mother said that she wanted someone to teach her how to hold the baby properly. I commented that she wanted me to hold her confused self, which felt like a new baby to her. She might be wondering who this person in herself was who was anxious about so many things, such as this actual new baby that everybody was concerned about—why were they, what was all of that about?

The mother agreed with me and asked me whether I thought she was anxious about the crying or about her confusion. I answered that it was probably both. I suggested that she observe the baby, who was trying very hard to imitate her while she talked. When she realized that Mark was trying to hold her hand, the mother was extremely surprised. She then told me that she was struck by the fact that I would talk to her and with her about her Down's syndrome child. I suggested that perhaps there was something in her that was not allowing her to see a child with Down's syndrome as a child who is an individual with special qualities and defects that are particular to him, and that this was part of her confusion.

The mother asked, "So Down's syndrome means that there are certain disabilities, and I must know about them as well as his particular lovely features? . . . Well, it is difficult because I see him just like any other baby—he has legs, arms, a head, etc. . . ." I then asked the mother, "Whose hands and legs did Mark's resemble?"

She started laughing and began to observe the child in more detail, comparing his hands to her own mother's hands and realizing that her child's legs were very similar to her husband's. By this time, Mark was making eye contact with his mother, moving his mouth, and requesting food. His mother told him that it was not time to eat but they could perhaps talk, and they started cooing.

The mother then returned to the point of remembering when she had started to feel anxious and confused, and she realized that it was on leaving hospital. She had been given a number of pamphlets outlining details of all the institutions that could help her because she had a Down's syndrome child. She had wondered what that meant—was it a thing, a child? If it was such a rare thing, why did it cry? And so much? Would she need all this help?

The mother then rang all the possible numbers listed in the pamphlets, but she received the same reply: that in time the child would grow out of it. Her despair grew with not knowing what to do. She had gone to the casualty department and requested some sedatives to stop the child from crying. I expressed her need of me to clarify her confusion, which seemed to have arisen from receiving the pamphlets. The mother agreed that she had been happy with the baby at the beginning, but that everyone's concern had made her aware of the need to be anxious.

We continued to observe the baby in detail. When the mother left, she said that something had loosened inside her. Mark was giving strong signals about wanting to be in communication with her. The mother asked if she could come again and have a chat with me if Mark continued crying. I said she could, even if he didn't cry, and we had four monthly interviews during which she developed observation of her infant's particular needs. Their level of communication was very good, and the child did stop crying continually. The mother seemed to enjoy mothering this particular child as much as she had enjoyed the first one. On each occasion she came with her 5-year-old, and they both shared Mark, observing, playing, and talking with him.

A two-year follow-up showed the mother's interest and enthusiasm in discovering Mark's personality and in helping him, and Mark showed a capacity for communicating at all levels. He was slow in walking but alert, attentive, and expressive facially.

CASE 67: ABIGAIL, AGE 9 MONTHS (CEREBRAL PALSY)

Abigail's mother complained of nine months of her baby's non-stop crying. An assessment period of five sessions was necessary. In the first session, the mother came by herself and arrogantly described how hopeless her situation was. When Abigail was awake, she would accept being held only by hanging on her mother's left arm; otherwise she would scream.

Their family consisted of a father and a sister who was four years older. This planned pregnancy had become complicated in the fourth month, when bleeding occurred. At the fifth month the waters broke, and the hospital attempted an abortion but without success. After two further months in hospital, the mother had a natural delivery, in the seventh month. She felt anxious and upset, as all this inconvenience had not been planned. The baby was born healthy, but after a month the crying and clinging started. At age 6 months, since she was slow in her overall development Abigail was seen by developmental paediatrician, who diagnosed her as having cerebral palsy.

The subsequent three sessions were dedicated to observing the mother–infant interaction, and both of them independently. It became clear that there was no social interaction. Even though the baby was breastfed, the mother did not look at the child. She held Abigail on her left arm, facing outwards, and the baby seemed to be a rag doll, looking up in the air, her signalling system both arduous and faint. The mother, who seemed to be annoyed and desperate, did not pick up anything from Abigail to start a dialogue.

Abigail made efforts to look at me and, when met halfway, responded with body movements and an intelligent look. She seemed unable to be held in anyone's arms, and she screamed in an inconsolable, pitiful way that appeared to paralyse the mother. No play or games were present. Abigail seemed to be part of the mother's left arm and body and would fall apart at the slightest change in her position.

After five interviews to assess what help could be provided, it became clear that two professionals were needed for regular help. The adult psychotherapist and I held six meetings with mother and baby: at first we held the sessions together, then we alternated fortnightly. The adult therapist's work was in listening to and supporting the mother's emotions. As a child psychotherapist, I focused attention on receiving all kinds of communications and signals from the baby, describing them, and working out (for the mother at the beginning, and with the mother after six months) possible meanings or deeper interpretations of the baby's needs, wishes, and pathological defensive behaviour.

A vignette of a session in the first three months

Abigail came in hanging on the mother's left arm. The baby, even though her body was lifeless, looked straight at me very briefly but intently and intelligently, thus giving hints of a potential to develop and of a wish to link with the therapist. The next move was for me to sit on the floor with Abigail. The baby would, with a twisted, dangling head, look briefly at me, half smile, and then look startled. I took this as some faint wish to request contact in a very uncoordinated way. Thereafter, I would hold both her stiff little hands and help her to clench and unclench her fingers, which would produce another twisted look and a half smile. Holding the baby's hands, I would talk gently to her about how nice it feels to be touched and held firmly, and her legs would jerk and stiffen in an uncoordinated way. I noticed the baby's overall joy and that she wanted her legs touched and massaged, even though the Babygro prevented direct contact. The mother asked me what I saw in the child. I observed that the baby had some determination to link with people, and with her, but needed to go through stages such as finding her own body boundaries, her own identity, and her mother's. The mother then asked me whether she could help Abigail.

I replied that Abigail enjoyed being looked at, talked to, nuzzled, and having her hands enclosed and her legs and body touched and massaged.

I felt that the mother could not be in tune with the baby because she had not got over the trauma, shock, and anger of her bad pregnancy, which had produced a narcissistic injury since it did not fit in with her self-image. However, my conversation with Abigail had helped the mother momentarily to understand the individuality of the baby, and in that way to facilitate the separation process naturally. At age 9 months, they had still seemed inseparable, since the child would not leave her mother's left arm once she was awake.

Subsequent work

After six months, the mother realized during her own therapy that she had had a terrible, frightening pregnancy, bleeding from the fourth month onwards, including two enormous haemorrhages that had caused her to black out so badly that the doctors thought she had died. She told me, "When I woke up, my parents were crying"—they too had thought she had died. This acknowledgment of the shock of her bad pregnancy and her near-death experience were interfering with her thinking and with her ability to tune in emotionally to her infant's needs. She then became realistically depressed and could mourn her expectations, cry, and face her actual experience with this child.

After eight months of therapy, Abigail became able to respond to physiotherapy and attend other helpful activities (toys, libraries, etc.), which had not been possible until then. It took another nine months for the baby to be able to separate and cry far less. This treatment continued for two years.

Follow-ups at ages 3 and 5 years and nursery reports indicated that Abigail was extremely physically disabled but had determination to progress and was lovable, was a good character to have around, and was progressing physically and intellectually and attending the local school.

Discussion.   In the last two examples of physical disability, Mark's and Abigail's communications were extremely brief and specific. For both mothers there was a "trauma" that had occurred with such intensity that it had created an emotional "blind spot", well repressed, with the result that they were unable to receive the specific message transmitted by the baby of certain "knowledge" of their incapacity or disability. These infants' continuous crying and inability to separate from their mothers provoked in me the idea that they felt invaded by a fear that they would be destroyed by an internal or an external danger. In both mothers, there was a complete absence of guilt and no sharing with their husbands, despite otherwise good and stable marriages. It seemed that these mothers considered their feelings solely their own business, and they were going to continue trying to help their babies in the hope that one day they would grow into healthy children.

What sort of mental representations did these mothers have of their babies and of their own experiences as mothers? It seemed to me as observer that they felt they were failures: they had tried everything.

They transmitted an inability to think or feel *with* the baby. Sometimes, as with Abigail, the narcissistic injury of a problematic pregnancy seemed to frighten the mother, making her impervious to the massive panic communications of the baby (whose impact was increased by the child's death-like physical appearance). It was possible to think that the mental representations of both mother and infant had been frozen at the point of their initial traumatic experience, and that their feelings had become repressed and inaccessible. The task of the psychotherapists was to reach and clarify the internal-world constructions of both mother and baby, allowing mental representation to develop.

In working with an infant who has a physical disability, it is possible to observe in detail the feelings transmitted in the interaction as it progresses at a very slow pace. In such cases, the therapist has to increase (usually for much longer periods than with healthy children) the detailed observation of the baby's messages. These messages are not only primitive but extreme in relation to panic, disintegration, tremendous hate and anger, lack of control, and endless need. In the observation of the baby (usually in the presence of the mother), I found it very important to be able to pick up moments of communication of hope from the infant in order to assess properly the potential for recovery and emotional development.

The therapist has to make a special effort in containing and staying with what is perceived and received by the infant as well as by the mother's phantasies. Sometimes two therapists are needed if the mother is very much in need of help. In such cases the two therapists can be seen as model parents with whom negative transferences can be worked out. It is then possible for mother and infant to create a healthy attachment and eventually learn to individuate.

A lot of time is spent in such parent/child psychotherapy in introducing the baby to the parent by describing the baby's specific signals and communications and the feelings these generate in the parents. Modelling or acting in the interview with the infant is rare but useful for diagnostic purposes. The therapeutic value seems to be in the transference of role and emotions in mothers who feel emotionally deprived or exhausted. They are, in symbolic terms, handing over the whole problem in order to watch the way the therapist handles it. The therapist verbalizes the mother's wishes to hand over the mothering of the particular baby, her ideals, and the possible primitive feelings of envy and aggression against someone who might be a better mother than she.

The therapeutic method is designed so that verbal communication of states of mind and feelings can be checked immediately against the changes in the interaction between the mother and the infant. Verbal interpretations of the unconscious motives of this mother occurred around understanding the initial traumatic experience and the uncontained negative and destructive feelings that seemed to be around. These negative feelings exacerbated the mother's death instinct and did not allow personal integration in herself, thus preventing her from helping Abigail to integrate her own corresponding feelings of trauma and death wishes.

When the infant becomes able to tolerate frustration and the mother becomes able to receive the primitive feelings from the baby (projective identifications), the base for having thoughts and learning from experience is set up. According to Bion's "A Theory of Thinking" (1962), "Inability to tolerate frustration can obstruct the development of thoughts" (p. 113); also, "A well-balanced mother can accept these [fears of dying] and respond therapeutically: that is to say in a manner that makes the infant feel it is receiving its frightened personality back again but in a form that it can tolerate" (pp. 114–115).

Conclusion

What arrested the development of the thinking function in Alex, Mark, and Abigail? Why were intact skills and intelligence attacked? Was it a way of coping with the disability? We can draw some speculative conclusions through the treatments of these and other children over several years and through early infant–parent psychotherapies.

It seems as though the real trauma that occurred was felt as a massive, sudden attack that damaged physical and emotional systems and produced shock not only in the disabled baby, but also in the family. In such cases the traumatic experience causes the personal relationships between family members to be frozen, thus leaving the child feeling fragmented and unable to face its internal pain, so exposing it to the insoluble feelings of isolation, delayed development, rage, and despair, as shown and communicated in the continuous crying of Mark and Abigail and in Alex's retarded, vacant behaviour.

It seems that the vulnerability of such a child and its parents can start vicious circles of perverse behaviour and other manifestations that fragment the family further and prevent their healthy development. The early detection of their distress could help the family and the child to mourn their unfulfilled expectations, face their now increased negative feelings, and develop the real potential in each of them.

THE BLIND CHILD
When the world falls apart: becoming blind at 4 months

This section introduces the idea of indirect infant psychotherapy. The work described was carried out by a paediatric physiotherapist, who was supervised weekly by a child psychotherapist. Monthly consultations were set up with the mother, separately from the weekly work with the infant.

CASE 68: ROBERT, AGE 4 MONTHS (NEUROLOGICALLY DAMAGED)

Robert was born normal, beautiful, and big after a problem-free, full-term pregnancy. The mother and father were middle-class, with the father in full-time employment and the mother being employed until Robert's birth. Robert's mother was feeling very tired and bored at home, but she was very happy about the child.

One evening she was arguing with her husband (about matters that have not been disclosed), and they decided to put the child downstairs in the lounge. The following morning, the father went to kiss Robert before he went to work and saw that Robert had turned purple and was having spasms. He immediately gave Robert mouth-to-mouth resuscitation and shouted for his wife, who called an ambulance. Robert was taken to hospital and fully revived, but at this point the parents were told that he would have serious disabilities, including being blind.

It seemed that the damage was neurological and that Robert would almost certainly have been a "cot death" had he not been found in time. The cause was not apparent—for example, there was no evidence of suffocation via blankets or pillow. The paediatric physiotherapist was called in to help the child regain mobility of his limbs through exercise, as they were extremely stiff and immobile. She began a regime of different exercises, but these were never continued at home. When she returned later in the week, his limbs were as stiff as on her previous visit. She tried to help the mother to exercise Robert's hand reflexes and arms, but the mother remained extremely angry. These factors were causing the physiotherapist anxiety, as she felt that she could not control the mother's anger and anxiety.

I was contacted by the physiotherapist and asked to help her think about the case. The mother had been extremely aggressive towards the physiotherapist, who was herself at the end of her tether.

We went through the stages of behaviour displayed by Robert: he showed very little interest, being seemingly in a world of his own, and very unwilling to cooperate. The baby did not cry while the physiotherapist was touching him or trying to help him bring back some life into himself, but he would not cooperate actively. The baby did not show improvement at the end of the hour of physiotherapy to help him develop holding reflexes and other positive reflexes, such as flexing arms and legs and hugging himself. However, the fact he did not cry indicated to me that there was some awareness on the part of the baby that an interested person was trying to help him.

I suggested to the physiotherapist that she should proceed even more slowly in order to help the child to feel an attachment to her first. This could be achieved by holding the child on her lap and cuddling him or singing to him for a while before treatment was begun. The physiotherapist talked a great deal about her intense wish to do so, but she feared that the mother would be even more annoyed. The physiotherapist also felt that she would not like then to leave the baby afterwards because she would feel anxious about his being left in such a dangerous situation.

We fully explored the details of her feelings, fears, and wishes and defences against them, and we also thought about, and wanted to explore, the relationship between mother and baby before his near-cot-death experience. It was necessary to explore the physiotherapist's emotions activated by this working situation for them to be a useful instrument of knowledge about the deepest emotions in the baby and in the mother.

We then thought that if she included the mother in the therapy, she could tell her that Robert needed the physical exercises, but before these, to warm up, he needed the physical closeness of a long cuddle and some time for exercising his other available senses, like smelling, touching, and hearing, to help him orient himself in space. The exercise of the muscles and his wish to do it had to come from an inner wish as well.

I suggested to the physiotherapist that she observe the child's reactions and her own reactions in detail and write them down afterwards for discussion with me. Her reactions to his reactions were very important to explore because they belonged to primitive states of mind in the baby, who had reactivated similar ones in her. If the mother wished to do the same, she could copy the physiotherapist. It would be interesting to see what happened and whether the mother would allow herself the experience.

I felt I needed to see the mother and baby and, consequently, met them with the physiotherapist in the outpatient department of the hospital. We explained to the mother that I was a psychologist interested in child development and that I wanted to see what the baby was capable of and how they were getting on. The mother displayed the same sharp, nasty behaviour towards me. I noted that the father was unable to attend the interview. The mother was young, very pretty, extremely annoyed and anxious, and in a state of paranoia towards the professionals.

I asked her what her feelings were about professionals trying to help her with the situation, and her answer was that she was extremely annoyed with life and with this happening to her. She felt that even though there were professionals trying to help, this was a lost cause. Her child was almost dead, and this was going to be the case for life. She couldn't cope with this, she couldn't give up the child for adoption, but she couldn't hold him either in her mind or in her heart. I noted that the way in which she held the baby was completely lax and distant, that there was no warmth in her body towards the baby, and that he lay there completely lifeless.

We agreed that we should consider some meeting whereby I would try to see if I could be of some help to her, because I felt that there was a part of her that was extremely annoyed that the professionals were all trying to help the child and no one was trying to help her with her anger. She agreed to this and requested that the meetings took place in her home, as she felt this might be easier since it was winter and the baby was in a delicate state. I agreed, as I thought that she might feel something different was happening if the setting was not the hospital. I also thought that it would be a good idea to go to the house in order to sense the atmosphere and observe her routines.

We agreed that I would see her monthly, while the physiotherapist continued twice weekly, and that I would keep in contact with the physiotherapist. This was accepted readily by the mother. We also agreed to pursue monitoring the different sedatives that the doctors were prescribing for the child, because of the fits he was having. The doctors were trying to alleviate the fits while still allowing him to remain alert. It seemed that, currently, the choice was between one or the other. Up until then, the mother had been very annoyed about any medication since she felt that the doctors did not know what they were doing. She was becoming increasingly more frightened by this, though.

The physiotherapist kept me informed and gave detailed accounts of the twice-weekly sessions she had with the baby and the feedback from the mother. We had many joint professional meetings to keep communications open and consistent, rather than giving different opinions, since the mother tended to play one professional against another. Hence the physiotherapist became the key worker in this case.

I was struck by all the trials the physiotherapist was going through with the child. We had to think about his possible mental state. He seemed to be in a state of shock and fragmentation, with too many professionals involved and an angry mother. It seemed more appropriate to give his body as a point of reference, and for the physiotherapist to serve as a model to the mother. So the concept of holding and giving him a bodily place on the lap, with soft conversations, seemed appropriate. He needed to feel held in this new state as a new-born or unborn child—held in mind and body and in the relationship following his near-cot-death, and brought slowly and at his own pace to a new mirroring one. Since his eyesight was nil whereas he had had sight before, accommodation and adaptation to his lack of eyesight had to occur through his other senses. The approach of the physiotherapist had, therefore, first to be psychotherapeutic, creating a relationship of holding with tolerance and acceptance that could be seen and shared with mother, thus awakening in her a wish to know this other world that he had to live in which had been forced upon him. The child and the mother needed to grieve what had been and to restart again. New attachments were necessary.

In order to help him gather himself together, the physiotherapist moved his limbs and massaged them despite his lack of response, holding him on her lap, and helping him to recognize her body and to encourage him to relax his stiff muscles. I told her to gradually try various methods of touching, observing when and how the child would react positively in order to enhance this and, at the same time, proceeding at a very slow pace in order to recognize the positive reflexes that could be increased and developed, as opposed to the negative ones.

I suggested to the physiotherapist that she should include the mother in these slow and detailed observations to learn about the baby, in order that the mother should feel part of this process and also begin to understand what the attention that was being given to the child was about. I thought along the lines that this child was, indeed, like a newborn with respect to the state of his body. I also thought that if this child had any memory, he would be able to recall his former freedom of movement as opposed to the frustration of the stiffness of his limbs.

I also felt that the mother's anger was paralysing for baby and professionals alike and was, therefore, inhibiting movement towards positive development. We discussed how overwhelming it would be for the baby to feel his mother's anger all the time, not just for an hour like the physiotherapist. Somehow, we would have to find some way of helping the mother to become aware of her feelings and to help her to keep them to herself. The mother was offered psychotherapy, which she did not accept. The father was very distant with respect to the situation and felt that he could not live with his wife as he felt that her anger and anxiety were unbearable.

When I visited the home, I decided to see mother, child, and physiotherapist in the same room. The physiotherapist engaged in activities with the child, and I tried to verbalize to the mother the difficulty in accepting this other infant near her. I also spoke with her about the possibility of guilt feelings and her despair about the damage that may have occurred to the child. I had to be extremely careful when talking about these three things, as the mother was highly sensitive and felt extremely persecuted.

I offered personal assistance to the mother, on a more frequent and regular basis, if she required this. I felt that she had a part of herself that she considered handicapped and that her anger was paralysing her. I also mentioned the fact that perhaps it was difficult for her to deal internally with elements of disagreement without being too upset.

Mother's monthly interviews

The first interview focused on the fact that I was available for her, to talk about her desperate feelings, that I was willing to think with her about how I could help her. Both the child and the physiotherapist were in the room; the physiotherapist felt more at ease working with the child, and at the end of the session she invited the mother to notice the improvement that the child had made and to think how she could help him further.

By the time of the second interview a month later, I had already had three other meetings with the physiotherapist, who felt that there was a sense of reflection developing in the mother. The child was now able to maintain some of the positive things gained by the end of the hour's physiotherapy.

When I arrived at the house, the mother seemed very busy with the telephone and other matters, and I felt left out. I mentioned that we could make an arrangement whereby she could isolate herself from external demands such as the telephone. The mother answered that there was no such time because she had no space for herself. She felt that only when the child was being attended to by the physiotherapist could she attend to anything else. At other times, the child would cry if he was not being held properly in her arms, especially if she was on the phone. I said that this could be something for the mother and me to discuss fully. I showed my concern for her lack of space for herself.

During this second session, which had been very interrupted, I said that it may be useful for us to explore the good and negative parts of her own personality. I mentioned the fact that Robert was involved in a slow process of exercising positive reflexes in regard to holding himself together and that it may be useful for us to look together at her own positive reflexes, behaviour, and feelings. She said quite straightforwardly to me that she had none and therefore she could not find anything. She also mentioned that she did not have time to waste in trying to find herself, because the only thing that she would find was anger, almost at her fingertips, and a great deal of anxiety. She concluded that she preferred to keep busy and occupied rather than looking into her internal world. I mentioned the fact that she surely did have good parts, and that these parts were obviously there because she had a very nice home, everything was in order, the child was physically well looked after, and there were indications of care and concern, which was a positive sign. I was not sure whether this was just a cover-up of her anxiety, but I said that if that were indeed the case, it was a good cover-up, a good outcome, and that obviously the words "good, bad, positive, and negative" were very much in her mind.

I did insist that in a month's time we would carry out that kind of exercise: while the child was exercising mental and physical muscles, we would do the same work in a parallel fashion. She became extremely thoughtful and said that it was funny that I did not look upon her as a nasty, neurotic mother, which was the feeling she got with other professionals she had met. She said she was prepared to meet in one month's time and do what I suggested.

During the three meetings I had had with the physiotherapist, I learned that Robert's mother had been the child of a professional mother who was very hygienic in the care of her children, but very cold and distant. Because of this, she felt very deprived of love and warmth, and that she could only survive by feeling nasty and angry. By this time, the physiotherapist was involving her in dealing with the child a great deal more.

When we had our subsequent meeting, the mother left the telephone off the hook and was able to sit with me in the same room as the child and the physiotherapist. She talked about her opposite, conflicting feelings and how difficult it had always been for her to cope with these and how unbearable it was for her to cope with her anger. She felt she would like to be like me and become an understanding person. This, in turn, made her angry, as she felt that I had something she could not have because of the level of her anger. She asked me how she could learn this tolerance, and we looked at all the other feelings that were around in the session, including feelings perhaps of not having enough, as I was extremely distant in only coming to see her once a month. Perhaps she had a very strong feeling that nothing was quite enough, that what I was giving was so little that it annoyed rather than pleased her. We did talk a great deal about her feelings of being left alone with a damaged child and self, and I thought that she was acquiring insight very quickly.

In the fourth interview, we continued the theme of her trying her best to help both her child and herself, with the physiotherapist becoming a helpful, mother figure for her and her child, rather than a persecutory one.

By the fifth interview, six months later, Robert was almost a year old and about to start standing up. He could not see at all, and the mother spent a long time crying about it. However, the improvement of the child was so noticeable that it was hard to believe. In the end, Robert's mother recognized that she had been greatly helped by somebody withstanding her anger and had been able to reflect on her character and on the painful traumatic experiences she had had. She decided now to have psychotherapy once a week, and I helped her to find a therapist.

The physiotherapy continued for another year, and I continued to supervise it once a week. It was interesting to observe how the physiotherapist had had to prepare the setting to facilitate physiotherapy, and this was achieved through a psychodynamic understanding of the internal state of emotions and needs in the child.

Discussion.   It was difficult at first for the physiotherapist to lend herself emotionally since she realized, through the supervision, that she was very possessive and at times found herself confused about when and how to proceed. The discussions of her sessions allowed her to understand how she was mirroring the mental state of the child and how important it was for her to stay in the state of maternal reverie and to speak about it. Once she got used to being projected into and to staying with and verbalizing the different states of emotions, she found herself being creative and innovative, intuiting exactly the right movement or stimulation for the child, even if this might prove to be the only one in the whole session.

This makes one wonder about the necessary relativeness of finding even the smallest amount of progress that can be remembered and the effect of identification from the physiotherapist's point of view. It seemed that, through the physiotherapist, for the baby there was a pull between death and life, a struggle that was felt as unbearable unless support and reflection were provided to the physiotherapist. The infant could then, through projective identification, live it through the physiotherapist and feel held and supported.

This experience, which started at the age of 4 months and was the main point of the sessions, slowly decreased over the next twelve months.

When Robert was 2 years old, he could walk, say words, and smile, and he started attending a nursery. His mother was working with him, following the example set by the physiotherapist, and speaking about her emotions and imagining what he was thinking. She had changed the furniture for soft, rounded corners.

The physiotherapist had to learn to bear and understand what was (or was not) being projected. In turn, this reactivated deeper or more primitive states in the mind of the physiotherapist as a reflection, or as her identification with the inner struggle, thus helping her to stay with the state of catastrophe felt by the child and becoming able to understand it, contain it, and come out of it, helping the child in this way to restart, grieving the past and developing new capacities.

TUBEROSCLEROSIS AND OTHER MENTAL DISABILITIES

Three films—*Rain Man*, *My Left Foot*, and *Children of a Lesser God*—have brought to the public new insights into the mental dynamics of the evolution of disability and the painful path that the family and the disabled child go through to overcome it. There are very few families, though, that do make it; for the rest, usually a troubled life lies ahead, as feelings and emotions do not sort themselves out and can remain frozen for a lifetime.

The aim of parent/child psychotherapy is to ameliorate this path in the life of such children and their families, through focusing on the individuality of the child and understanding the deeper emotions at play in the parents and/or family.

The cases discussed here involve tuberosclerosis, general retardation, and macrocephalus. The work in the case of the latter—a macrocephalus baby who recovered despite a prognosis of death—was done with a specialized foster-mother, who felt it important to pursue her instincts for neutralizing bad habits and tendencies the baby had acquired, for attuning, and for bonding with the baby.

CASE 69: NADIA, AGE 2 YEARS (TUBEROSCLEROSIS)

The referral was made simultaneously by the paediatricians, the GP, and the health visitor, who said that the girl was biting the mother and was aggressive towards other children in the park. The mother felt upset and was very cooperative in providing information and attending the sessions punctually.

Both parents came to the consultation with Nadia, who looked big for her age and showed her disability, with her tongue hanging out of her mouth and saliva dripping, her finger in her nose, hair uncombed, screaming and seemingly quite uncontained by her parents. She would kick them and throw everything around, including my diary from the desk and toys from a box.

Her parents asked me what to do about her behaviour, which they had been told was part of the syndrome, and they said that I should know what they were talking about—had I spoken with her paediatricians, did I have experience of this pathology, how many such children had I seen. I said that since the referrer had been one of the paediatricians, I had spoken with him about predictable behaviours. He had said that such children could develop aggression, but not to the extent he had seen in this child. That was, in fact, the reason that he referred her to me: to find out what was making her behave like that. The paediatrician had explained clearly to me that tuberosclerosis is a genetic illness where tumours develop in the brain and continue doing so despite surgery. The development of new tumours continues slowly, and by the age of 12 years the child is retarded, with death likely from age 18 years onwards. The child becomes progressively more and more disabled and then dies. The paediatrician mentioned that he usually does not need to refer such children, because they start presenting difficulties in behaviour management only when much older. He had advised these parents not to have any more children, since this is a hereditary condition.

I felt that the parents were annoyed, exhausted, and full of emotions that made it difficult to start the work. I explained that I would explore with them over a number of sessions what exactly was going on with Nadia and with them.

It turned out that they lived far away and had come for just the one interview, thinking that I was going to solve everything there and then. I felt that everything was worse than I expected. The father was commuting to London anyway, and the mother felt really annoyed. Her annoyance was now directed at the professionals and why they had not told her about the number of sessions, about more work for her to do, having to explore her child (as if she didn't know her), and that the professionals were always talking rubbish—first they didn't believe her about her daughter screaming all day and fainting, because when she arrived at the hospital the girl would be awake, and, if she stayed in, it didn't happen. The mother then shouted, saying that I looked as hopeless and idiotic as the others; that she was alone in the middle of nowhere, with a child that was a monster, and others kept trying to convince her that it was just her imagination—and after all, she was an intelligent person who had a nice job managing a post office, had planned this pregnancy with care, saving money and pushing her husband into a better job for the betterment of the family. And she had been treated like a moron. Until one day the girl had not awoken after fainting, and then the paediatricians finally took it seriously and investigated it.

I sympathized with the mother, saying that it seemed very sad that she had had to suffer so much before being heard and helped. The word *help* triggered lots of feelings. She asked whether I really knew what it was to help parents in her situation. "Everything is so mechanical, so cold, nobody sympathizes really. Either people are intellectual and studious about it, or they panic. Help?—what is help in despair? Does anybody cry with me?—no, they just pity me. Now: you will tell me what you know about managing this girl, and then we leave."

I said that I could see how little she had been believed, and how long and lonely had been the path of discovery of what was wrong. I could offer management through talking about Nadia's individuality and their feelings about her, but that this was not short-term work. Many months of hopes and building their image of the daughter and the family had first to be revisited, followed by as many months of disillusion, fear, annoyance, and family disappointment.

Where were her parents and her husband's parents in all of this, I asked. The maternal grandparents lived by themselves in a little village and were helpful. They did not, however, want to look after Nadia, because she was so unmanageable. The theme of her illness and shock to the family had never been discussed. The mother was an only daughter. The father's parents lived in another village and visited twice a year.

They gave all this information in a matter-of-fact way and asked what the importance of it really was in any case. By this time, Nadia wanted to play with me and was putting toys on my lap and making noises. I realized she was very delayed in speech, and I tried to play with her. The cuddly toys—a bear and a rabbit—were smacking each other, and she laughed; cars were colliding, she laughed; she pulled my hair and waited, and I felt furious. So I said to her, "And what is your story? It seems you want attention all the time, and play, and find my talking to your parents annoying." She walked clumsily to the door and wanted to open it; I said that it was time to tell each other things. I closed the door and she had a temper tantrum, through rage and impotence. I said that she feels rage about not being able to do things like the grown-ups, like other people, and it is horrible. She screamed, kicking me, and I put a little chair between us—I realized that I had not got the message of the animals and the car quickly or accurately enough. I said, holding her hands across the little chair, "You and me are finding it difficult to understand each other. You feel people always collude with you. It might be your way of perceiving that is different from ours."

I then talked to the parents, saying that Nadia might perceive reality and relationships differently from us and that there was no feeling of harmony in her. It had become very difficult for her then to understand what we wanted her to understand, and it was very difficult for her mother to get on well with her. It must be very frustrating to have an only child who from birth is difficult to understand and where there has been no feeling of togetherness.

I was amazed by the little girl's awareness of discrepancy and seeking help through misbehaving. It was this that had led them to consulting with an infant specialist.

I said to the parents that it had been difficult and painful for them to bring her up, and it was difficult for her to be so aware of the frustrating relationship. That is why it was important to try to understand what might help her to perceive them in a more human way. I didn't know how to help them in just one hour. I could only offer weekend meetings, spaced out to give time for reflection and for tasks and goals to be achieved; meanwhile, I wanted to know how having this kind of family had affected their personal relationship. They were mute. The mother said, after a while, that she could not see the connection between Nadia's behaviour and themselves.

I said that everything was related and that we needed to try to integrate all areas for a better functioning of our selves. The mother became very defensive and said that she did not want to talk about it. I said that it was painful to see how many areas of life become affected, but when we talk about it, sometimes we can feel that they are related to one factor and perhaps to a disappointment. Some people, after a bad delivery, have a bad relationship with the baby and the partner who produced it. When the start of a new relationship was difficult, as it had been with Nadia, it probably affected other relationships—with parents (through not feeling good enough) or with partners (through shared guilt or blame)—and all the wonderful plans would be marred by the reality and seem awful, and the gorgeous expected baby would become a monster, and despair would grow. Perhaps at times life would even seem not worth living.

The mother then agreed with me and arranged dates for when she could come for consultations, and the father would bring them.

Treatment

By the second appointment, the family was thinking of moving to London in order to get more help for Nadia—a special school, a speech therapist, a physiotherapist. They were talking in a lively manner about it, and I had the feeling that they had gone from despair to feeling powerful again and that they could make plans again.

I asked the reason why they had moved to the village where the grandmother lived. The mother said she wanted companionship in bringing up the child. She hadn't wanted to work while having children, and they had thought of having two or three. The pregnancy had been good but the delivery too long and painful. She now had no wish to have more. Slowly, everything had changed. The baby screamed a lot; she felt anxious and didn't sleep much. There were lots of arguments with her mother. And the husband's absences in London four nights a week felt too long.

I imagined the parents' shock after planning what they felt would be an idyllic family and it not turning out that way at all. They wanted to live in a house, but London suddenly appeared as a necessary alternative rather than a wished-for one, and they were considering it seriously.

Nadia was looking a little tidier and was trying to speak, making conversational sounds. She started knocking a cuddly toy around, and I brought up the delivery experience. I thought they were related to the teddy-bear being knocked around. It might have been extremely annoying to have so much pain during the long delivery, with nobody to soothe her. For the parents, life with a child seemed very different from their idyll. I wondered how much of this anger was transferred to Nadia from the very beginning. At the time of birth, what had the father seen and what had he done?

He replied he had been frightened and did not know what to do. He had been waiting outside the delivery-room, with no thought of danger, just annoyance. His wife had had to have many stitches and had suffered discomfort, exhaustion, and anger. She did not want to see the girl immediately, who instead was held in the father's arms. He felt good. At this point in the interview, Nadia went to him and sat on his lap.

I felt that their story of self-deception and disappointment started then, and it was important for them to confront the reality. The first relationship of mother and daughter had been very awkward. The supportive father was there, holding the baby, but the mother had left in rage to recover her own strength. Breastfeeding was easy and was used as a comforter, much more than necessary. Nadia's screams started to make the mother frightened. She then realized that there were vacant-like states in the baby. The husband's absences now seemed eternal, the house became a burden with the screaming child, and she had fainted at age 3 months but the hospital thought it not serious. Medical examinations proceeded in the months that followed. No epilepsy was diagnosed. At age 8 months, Nadia fainted again but did not awake from the faint by the time she reached hospital. After a further series of examinations, she was referred to another hospital, which diagnosed tuberosclerosis.

I mentioned to the mother that those months of not being believed and so much uncertainty must have left her deeply wounded. She agreed and cried. She asked me whether I thought it was important to review all that horrible period, and I said that it was very important.

She then recalled how she had fought with her baby daughter and with her mother and with the professionals. How could life be so cruel? She had never liked being an only child, and here she was with a daughter who had an illness and so would have no siblings. And she saw her husband coming and going, leaving her feeling alone with the mess.

The father said that, while wanting to be home with her, all he could do was telephone his wife from London. He felt that it was not up to him to change their plans. He was happy to think that she now wanted to come to live in London, but he would not push it.

Nadia played with me a little, and I felt concerned about the distancing behaviour between mother and child, as if they bothered each other. At times it seemed very disturbing.

The mother's internal objects seemed to follow an intergenerational link of self-hate for passing on recessive genes and then being unable to offer any help. Despite a kind and containing father, the little girl had had a bad start with an upset mother and with her own brain which was already not functioning properly, being burdened by the growth of tumours.

We had nine sessions, at fortnightly intervals. After the second interview, the family had moved to London and were put on waiting lists for the speech therapist and physiotherapist. This delay was a cause for further annoyance to the mother, who had thought that London services were so good and speedy, again idealizing the situation. I discussed her tendency to make plans that she thought would work fantastically, and how disappointed and annoyed she generally felt afterwards.

We went on to observe Nadia in terms of her behaviour and needs. The mother said that Nadia was a very stubborn little girl who could get away with murder because they felt pity for her and gave in. I commented that, from pity, she had become a monster for them and for other people. Perhaps we could think together about what might make her more contained in her behaviour. Her syndrome does not come with such chaotic behaviour, and this must be as painful for her as for them and other people. Nadia now asked to sit on my lap and touch my face. I allowed that to happen, and the mother started crying for herself and the little girl. The father was choked with so many feelings he couldn't express, about how to start, where to start. His wife had so wanted a nice family with three children, and what she now had was misery.

I said we would try to put words to feelings and go on to talk about and face all that came to her mind. The father was enthusiastic about this possibility, since he felt caught in a plan he could not change, one that only circumstances and his wife could. We had to talk about this dynamic in the marriage and its effect on the little girl.

The sessions were very much about observing and talking about the dynamics of the family, observing each of them individually, their needs, their communications and limitations. Whatever was projected onto me, or transferred, was fully discussed, without the previous fragmentation and annoyance all round.

Nadia began to show a liking for calm play with dolls, imitating and dramatizing medical proceedings, and needing to act and talk about anger, about mother, about the way things used to be, about the ways she saw things—her head, her living space. For example, she would put PlayDoh around the head of dolls or teddies; sometimes she would put it on their heads imitating wires, or bumps, or on their face or legs. I wondered whether that was her internal perception (or awareness) of the tumours, or her external perception due to her strong feelings towards her father and mother. There was a lot of curiosity in her and about others.

It seemed a great attraction for her to tell us or show us about her ways of going about setting a table or dressing up the dolls. She would spend a great deal of time caressing each utensil or item of dress. Her mother acknowledged that she herself was a quick person, and it would be very important to acknowledge Nadia's rhythm and preferences as being very different from hers. The mother's tone of voice and attention given to Nadia became softer and more genuinely interested. She now even found Nadia endearing. Nadia started at a nursery for normal children, her overt aggression disappeared, and her mother got a part-time job.

The father came alone to the ninth session because the mother had an interview for a new job. He was very thankful to have a different kind of family. He had never expected to learn to talk about feelings—in fact, he was always frightened of feeling anything. He recognized that he came from a family where "you just don't talk about feelings, you live your life the best that you can. And if there are distressing experiences, you just get on with work and whatever happens and whatever you have to do." He said that the family had learned to speak another language, where you can dare to question, to face nasty reactions, and to acknowledge what you like and dislike, what is your fault and what is not. With Nadia, he and his wife felt terribly guilty of having produced her, terribly sad that they were never going now to have what they wanted. They had got annoyed and distant with each other and hated Nadia, without realizing it. Now he saw Nadia as a physically ill child with a personality and characteristics of her own that were interesting and positive. She was now seen and treated by them as a human being, and as parents they became more human as well.

We agreed to a follow-up session in six months' time. All three attended. Nadia looked pretty, with her hair combed and her mouth closed when not speaking, and she articulated words clearly. They had continued the path of trying to put their sensations and feelings into words and observing themselves and Nadia in different situations and their reactions to these. They thought that perhaps they were not living as comfortably in London as in their former village, but inside themselves they felt much better.

The mother said that Nadia was maturing nicely, that the situation was difficult but not impossible; she felt grateful that I had given them the opportunity to come back after six months to tell me how things were going. They felt "kept" in my mind and by the feeling that I was available.

Discussion. I have treated and supervised the treatment of a number of children with tuberosclerosis. In all these cases there has been tremendous upset in the parents at having created a defective child from recessive genes and then being unable to do anything to stop the process. Their distress leads to them using distancing behaviour that represses the expression of their feelings about the child and between themselves. Soon they become unaware of positive growth. The tumours that grow in the child's brain seem to make the child not human—a monster—and the parents lose sight of the child's individual personality. The child reacts angrily, and serious behaviour difficulties often arise.

Nadia was greatly wanted, expected, and idealized as a baby. But she hurt her mother too much at delivery, and immediately afterwards the mother felt insulted and the baby felt abandoned. The mother began their relationship feeling cheated and so did not react positively to the baby's cries. A vicious cycle of bad treatment, distancing, and retaliation had been started, affecting the development of speech and trust. The father was away most of the time, so there was no mediation to stop mother and daughter from getting entrenched in this negative mode of relationship.

So the therapist needed to establish a very different kind of relationship with them, one that would not mirror the distancing fear between them. It became important for the therapist to take on the three complaining parts: the silent father, the annoyed distant mother, and the aggressive child. Each of the three had elements to explore that would complete the picture of the monsters or ghosts in this family.

The mother, an only child, had had fantasies of an idyllic family with three children, living in the countryside. But the reality of the delivery, the pain of the stitches, and the crying baby made things go from bad to worse, so that she could not integrate the pain and difficulties.

Nadia felt wrong-footed from the start, with no patient, understanding mother, no father or grandmother—just she and a new world, with a disability not yet known about. She resorted to crying, and her misery filled the mother with a persecutory guilt from her injured narcissism. It became difficult for them to start a dance of understanding each other, and Nadia's emotional, cognitive, and social growth became impaired. She seemed not to like anybody and was not liked by anybody. Her increasing frustration was fed by anger and hurt. These feelings were not acknowledged or expressed, and her appearance of not being contained herself was evident in her tongue hanging out, her spreading everything around, and her hair being messed.

The therapy had to allow attentiveness to her, without further annoying the mother. An alliance was made with the mother in seeking to know about this monster. The work encompassed each member as important and representing something to the other. Bit by bit the therapy proceeded, slowly incorporating personal elements that had been fragmented and projected only into the different persons with whom they had conflicts, then reintegrating—or integrating for the first time, as in the case of Nadia—the individual aspects of their personality.

CASE 70: TIM AND ARO, 2 & 3 YEARS OLD (DELAYED MENTALLY)

I supervised two separate cases of tuberosclerosis, aged 11 and 12 years, in which both sets of parents had subsequently decided to adopt babies, from Bosnia. The consultations were organized because the way the parents were handling these babies—Tim and Aro, aged 2 and 3 years, and both of them extremely delayed mentally—was worrying to Social Services. In fact, the parents had made heroic efforts to acquire these children, but once at their respective homes, they were sleeping either with the mother or with the father and were being bathed with one or the other parent, and some rituals had been established that were making people concerned. In both homes, the child with tuberosclerosis was deteriorating, but the energy of the parents was totally focused on constantly doing things for the little one, on the grounds that because it was adopted and had been deprived, it needed attention all the time.

In reality, it seemed as if these parents had not taken into account the human needs of their disabled child nor their own feelings about the adopted child and its impact on the family. The parents wanted to deny the frustration generated in them by their ill child, and they had worked out their guilt by adopting a disabled child. One father had (literally) fallen in love with the adopted child, a girl, chosen by him and with whom he was sleeping and bathing, and there was great concern about possible sexual abuse. It appeared that these fathers, instead of questioning their own and their wives' motives, wanted to punish themselves and their wives, or to gain sympathy from other men for having produced a child that started deprived and became increasingly disabled. They then over-intellectualized about how good they were being by providing a sibling to their ill first child.

In my experience, little or no account in families such as these is taken of the baby's individual needs, nor is there an opening up of their true feelings about the fatally ill child. The congenital illness awakens so much guilt and so much resentment at having to limit their family. These parents divert the pain and dismay of their unplanned reality by twisting other feelings, and unconscious feelings of revenge get set up against the ill child and sometimes against the mother (as the producer of the child).

CASE 71: CHRISTIAN, AGE 6 MONTHS (MACROCEPHALUS)

The professional involved in this case, which I supervised, was a trainee in mother–infant psychotherapy who visited an excellent foster-mother specializing in babies who were going to die. The child had been diagnosed as macrocephalus and had undergone surgery to drain the encephalitic liquid from the brain. The baby was losing weight, seemed dispirited, and was deteriorating. The mother (single, 23 years old, with no other children) was tired of visiting the baby in hospital. She was told that the child was not going to live beyond 9 months, and she decided to give him to a foster-mother to care for. The foster-mother, Ms F., was accustomed to receiving babies in this state and agreed to have him, but she decided to consult a specialist to see whether it was possible to make the baby's life a bit more pleasurable. There was something in his personality that made her seek something better for this baby.

On examining the trainee's observation material, it was pretty obvious that Ms F. felt a vitality in him that had not been addressed. In spite of the weak limbs and the loss of weight, the child followed Ms F.'s movements and voice with his eyes. His eyes would shine if he was picked up, and he would happily nestle between her breasts as if searching for a cuddle, which Ms F. was ready to provide. She did not know whether she should be stimulating him or not, or whether further activity would be tiring, since his physical appearance was so appalling. However, the gratifying responsiveness of Christian was a good indicator of his wish to attach to Ms F. There were tiny signs of his calling for her attention: when awake and alert, he would move his little fingers, or pull the cover sheet, or attempt conversation by moving his mouth, making almost inaudible noises.

Christian's overall development was very retarded in relation to his age, and he mostly lay on his back. There were no neck muscles, back arching, movements of his arms or hands, no holding, no movement or capacity to be on his stomach. We decided to help Ms F. to look for small signals of his and her own happiness as a guidance for pursuing an activity. She would look enthusiastically for the tiniest signals, repeating the actions that were liked. Awareness of their importance made Ms F. very committed to doing and providing the right experience, even if it was going to be the last one for this dying child.

The dreaded ninth month arrived. Christian was putting on weight and was sitting up; his monstrous appearance was now softer, and he was endearing to whoever was with him. The doctors found this progress puzzling, and they started giving him appointments further apart. Ms F. decided she would not foster any other child until Christian died, since he had demonstrated to her that he liked games, attention, and talking.

Ms F. was advised to proceed slowly and steadily while carefully observing Christian's likes and dislikes, obvious needs and more hidden ones, stimulating him at times and in ways that were appropriate, but without following general rules. For example, Christian did not like massage, but he did like jazz and classical music played on the piano; he liked sweet but not savoury dishes, so it was necessary to think of ways in which meat could be sweetened until he had got used to its texture. The same exploration was done with scents: he preferred pine to any other scent, and I wondered whether this was related to antiseptic liquids he might have remembered from hospital. His reactions to visual and tactile stimuli were similarly explored by Ms F., with great sensitivity.

When Christian reached the age of 2 years, Ms F. began to worry about his living situation as she no longer thought he was going to die. She wondered about his mother, who did not want him back as she had had another, normal baby. The mother was concerned about taking on a child who "didn't do well with her, and is doing well with Ms F." Ms F. then decided to focus on her own and Christian's needs, and she adopted him. He was now presenting very little motor and cognitive delay, though he would need continuing medical surveillance and care.

Discussion.   One questions the possibilities present for Christian and his mother with such a bad start to their life together. Ms F. was not responsible for Christian's abnormalities and (unlike his mother) could forge an attachment with him untainted by guilt. What made Ms F. ask for help? Did she feel that she had taken on a baby who was going to thrive? Did the mother lack the maturity, strength, and family support needed for the continuous surgical/hospital interventions? Did the system of hospital care lack a structure for counselling and working with the mother's feelings—the anxiety, stress, annoyance, exhaustion, mixed with love, expectation, and hopes?

The reality showed a mother who, as a single parent, was extremely ambivalent about having a baby. Once she accepted the pregnancy, like most mothers she naturally expected a healthy normal child. The shock rendered by Christian's condition and subsequent hospital treatments and interventions militated against her forming an attachment to him. Too many negative feelings undermined her love for him and eventually killed it. The baby was going to die, but the bond had already been severed. Meanwhile, Ms F. attended to Christian's needs and so developed an attachment to him, further decreasing thereby the attachment between the mother and him. Instead, the mother immediately went on to have another child to fill the gap created between the unborn child she had imagined and the reality of Christian.

I would like to digress briefly to discuss unconscious communications between mothers and unborn babies. Christian's mother chose his name before the birth, and if the baby had been a daughter, she would have been called Christina. The mother thought of the name because of the reference to Christ, who had survived death. She explained that the baby was almost aborted, but had survived. What interested me was the quality of resilience attributed to the foetus which seemed to have helped him to survive a traumatic birth and treatment. The mother, realizing that she could not cater for his needs, gave him away and did not change her mind even when the child began to improve. He had, in her heart, "died".

Ms F.'s attitude to Christian supports interesting speculation about the function of positive emotions in helping the body to recover its natural thrust towards healthy development. Discoveries in the fields of neurochemistry and neuroendocrinology offer explanations at a physical level that help us to understand such miraculous recoveries in babies (newborn, or early in infancy) who are expected to die. In his book *Affect Regulation and the Origin of the Self* (1994), Schore explains the production of opiates and beta endorphin as being induced by the quality of the socioemotional, imprinting, and attachment developmental processes: "In face-to-face affective interaction, the emotionally expressive face of the imprinting object, the mother, induces alterations in opioid peptides in the child's developing brain. The mechanism of this psychoendocrinological process involves the caregiver's regulation of the infant hypothalamic production of corticotrophin releasing factor (CRF) . . ." (p. 145)

In Christian's and similar cases, the caregiver's role facilitated attachment and stimulated neural connections that are vitally important in the first year of life. Nerve cells that do not get connected in the first and second years of life are destroyed by an autodestruct mechanism, a specific enzyme that kills the cell. Also, if children are born with, say, cataracts and are not promptly treated, they become permanently blind, since sensitive brain cells have not been activated by the right stimulus. In general, the brain is more forgiving in a child's first year— hence the crucial importance of early intervention, as in the case of Christian.

It has also been found that about two-thirds of babies infected with HIV in the womb later fight off their mother's antibodies and become HIV negative. There was a case presented in *The Denver Post* newspaper (Schrader, 1997) about a foster-mother who takes in infected babies and toddlers—discarded victims of drug-addicted mothers who inject. These children not only are infected but are addicted. The foster-mother commented that being a mother of these children is a more intense job: "for months you watch them draw every breath and you hold them as they shiver with night terrors." She has to give them eighteen daily doses of medications, including drugs to help them battle against panic and secondary infections and to help bolster their immune systems. One child was given to her at birth weighing 4 pounds and was expected to live thirty days at the most, since he had been infected with HIV and was addicted to PCP, heroin, and crack. Doctors tested the child's blood every week for HIV antibodies, and at age 18 months he had sero-reverted, meaning he was HIV-free. By age 2 years, he had been adopted by the foster-mother.

This story confirms again the important role of the alternative caregiver in the first year, when mothers of disabled babies are absent, unwilling, or unable to go through the process of painstaking exploration of their individualities. Positive effects may be seen irrespective of whether the disability is congenital (various syndromes, or deformations that require surgery), traumatic (delivery, infections, biochemical vulnerabilities, abuse), or transmitted (drug/alcohol addiction, etc.).

HOME VISITING: IN THE FACE OF THE GORGON

Home visiting with high-risk babies and their parents can be experienced as facing gorgons, following the mythical image of the Gorgon Medusa, "whose looks turn any beholder to stone"—or, I would add, that make people freeze through fear or impotence.

Home visiting is specialized work that is usually not practised or discussed in the psychoanalytic world. However, it is important to think about it and to realize that the enterprise includes facing gorgons: *the enormity of primitive experiences that are related to more basic levels of communication.* The work has to tune to the level of exploring and being immersed in the "nameless dread" of early intergenerational experiences between babies and a possibly wilfully misunderstanding mother, whose thinking may have become impaired by a continuous need to avoid or modify a frustrating external reality and who believes that she is in the right and "others" are persecutory.

It might appear that gorgons would threaten and distract any thorough thinking rather than enhance it, but I question this attitude and its attendant myths. In thinking about the technical complexities attached to such work, we are facing not only the patient's gorgons but the domestic ones as well and therefore our own gorgons (reactivated in us) related to them.

Context of work

Since our resources are scarce at the Infant–Parent Clinic and our training lengthy and specialized, we try to maximize our services through indirect consultation or direct work. Sometimes the family work has to take place at the patient's home, even though such psychotherapy or psychodynamic-based therapy is difficult and costly. Thus, we may visit high-risk babies once a week and involve other agencies if the danger calls for it.

The cases that required home visits included 3 in 1,000 psychiatric mothers who refused to attend a consulting-room when their child was failing to thrive; 1 in 1,000 babies who were physically too ill to be taken out of their home, especially in winter; 3 in 1,000 families where there were four or more children under the age of 5 years and the family had no car; 4 in 1,000 families where there were one or two children with physical disability or another child under the age of 5 years. The comparable figure for babies in maternity wards, special-care baby units, or other hospital wards was 10 in 1,000. The proportion where a home visit was needed as part of an assessment was 5 in 1,000, or, where the mother was not well physically (after a Caesarean or other surgical operation), 7 in 1,000. The total was 33 out of 1,000 cases.

Purpose of home visiting

Home visiting is integral to the training and duties of staff in medical careers: general practice, psychiatry, nursing, physiotherapy, social work, and so forth. This is not the case, however, in psychoanalytically oriented psychotherapies. Yet, when working with parents and high-risk babies, where early intervention is crucial because of the speed and importance of early development, we cannot afford to miss this opportunity of being allowed into the house to confront and contain the gorgons and so facilitate the process of healthy growth.

I shall discuss some of the perils of working clinically with infants in a psychoanalytic frame of mind when in an unstructured interview situation. Home visits do provide, however, a great opportunity for change. In such situations, the psychotherapist has to consider three factors: aims, setting, and technical instruments.

1. *Aims.*   The aim, as in all therapies, is to facilitate normal development. Work with infants and their parents who cannot come to a consulting-room or clinic is special because for them the past and present have fused.

By being allowed in, we are given an opportunity of looking, feeling, and even smelling them and their difficulties. We try to offer a model of tolerance, space, and time for them exclusively, which is felt as goodness. Most of them have never had such an experience, being very needy and with perpetual conflicts that they may or may not even acknowledge.

It is not for us to tell them what they need. We can patiently assess while finding out whether they need us or another agency. The aim is to attune to the family, to be able to reciprocate and find a common language, like the first relationship between mother and baby. So we can aim to have a relationship with respect, amusement, surprise, and containment and, on that familiar base, serve as a model for them. We may then find that because of past associations or negative representations progress is being stopped or blocked.

Home visiting is like going into the patient's unborn self and, by being face to face with the untried capacities and feelings, letting them have a different experience, of facing unspeakable terrors and hope. Together, we create this positive containment to transmute the negative experiences. This new way of relating includes sensations, actions, and words that might at times mirror theirs. We may start reciprocating behaviours and states of mind so that they can understand what is going on.

2. *The setting.*   The psychotherapist usually has to create a setting to do the work calmly and thoroughly, perhaps providing the first good model of containment for the family's gorgons. Space and time are needed to think with the family about their anxiety and pain. For this purpose, we organize a room (or space in one) for the interview, requesting that it be the same for all visits.

Ideally, there should be one or two comfortable chairs, no electronic devices such as music players, radio, or television, no telephone to shatter a calm, intimate atmosphere. In such an ambience, reflection on the verbal and nonverbal contents of the mind will allow the therapist and patient to retrieve lost links from the past to the present which are important to the understanding and resolution of the conflict and problems.

However, the possible disturbances are many—too many children or other people around; a TV constantly on, somewhere; a telephone ringing and conversations going on; people coming and going; smells that are not nice; or the house may be in a state that is difficult to bear. All this makes it difficult to concentrate and have an ideal setting for working on deep unconscious material. We really need to prepare to take in all of this "disturbance" as communication from the family which provides important clues for understanding it and altering interventions accordingly.

The setting seems to become part of what the analyst/therapist offers to the patient—an attentive, exclusive space–time in the mind. The danger of not being in the psychotherapist's consulting-room is that the therapist may feel unprotected from and intruded by the patient's physical reality. Whether the therapist can maintain his or her own secure base while in an alien setting is dependent on retaining a good internal analysis of his or her own fragility and internal world.

Figure 7.1 represents the professional in the home, with baby, father, mother, and siblings and with activity of all kinds going on. The Xs in the circles stand for the threatening mental representations—the gorgons—which are unconscious and which we all have, whether elaborated and known or not. These may also be reactivated in the therapist by the situation. So we try to imagine a safe and secure setting that the therapist can create in the home.

The therapist offers a space and time of his or her mind which is not physically visible and is only psychologically felt. The therapist has to hold on to his or her inner good object and believe that he or she can withstand the physical and psychological disturbances of the home, which sometimes intrude on the innermost areas of the therapist's mind in the most insidious ways. The therapist has firmly to acknowledge the resistance in the home at the start, speak about it, and create an atmosphere that helps him or her and the patient to feel, reflect, think, and work in an alliance. In this way, the therapist can take the chaos in the mind of the patient and work with the resistances to thinking that appear again and again.

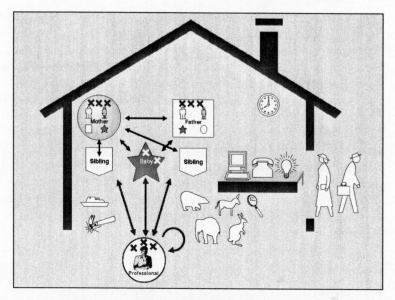

Figure 7.1.   The professional in the home setting.

If the therapist becomes identified with the gorgons and cannot think and begins to feel persecuted, the work needs extra reflection on the transference and countertransference, often with the help of supervision or discussion with colleagues.

3. *Technical instruments*.   The *transference*, as a re-enactment of past experiences in the present, occurs in home visiting as in any other situation. A person transfers all the time, even the feeling of not having a past. In our consulting-room we are allowed to work from the patient's beginning, and generally we rely on words as well as all the other kinds of communication.

But what happens when the past is all in the present? Rather than observing ghosts or gorgons, we may have become one of them, through the confusion of the family's everyday trauma of living. We are entering into a dynamic where, after a large number of professionals have already been involved with the family, it is difficult for our identity and role first to be separated from the other professionals and then to be maintained.

This experience for the therapist is similar to a baby's first experiences, which the mother has to contain and digest for the baby. It differs, though, in the sense that the patient is not moving forwards but is stuck and stale, through force of habit and known behaviour.

We confront different situations: one may be that the family did not request help, but it has been offered by professionals or through a programme. In such cases the initial attitude can include suspicion, persecution, or pride. These same attitudes could be awakened in the unconscious of the therapist, who might identify with such phantasies and behave in a way that reinforces the malady. If reflection on our attitudes and reactions reveals elements that have penetrated unconsciously into our mind, we can discover very important data about the dynamic in the family and in each member. The baby, the mother, the father, and the other siblings all act their story. We are there to explore, verbalize, and cope with disgusting or appalling situations.

The *countertransference* continues to be our most important guide for understanding the unconscious of the mother/father and the baby's mental states, through our unconscious perception of conflict.

We react to the transference of the parents and the baby, to their attitudes, their smells, and their house. Body reactions and images come to our help or mislead us, so it is important to keep a close observation of how we feel, think, talk, and finally act and react. For this purpose, we have to create the best possible conditions so that we can receive the monsters that are immobilizing the family. At times it may seem too many or too much, but if we tolerate the situation, new perceptions are possible through transforming the patient's reality— past and present.

Strategies for intervention

The baby's own hope and force of development are used with freshness and flexibility, helping the mother to understand it in spite of her past and present difficulties.

—We contain and understand the situation with slow and steady development of a better relationship.

—We model by making an effort not to become part of her persecutory reality but being committed and reframing the behaviours more positively.

—We speak for the infant to inform the parents how their baby might perceive/feel the situation.

—We work with our understanding of the contents of the mother's mind and contents of the baby's mind.

How do we say what we say to the patients?

A core interpretation given prematurely might be felt by the patient as further rejection and as the therapist's incapacity to contain. But "acting out" by the therapist can also show the patient's capacity for overwhelming the therapist with what is felt as too much. This might be a recurring pattern from the past: either the patient needs more containment than usual or the mother was unable to receive or contain primitive elements from the baby. The tendency at times is to get hooked with the transference of the mother and become unable to move away and contemplate the transference of the infant. We know that in a home visit we are there because for some reason the mother is unable to attend the consulting-room. The baby might greatly contribute to the ability or inability of the mother to move forward, representing an important present conflict rather than a figure from the past revisiting the present. If, however, we are able to step back and relate to the baby and feel what the baby is projecting and what it is transferring, we might facilitate the relationship and mobilize the mother out of her incapacity, making it possible for her to move to a different relationship with the therapist.

Changes in the way of thinking can occur rapidly in the relationship and in the individuals, since where an infant is involved there are possibilities of quick disentanglement and understanding of the causes of difficulties.

CASE 72: LOUISE, AGE 6 MONTHS (FAILURE TO THRIVE)

The mother was agoraphobic and chronically depressed. The darkness and deprivation of her council flat was immense. Louise, age 6 months, was failing to thrive, being totally unstimulated, and would only play with a rag doll. Her "absent mother" had left her with a constant grin on her face and no other visible signalling.

I felt flooded in a suffocating way by images of murder, abuse, and total deprivation. These were difficult to put into words in a way that would not be felt as strange or persecutory.

Louise was observed lying in her pram seemingly lifeless, underreacting greatly, with only a fixed gaze and grin. Her looks reminded me of the Spitz babies in institutions, victims of hospitalism, where no first object had been found and general retardation with fear of dying may occur. At 6 months, the baby was still at birth weight, and her lack of movement and stimulation was affecting her badly. However, when I moved near and spoke to her, Louise would make faint moves towards her line of vision; after a while she moved both her legs and arms.

The mother talked incessantly without relating to the baby. After a while she was asked about the personality of the baby, and she realized she did not have a clue. She explained that the baby did not pick up her strange states of mind because Louise always smiled when she was crying. My further comments on the baby made her start to observe Louise while I was speaking.

The smell of the room was sickening and stale, as if the baby had thrown up. Then the baby started to defecate, and the smell in the room became even worse. The mother mumbled about her paranoid feelings—the neighbours were all against her. I suggested that Louise be cleaned, and as soon as she was picked up awkwardly by her mother, she moved her legs up and down. I started a description of Louise, acknowledging the mother and her likes and dislikes. The mother changed her without looking at her, and, when I talked, the baby would look in my direction. I continued my description of Louise's interest in human voices and in her mother— the uncoordinated movement of arms and legs indicated that. Perhaps the baby was making an effort to demonstrate that she was different from her indifferent and depriving mother. We then talked about the importance of relating to Louise differently; the mother looked at me surprised, as if she did not know there were different ways of relating to people—and to babies.

The mother did not seem to listen and continued to mumble about life. I listened to the horror stories of her childhood and early adolescence, with sexual abuse by her mother's different boy-friends. Through this symbolic holding of the mother, I tried to understand her tortuous, painful past and pick up clues from her abused infant-self to allow her a new birth and existence, rather than the garbage bin she had become.

After a while, the mother started holding Louise awkwardly and fed her with a half-full bottle that was on the table. My holding through listening slowly gave the mother courage to face her horrendous past as well as looking at Louise's real needs. In the third session, when asked about the scars on her arms, the mother had a flashback to meeting an ex-boyfriend in the park, who attacked her viciously with a broken bottle and left her bleeding and almost dead on the grass. Her agoraphobia had started soon afterwards, and this link helped her greatly to work through the "contents of her mind". She showed amazement at my holding her and her story in my mind.

After the third session, she came to my consulting-rooms. Louise began to put on weight, and the relationship between mother and baby started to bloom. A new experience of being safely held in a psychotherapeutic relationship helped the mother to form a different relationship with her own baby-self, so she could mother Louise more effectively.

Discussion. We can see in the case of Louise how the countertransference from each of them was taken up in the process of work by the therapist giving attention to both the mother and the baby and discussing the impact on them. The role of listening and understanding what had happened included clarifying and inviting reflection. It also included modelling for the mother through suggestion and nonverbal communication with the baby, such as gestures, movement, and toys.

The persecutory neighbours had been created in the mother's mind in as invasive a way as the sickening smell of the room, which she did not seem to mind. An indication that her fears and her situation could change had to be demonstrated to her by an active request to clean the child and freshen up the room.

Until then, there had been many professionals involved and concerned, who were kept fragmented by conflicting information and messages. It seems that too many workers spoil good containment, just as too many cooks spoil the broth. In order to understand a case, a professional has to be able to contain within him/herself all the information from all levels in order to be able to connect fully. This requires time and acknowledgement of the terrors involved in the failing-to-thrive child and its consequences (death or permanent damage), the mother's fragmentation, the diverse information of different workers involved, and the sickening reality of her everyday life.

For moving a person who is frightened at home from the state she is in into another one, it is helpful to attune to her mental and physical reality with comments that will cater for her immediate and practical needs, as with an infant.

I believe that the babies who are referred to us, and are so worrying to primary-care professionals, are already carrying hope within themselves from the attention of so many professionals. To reduce the "team" (or the group) to a single professional makes home visiting an important but lonely and burdensome job. But we can see, as in the case of Louise, when finally the workers were reduced to one who was linked closely to the health visitor, the very important work of containment and slow understanding could take place.

Home visiting should be carried out by one worker, under supervision by an infant specialist who can support and allow other perspectives. Once the case is resolved in its crisis or urgency, other professionals can be brought in as necessary. This model prevents further splitting and leaking of the elements that help growth.

The therapist's aim is to understand what is not allowing healthy growth in babies and their parents. To understand this it is necessary to be able to integrate the different levels of communication, the behaviour, and—beyond behaviour—the internal causes of the situation. Good integration of information and activity in each case requires time and containment by the therapist of the contents of the mother's mind, whether good, bad, or horrific, as she acts and tells her own story. The courage to do such work needs to be well supported, not by numbers of professionals attending the case, but by the depth of the work done and the quality of the supervision.

I have visited many infant/parent programmes that do home visiting by young and inexperienced social workers, paramedics, and nurses. They do have positive results, as studies in the United States and in the United Kingdom have shown, as any intervention is better than no intervention. It should be cost-effective to provide sound psychodynamic clinical training in infant mental health over a two-year period, as occurs at our Infant–Parent Clinic. Some programmes, however, offer brief training of only a day or two to deal with gorgons in the family with ongoing in-depth group support, as if courage can cover up one's fears and help denial. Unfortunately, as has been studied by Isabel Menzies Lyth in her work *Containing Anxieties in Institutions* (1988), if fear is not acknowledged and fully worked through, it gets transformed into somatizations, malpractice, and other ways of unconsciously escaping.

A nation's policy-holders should be aware that in thinking about the cost-effectiveness of short- and long-term services for infants and their parents, it is cheaper to pay for a psychotherapist or *specialized* infant–parent psychotherapeutic health visitor or paediatric nurse to do early psychotherapeutic interventions in health clinics or home visits. The alternative is costly time spent by the mother in psychiatric institutions or special units, with the child needing state care and at risk of further emotional damage.

CHAPTER EIGHT

Borderline and psychotic mothers: moving to insightful parenting

The extended psychotherapeutic work necessary with mothers in an extremely vulnerable state arises from their sudden or chronic disorganization of thoughts. If proper work cannot take place, the ground must be prepared by making emotions sufficiently flexible. "Proper work" is usually taken to mean making conscious the unconscious and helping patients reach an understanding of what is happening in their lives and why it is happening. However, I consider that preparing the ground is in itself proper work, because we have to contain their transference of chaos, fear, panic, persecution, or distress and be in it with them, by acting as a different kind of mother from the one transferred.

The state of disorganization does not allow good integration at a rational level; containment by the therapist, with a description of that attitude to the patient, gives the patient the feeling of strength and sympathy emitted from the therapist. Therapists sometimes lend themselves as containers; at other times they lend capacities to think or function. It is from the continuity, availability, and flexibility of the therapist that the patient finds her identity and learns to understand and integrate her experiences. In due course, the work ends when attachments and separations have been properly exposed, experienced, and assimilated.

The issue of psychotherapy with severely disturbed mothers who require psychiatric containment, either in hospital or through heavy medication at home, is controversial. We will try to evaluate whether any psychotherapeutic work can be done, and how mothers can learn to relate to their babies, whether in crisis periods or chronic illness. Since mothers and babies are very vulnerable, a great deal of thinking is necessary to find strategies that could be applied to the crisis or mental state and, from these, to develop a base from which the mothering can develop.

In the psychotherapeutic field related to puerperal psychosis and other mental illnesses in pregnancy, there is great discrepancy between what is wished and what is provided for the patient after the birth of a baby or who has an infant to look after.

There are some myths to be dispelled:

- that *mothers need to attend the consulting-room*—if they do not, then they are perceived as not making the necessary effort to be helped
- that, for psychoanalysis to be possible, the patient has to be *able to verbalize* her conflicts in order to be able to work through them
- that the *timing of the intervention* can be known in advance (but in cases of severe mental disturbance and the birth of a baby or the existence of a little child, when is the most appropriate time to intervene?)
- that there can, ahead of time, be a *specific focus of the work* (but we need first to assess the psychoanalytic understanding and potential of the patient so as to be able to focus the intervention; this requires attunement to her circumstances at the time and handling the case with great sensitivity and caution, since mothers and babies are always vulnerable, especially in the case of evident mental disturbance).

It is important to rediscover the flexibility of psychoanalytic thinking in different settings, whether in a premature-baby unit where the difficulty may have arisen or in a home or hospital setting. Referrals/

requests for help may come from the staff of a unit, from mothers, or from their relatives.

The cases presented in this chapter relate to various kinds of difficulties in mothers who have been schizophrenic, borderline schizophrenic, or borderline paranoid schizophrenic or who suffer from postnatal depression, bipolar disorder, or puerperal psychosis. The importance of naming the different referrals received helps to differentiate the different treatments arranged, rather than classing all patients as "mentally ill mothers". This general label seems to get in the way of their being helped by psychoanalysis, as it suggests that they need inpatient-unit or home help from psychiatric nurses, health visitors, or other professionals, but not from psychoanalytic workers.

Referrals by agencies occur in cases where mothers abuse their children physically and/or emotionally and such abuse cannot be stopped, or where mothers display chaotic behaviour and arouse concern about their child's poor emotional development. Sometimes, mothers with physical or mental disabilities are referred by the court for assessment of their parenting capacity, usually when there has been a history of difficulties. Most of the cases reported in this chapter were referred by health-care providers or Social Services, with very few self-referrals.

Mother–infant psychotherapy

There are times when a mother and infant do not attach or bond, or reciprocate mutually, yet they wish to have a good relationship. In such a situation, an infant psychotherapist may be asked to help. The cases we are discussing here, though, are not about mothers or infants who have some general difficulty, such as feeding, but about mothers who have a severe disturbance that is adversely affecting the baby's development and causing behaviour that is of concern. We need to take into account a number of considerations: Can the mother react to the baby's needs in spite of her difficulty? Is it possible to trust her criteria of reality as against her hallucination or psychotic states? How safe is the child? How is the child's development being affected? How safe is the mother?

It is in all cases important to observe the behaviour of the infant, the interrelating (or not) between the infant and the mother, and the quality of this interrelating. Both mother and baby have mental representations. In the mother, these representations come from her past experience and relationships, her economic situation, her culture, and the images she has of this particular baby. In the baby, there are mental representations of the care it has received thus far, including what happened to it before birth, especially in the case of referral from maternity hospitals. It is necessary to investigate all this, since mothers (or fathers) who abuse start to do so before the baby is born. The traumatic past of the baby can therefore be reflected in behaviour that is of concern at the time of the consultation or in the resilience that the baby shows.

There are also babies with inborn factors of vulnerability, which others have called inadequate constitutional protective barriers; such babies have little capacity to comfort themselves or tolerate frustration. This, in turn, generates a mental representation that could feel persecutory in relation to whatever the mother actually does to the baby. Babies may also experience deficiency in autonomy or ego, in terms of how quickly after birth a baby feels competent. Again, this will have a repercussion on some representation in the baby's mind as to what it is (or is not) able to obtain. Other vulnerabilities experienced by the baby can produce stronger, vivid mental representations that will need further exploration by the therapist.

All types of mother–infant psychotherapy practised at our Infant–Parent Clinic focus on the mother's mental representations of the particular baby, the father's mental representation and attitude towards the mother, and the baby's mental representations of itself, of its parents and other caregivers, of the world around it, and of the kind of holding, care, and satisfaction of its needs and temperament.

The following classification of infant–parent psychotherapy is based on our study of over 3,500 cases. When the problem lies in a severe pathology in the mother, treatment might include:

1. *Crisis interventions*—usually one or two sessions at the peak of a problem that seems insurmountable. The focus is on resolution of the immediate crisis and helping the mother to understand the baby's situation as much as possible. [20% of cases]

2. *Elaborative work on personal insight*—work with the unconscious phantasies, coupled with the classic work in mother–infant psychotherapy (e.g., Cramer, 1995; Daws, 1989; Fraiberg, 1980; Lebovici & Stoleru, 1983). The aim is to make conscious the unconscious reason for the mother's failure to understand her infant. [60% of cases]

3. *Development of the mother's relationship with the infant*—development of the relationship based on the understanding of the individuality

achieved by the infant despite the personal disturbance of the mother. [borderline psychotic mothers: 16% of cases]

4. *Creation of and maintenance of a "good-enough" caring relationship with the infant*—development of the relationship through building a network of relatives and/or professionals who can support and monitor the child's development. [mothers mostly in psychiatric care either in institutions or living at home: 4% of cases]

In Interventions 3 and 4 in particular, even though we observe, perceive, and develop some understanding of the mind of the mother, we put her deep-seated problems aside (though with due respect for and acknowledgement of these). Instead, we concentrate on helping to bring out the different possibilities for the mother–infant relationship, for the infant's representations of the mother, and for the structure of the internal world of each of them. If the baby has a disability or malformation, or a sensory or emotional sensitivity that needs explanation, the therapy will focus on describing this in order to facilitate the mother's better understanding of her baby.

Clinical material has demonstrated the need to be able to move from one strategy to another, because when a severely disturbed mother is referred or presents for consultation, it is very important that the baby's deterioration is monitored. In general, troubled babies present symptoms, which is why they make such an impact on the system, in order to be helped. There are many causes for children failing to thrive, and psychiatric disturbance in the mothers is often a factor.

It has been shown that most mothers who are severely disturbed or psychotic produce children who become disturbed at some age or children who become psychotic before the age of 4 years. In a study on psychosis in the first four years of life, Massie and Campbell discovered that either the mother or the infant could be shown individual ways of dealing with the other person. Massie created the Agitated Behavior Scale (ABS) to show infant behaviours under stress, in order to assess their vulnerability (Massie & Campbell, 1984). He looked at whether the difficulty arose initially within the infant or within the mother.

Massie also looked at two extremes of behaviour in the mother— from the mother who cannot separate from her child, to the mother who never looks at, talks to, touches, or holds her child. For Massie and Campbell, it is of utmost importance for the paediatrician to evaluate these two extremes during the interview, as they can be a warning signal of needs and can let professionals know whether the mother may be interested in engaging in some sort of work. For example, with an overanxious mother who panics at everything and thinks the world is falling apart, although there might be no explanation forthcoming for the causes of such behaviour, nevertheless it is important to try to discuss this with her. From the case of the "absent" mother—the one who is never around—to the clingy mother who cannot separate or is always laughing and smiling, we can see a gradation. It is similarly very useful to realize the extremes of a child's severe disturbance in cases where the child never looks at the mother, or the child needs to have control over the mother, fixing her in front of him.

Setting

Before the assessment of mother and child, I take a great deal of time to prepare the setting. Consultation in a hospital/institution often must take place in a room (usually the Sister's office) where there are many electrical devices, such as answerphones, telephones, fax machines, and so on; all of these have to be muted. It is vitally important to create a space, similar to the mind, that permits concentration, free-floating attention, and unilateral and parallel thinking as well as privacy.

Consultation does not always take place in hospital. There are cases of schizophrenic, chronically depressed, or agoraphobic mothers with "failure-to-thrive" babies about whom the health visitor and GP become extremely concerned. The mother will not leave her home for two reasons: refusal and/or an incapacity to go out. I then conduct the initial interviews in the home. I consider that very useful work can be done through home visiting, since it is necessary to assess the mother's resistance to starting a new encounter that may change the difficult but familiar state of affairs. Going to where they are suffering—whether their home or the hospital—makes a real difference.

The problem, as described more fully in the final section of this chapter, is that home visiting is full of gorgons, where the mother's chaos combined with the usual domestic chaos intrude on the therapist's capacity for reflection. This has to be expected and taken as important information about what the patient is prepared to share and make good. Home visiting can monitor both the impact of our work and the mother's capacity to take it in. In the home, a minimum space has to be created: a dirty or cluttered chair should be cleaned or cleared if no other chair is available, the TV or radio switched off, the telephone unplugged, and persons not relevant to the case asked to leave the room. Where there are other children being cared for by the mother, it is better to see and feel the atmosphere of the house and how the mother handles and protects the baby.

Whether the setting is the hospital or the home, with known out-of-control cases I ask for someone strong to be outside the door. Also, for a first meeting I ask for a colleague known to the family to be present, so that I can safely dive into the emotional atmosphere even though I know that it will be very tough, that I will have to bear their transference of conflict and disturbance (past and present) and my counter-transference (the repercussion in me of their actions and verbalization).

Technical instruments: transference and countertransference

In every situation, all of us are putting or transferring our experience from the past into the present. We all transfer in normal circumstances, colouring our present experience with experiences from the past. In psychotherapy, when the experience from the past has been integrated and is consistent, it is easier to understand the behaviour of the patient and to try to help him or her realize what his or her past experience has been.

The more disturbed the patient is, the more difficult it is for the patient to be in any present situation without being invaded by past experiences that are unintegrated and do not make sense. The problem with psychotics or borderline psychotics is that their change from theme to theme is extreme and is often difficult to follow and tiring, while their level of reactivity is also great.

If a psychotic mother has a baby while in such a precarious state of mind, it is important to help her focus on the child and the child's individuality and let her state of mind settle in her own time. The mother is likely to be in a fragile mental state precisely because the baby has reactivated her old pathology, and it would a fallacy to believe that we are able to help her with this during the brief period of infancy. However, we can try to help her to establish a relationship with her real baby and not leave her persecuted by the baby of her fantasy.

This massive transmission of feelings, with no clear narratives and logical movement from the past to the present and to the therapist, produces a reaction in the therapist that holds important information about the state of mind of the mother. Even if the therapist is in psychoanalysis him/herself, and is very experienced in human rela-tionships, in cases involving mother and infants there are always further feelings and reactions awakened in the therapist that he or she can learn from. These reactions can be visceral, sensory, and mnemonic—mental representations of previous feelings and relationship. In cases of severely disturbed mothers and babies, there is an added difficulty because of the primitive quality of the feelings so activated, usually linked with life and death, surprise and fear, shock and disappointment, bliss and hope. In cases of severe mental disturbance, there is an added belief that the worst is about to happen, or damage is irreparable; levels of despair and hate or anxiety are felt as unmanageable and pervasive and destructive of all capacity for a new beginning.

The psychotherapist and other professionals can feel hopeless under this avalanche of negativity which does not allow integration of experiences. For a mother the turmoil of mixed feelings following the birth of a child becomes almost impossible to articulate and explosive in quality, allowing no coherence of expression, boundaries, or peace.

This may be one of the reasons why there is very little discussion about the different strategies for such work, since it feels almost too difficult to tackle. On the one hand, a therapist can experience attraction and omnipotence at the idea of helping such chaos; on the other, there is terror and repulsion. The therapist feels the split and the impotence and despair communicated by the mother's pathology. The therapist can be trapped in these patterns, unaware of the internal pressure communicated by the mother and the baby. They do not understand their compulsive feelings, and sometimes the therapist cannot contain these either.

What is required from the psychotherapist is to be more reflective than usual, because of the amount of negative, disintegrative, and rejected impulses coming from the mother and child to the psychotherapist, in the hope that the latter will hold all these experiences and feelings with them. The mother may need to learn to reciprocate, be aware of others, share states felt as unbearable, stay calm when everything seems to be going wrong. She may not be able to speak about all this negativity, but this may not be so important just yet. A psychotherapist who can attune to where the psychotic mother and baby are without running away or feeling contempt, helplessness, arrogance, fear, or other negative feelings towards the work and him/herself will be able to create a digestive thinking apparatus and share it with the mother as a model of identification.

The fact that we are all human and have, in some way or another, all been rejected in the past can present advantages and disadvantages.

The experiences of the psychotherapist sometimes do not allow him or her to be containing and to metabolize such experiences for the mother. Thoughts may appear such as: "Oh well, these people are untreatable," or "These people cannot think and therefore cannot formulate thoughts, so my time is wasted," or "You have to take this interpretation and think about it, because I know, and you don't; if not, you will always be ill"—this latter was reportedly said to a mother by a psychoanalyst next to the incubator in which her neonate was dying because he didn't have proper lungs. Basically, I think that because of their own vulnerability and ignorance, there is an impediment in some psychoanalysts and psychotherapists to taking in the gravity of a situation, so that they cannot hear the true desperate calls from a mother for help.

Some desperate calls are made by the babies: dying through failure to thrive is a cry for help—otherwise the baby is dead. This does happen, but sometimes it goes unnoticed. This also happens with mothers: many attempt suicide or succeed. So a mother who is actually presenting herself to a worker is seeking help and still shows some hope.

Referrals

If a referral of a very disturbed mother is made via a health visitor, GP, or medical officer, I might invite the referrer to the initial interview too, or I might go to the referrer's office if he or she feels that the mother is too frightened or persecuted to come to my office, even though they might be accompanied by their husband or friend. This is done with the prior agreement of the mother. It is, after all, referrers who are primarily responsible for such mothers in the community, and it is useful for them to know what happened at the interview. However, there are cases where the referrer does not want to be involved, or the mother does not wish be. The point is for the psychotherapist not to act out a long story of resistance but, rather, to get everyone together and allow possible understanding by simply containing anxiety from both sides.

Verbalization

The topic of verbalization in psychoanalysis has been questioned when the patient is in a coma, or sleeps in a session, or is not able to articulate phrases because of the lack of logic or grammar as a result of mental retardation, neurological damage, or psychosis, or where a child is too young to speak. Successful communication in such cases depends on the art and skills of the particular psychoanalyst or psychotherapist.

A typical example would be a mother who has had a baby but is unable to speak about her problems because she is in a psychotic breakdown or state, or because of mental retardation or physical damage of some kind. She needs to be able to communicate in a way that makes sense in order to care for her child. For this purpose she must be able to communicate with the baby and respond to the baby's primitive communications to her.

As a basic level of verbalization, the relatives of the baby can start the communication of the mother's wishes or needs. The husband, mother, or sister of the mother might call a professional and ask for help for her. This can be taken as a communication of wishes from the mother that, though not verbalized by her, have been picked up by the relative and transmitted. If treatment is initiated with which the mother complies, the communication can be taken as coming from her and psychotherapeutic work can start, with appropriate delicacy, sensitivity, skill, and respect.

This primitive indirect communication contains unconscious material transmitted by the mother to the relative who made the referral. This material is so compelling that it may sometimes, because of the sense of urgency emanating from the mother, make the professional act out instead of reflecting. The therapist needs then to examine, reflect, and consult other colleagues who might be involved. It may be necessary to visit the mother, whether in an institution or at home, to see and feel what is she is experiencing. A psychiatric opinion would need to be sought if the mother is not already under a psychiatrist's care, and inpatient facilities may need to be held in readiness.

The process of assessment for psychodynamic understanding of the mother–infant relationship can now be started. This requires a number of sessions to explore with the mother her difficulties in mothering her baby and her real capacities to care for the baby in a good-enough way. We then monitor what she does with any insight she may have gained in the interviews, seeking manifestations—through her verbal and nonverbal communications and her behaviour—of the therapy having made a difference to her. Since many patients will have seen psychotherapists or psychiatrists previously and seem to know the jargon and the rules of the game, they can delude the system. The fact of a patient having a baby in her care must make the assessor weigh her statements concerning care against obvious signs of neglect in the baby and in the mother herself.

The parallel observation during the assessment is the physical and mental state of the baby. As we will see in the case of Sarah, she was brought to the third and fourth consultations in short sleeves on snowy days. However, the mother was attending the sessions punctually and felt grateful about the insight gained about herself.

Assessment continues with an observation of the network of care surrounding the mother—are there any friends? husband or father of the baby? siblings or mother nearby? day care? others? If there are none, we look into the possibility of creating a network of local workers, linked with a psychiatrist and a hospital. In the United Kingdom, there are very few hospital units that cater for psychotic mothers and babies. This task calls for more creative thinking around how to help them remain safely in the community, if at all possible. There are mental states that, given their gravity and the risk for both mother and baby if they remain together, require treatment in an inpatient unit, even if this means the mother and baby having to move from the community or town where they are living to wherever a suitable unit might be located.

The outcome of the assessment must convey the mother's state of mind regardless of clear or proper verbalization by her, with a prognosis of the effectiveness of solutions sought to help the case. There might be a first stage in which the staff of the hospital are helped to contain the strong feelings transmitted by the mother and the baby, and a second stage in which the husband/partner, relatives, and helpers (child-minders or nannies, depending on the patient's socioeconomic status) hold group meetings to form a kind of collective mind to contain the ill mother and the baby. This forms, in due course, the scaffolding of the mind for the mother to hang on to when she begins to be able to think or to feel about the baby or her situation as mother in spite of her unbalanced mind and uncontrolled anxieties. It is then, in this third or even fourth stage, that the mother might be able to talk about her experiences. Only after these have been contained and carried consciously by the staff and the relatives can she finally feel them safely. The fact that they have been carried by others and by the therapist makes them more bearable and safe for the mother to internalize them with appropriate boundaries and containment. All this also helps the mother–infant relationship.

Timing

A crucial question is the timing of a particular intervention. It is important to consider at what point a mother can be supported psychologically or helped to gain insight into her emotions. Psychological or emotional support is always positive, and there is very little doubt about its usefulness. The question remains, however, whether the mother will feel persecuted instead of supported by the therapist. A regular, predictable professional presence at times of crisis must be available to gain further understanding through the experience of being with the patient during the most critical period. This does not mean that in the throes of an acute episode of anxiety the patient will want it put into words to understand it. Rather, it means that the psychotherapist should support the psychiatric work and provide a good model of containment of profound states of despair or personal turmoil. The psychotherapist has to learn about the limitations of talking cures and the importance of working as part of a team with the professionals who can help to stabilize desperate states in order to provide a secure base for thinking, feeling, and caring for the baby.

The time to consider interpreting unconscious reasons for behaviour is when a steady pattern of control over emotions has been demonstrated for more than a year, the prognosis for the mother is not severe, and the baby is showing good overall emotional, physical, and cognitive development.

In states of psychotic anxiety or delusion, the presence of the psychotherapist as a steady ally to rely on provides the best complement—if the patient accepts it—to medication.

Focus

Focus is the area and content of the psychotherapeutic work to be done. It is the next stage to think about after thorough assessment of:

- the internal state of the mind of the mother and its possibilities and capacities at the time of the assessment
- the physical and mental state of the infant
- and, afterwards, through team discussion, what structures of help might need to be created.

In general, I prefer to focus on small goals that are coordinated within a general plan, to be achieved in, say, fifteen or twenty steps. These goals can range from the mother simply answering the door after the third call (rather than never) whether in an institution or at home; to allowing a system of relatives or workers to help and to supervise; to allowing the child to be looked after during the day by a specialized or supervised child-minder and attending a day centre; to gaining, after two years or more, insight about causes of anxiety and finding a way to help herself. The coordination with the psychiatrist and his or her team in the hospital or in the community is extremely important in order to maintain changes in medication, routines, and goals of treatment. The psychotherapist has the important role in the containment and monitoring of the other professionals and workers involved, since frequently these workers mirror the pathology in the patient's pervasive system, which needs exploration and utilization for better understanding of the patient rather than them acting out the primitive mechanisms so triggered by her illness. In this way, gratification at achieving positive results for all generates a good feeling about it, and this encourages further progress and affirmation of the mother's competence.

Interpretations

Interpretations are made when the attachment of the mother is secure, regular, and lasting. This does not mean having a high frequency of sessions, but providing sufficient space and time where the proper digestion of experiences and reflection of thought can become possible.

Examples can at this stage be made of the effect that past experiences are having on the therapeutic relationship; this effect would be acknowledged, emphasized, and then set aside. The same procedure is followed in other complex areas—for example, the primitive internal feelings generated in the professional team, which are acknowledged. I do not use countertransference interpretations with markedly disturbed patients. It may produce confusion, rather than clarification, given the level of concrete thinking in which they move. I tend to use the countertransference as information for myself, which I retain and use when I consider it appropriate in a given interaction. It is like putting some sort of damper on the process, making it much slower and taking the need for containment more into account.

CASE 73: MS M. (SCHIZOPHRENIC) AND JOANNA, AGE 9 MONTHS

Ms M. was schizophrenic. Joanna, age 9 months, screamed constantly. The consultation was arranged in conjunction with the medical officer. The baby would cry in panic at the sight of any person, outside or at home. At times her mother would force the baby to socialize by taking her to a sale or parties or a mother–toddler group. Whenever the baby was faced with adults or children, in the street, park, and so on, she would immediately cry and hide herself, and it would be impossible to separate her from her mother or to calm her down. The mother felt she could not leave her with anybody, or go out, or speak to friends. The mother thought that perhaps she was being overconcerned, but she was at the end of her tether.

The mother was 24 years old. She had been hospitalized for a year at the age of 20, as she had had a schizophrenic breakdown. Afterwards, she met and married her husband, and a year later Joanna was born. Ms M. was still medicated as an outpatient and was concerned about having damaged the baby already. The whole attitude of the mother was very defensive and aggressive. In a way, this made one feel hopeless about maintaining a therapeutic link. How was a helpful intervention going to take place? Who was the patient?—if the patient was the one presenting the symptoms, then it was the child; if the patient was the one who felt pain and distress, then it was mother *and* child. The mother and the baby were presenting the problems in different ways—the mother as if an angry, split-off part of herself was not allowing her to understand her daughter. She reacted in a very persecutory way and made it clear that she did not want help for herself but for her daughter. I felt that she had a functioning self that had been constructed on top of a fragile ego that would disintegrate if defences were not respected. It seemed that she was not prepared, nor did she wish, for any work with herself; what she wanted was relief from her emotional burden. The mother occasionally presented a more depressive part of herself, which allowed her to be concerned and seek help. This enabled our work to develop.

The plan was to work on the relationship between the mother and the baby through acknowledgement of the feelings awakened in the therapist by the behaviour and feelings transmitted by the baby. Attempts could then be made to convey to the mother those feelings communicated on a nonverbal level by the baby. Thus, the mother would hopefully be motivated to learn the capacity to verbalize primitive feelings to the infant in a way that would be less overwhelming for Joanna. Normally, the function of translating bad and good experiences in the baby is done automatically by the mother. The "mother's capacity for reverie" (Bion, 1962a) is that state of mind which is open to the reception of any feelings from the loved person and is therefore capable of reception by the infant, projected by the identification. Given the disturbance of Ms M., it was planned that the medical officer was going to be a "co-thera-pist" or a "co-patient", serving as an intermediary between the mother's difficulties in expressing herself and her emotional states and helping her to receive and to understand the contents of the interview. Dr A., the medical officer, understood the family setting well, having been the mother's medical officer when Ms M. herself was a baby.

Ms M. had been adopted along with eight other children by a single woman. All of them were extremely disturbed, going in and out of hospital with psychotic breakdowns. Ms M. was the only one who actually had children— Joanna first, then another child four years later. She had already formed a very good link with the medical officer, who knew her mother as a very strange person and who had cared for Ms M. physically. Later on, Dr A. helped her to understand, digest, and even remember some interpretations of unconscious causes of her behaviour. Interpretations of this kind were made very sporadically, and her reactions and subsequent behaviour were observed carefully.

First interview

When Ms M. and Joanna came into the room, Joanna hid her face and began to cry. Dr A. commented very gently on Ms M.'s con-cerns, as doctors do—"You see, this person comes to see me be-cause of . . ." and so on—because this is how they usually related, and so I let them continue, but Dr A. did not know that I expect patients to explain their concerns to me. Mrs M. said that it was impossible to talk. This made her cross and desperate because Joanna was crying all the time. My feeling was that Joanna was frightened, and that the mother's reaction was very abrupt and angry. I said that Joanna was transmitting to me fear in seeing an encounter with us, new people. Ms M. replied angrily that she felt annoyed that Joanna did not help herself. Sometimes she thought that this was manipulation. I felt very strongly that Joanna was frightened of us. Her whole body was crouching low, held in her own arms with her eyes closed. I explained that we could look together at Joanna, at her body and expressions, and we could try to feel what she might be feeling.

"Mummy," I said, "what is this all about? I am scared, I don't want to make you annoyed. You know, Mum, I am very little and easily frightened. Perhaps I am different to what you expected of me. I love and need you, Mummy, but I can't be what you want me to be. Help me to be myself, to become strong—you can help me." The mother looked surprised, expressed her amazement, looked very thoughtful, and said that she never imagined thoughts going through a baby's mind. Joanna stopped crying, did not look at us, and remained cuddled in her mother's arms, under her cardigan, until the end. I said that Joanna felt relieved. During the rest of the interview we elaborated on these points, mainly on the idea of Joanna being different from other children, and her mother's need to know her individuality. We made it the focus of our work. The mother was pleased because she had felt so disturbed and desperate and extremely paranoid. She had no model of care to identify with and only felt suffocated in persecution.

When the brother was born, Ms M. talked a great deal about the differences. In fact, the boy seemed from the beginning clear in his requests, with a stronger capacity to wait and tolerate frustration, and he was able to put up with the mother's paranoia without disturbance in either party. The question is whether the previous mother-and-child experience and continuous support created this stronger child in the mind of the mother, which she could then reinforce.

The reality was that the mother discovered Joanna's individuality, and this helped the child to develop healthily; while the mother came to accept that her ideals were not necessarily being met, a good-enough mothering was nevertheless developed. Joanna and mother were seen fortnightly. Ms M. subsequently wanted to have full psychoanalytic treatment five times a week, and she was referred by her GP. We maintained monthly follow-up interviews with mother and both children. After a year, she attempted suicide on several occasions, requiring long psychiatric hospitalizations. The husband had to manage with a nanny's help, and we then made home visits to work with the children's phantasies and the husband and nanny. After the fourth incident, in which the mother threw herself out of a second-floor window, psychoanalytic treatment was stopped completely, on psychiatric and GP's orders. We continued once-a-month integrative work with the mother and children until Joanna was 8 years old and the brother 4 years old (two years after individual, intensive psychoanalytic work stopped). Ms M. is still under medication and will be for the rest of her life; she tried several times to stop, but she felt so unwell she willingly restarted again. She then became responsible for taking her medication and discussing with the relevant professional any changes she wants to make.

Joanna is now 16 years old, a very well-balanced, intelligent girl, in a secondary school of highest academic standards, and she is extremely sociable and very outgoing.

Discussion.   The setting changed several times. At the beginning it was the medical officer's office; three years later it was the mother's home but without her there, just the people who were holding the fort: the father, the nanny, and the children. We then went back to Dr A.'s office, and the follow-up had taken place in my office. The setting was kept as the space where we could attune to all their needs (mother and baby, first, and both children later), contain their feelings, and create a mind for feelings, thoughts, and perceptions that she could take in gradually.

Interpretations of contents of the mind were carefully phrased and thoroughly thought through before being expressed. They were talked about, explained, and shared between the three of us (myself, Dr A., and Ms M.). I always sensed an extreme fragility in the mother and an immense fear of been intruded upon and forced to undertake impossible tasks. The search for and receiving psychoanalytic treatment at the time was felt by the psychotherapists as a golden goal achieved. We felt that in three years of work done so carefully by us, she had wanted finally to change her internal objects, or the inner view of herself and contents of her mind. It was an important lesson for psychoanalytic professionals about how much a patient can take in and the necessary conditions for individual intensive work.

In this setting of three adults (plus the baby), Ms M. built an ego and developed a healthy-enough mind. Her experience of her own single mother, full of little children, and her difficulty in integrating experiences had not allowed growth and became pathological. Ms M. had been adopted, and it felt unbearable or impossible for her to attach to her baby, who in turn became persecutory. She went with her baby to ask help from her own baby's doctor, who attuned well to her unconscious need, as Dr A. set herself up as an auxiliary ego and re-did what her mother should have done: translate raw feelings into bearable ones. It was necessary with two therapists to be even more careful and to monitor countertransference acting and reactions constantly.

Timing was learnt during the different treatments by the psychiatrists, community workers, and ourselves. The father in this case, as with many other psychotic/borderline mothers, is much more important than in mildly disturbed mother–infant difficulties. The sort of person that he is—whether he is disturbed or whether he will be supportive of any work that can be done—is also important. Mr M. was a well-balanced person who, when the mother first made the suicide attempts, engaged a nanny to help with the baby and the other children, and he was in general very supportive of the mother.

Ms M. wanted to live without medication and have psychoanalytic treatment. She did so, but started again attempting suicide, and she had to cease a psychoanalytic treatment that was going deep into her anxieties without taking into account her difficulty in integrating the new knowledge, given the strong defences of her habit from early on of splitting her experiences into unrelated fragments. This happened because of the degree of early trauma in her life. Mother–infant psychotherapy had to help integration through allowing attachment, together with her child, to the therapist.

The differences in treatment—between psychotherapy and psychoanalysis—were due to the psychoanalytic use of setting, transference–countertransference, timing, and focus.

In mother–infant psychotherapy, the search for a solution is based on how to help mother and baby create a good-enough relationship that can be tolerated, building a foundation for development to be possible and for amiable and positive object relations to exist, and to hold the destroyed or unintegrated negative experiences and fantasies. In intensive regular individual psychoanalysis, the patient has to have a functioning self that brings the patient to speak about his or her difficulties and is able to transfer and receive back interpretations of unconscious conflicts. Unfortunately, Ms M. was unrealistic, being very disturbed, with a damaged ego structure, so that it became too painful and unbearable for her to reconstruct it. When she finally began taking medication again, the suicide attempts ceased, and she managed to continue accepting help with the mother–child relationship. Her husband was a very important factor in this case.

Also, in cases like these, it is very beneficial if there are parents, sisters, or relatives around. Severely disturbed mothers usually do not have friends or a family system around them; sometimes they have no husband, or their husband is also psychotic. The cultural background also plays a large role in regard to emotional responses in the mother. It is important for all these factors to be taken into account in order to assess whether, or how, such mothers can be contained.

Psychotherapists, community professionals, and psychiatrists can make an excellent team to look after a patient when they communicate well and stay in easy and good contact. But this is difficult and costly. It may be that it is so difficult because to meet is to share the more destructive and persecutory anxieties of the patients, and it becomes painful, tiring, and hopeless at times. The problem then is that the more we split, the less the patient gets better, even though the professionals feel freer and better.

Babies cannot wait. In helping mother and baby, sometimes professionals can hang on to the hope that the mother had in having the baby, and they can bring out the potential that might otherwise never be discovered.

CASE 74: Ms D. (PREGNANT, WITH HALLUCINATIONS, UNABLE TO SLEEP)

A GP referred a woman who was eight months pregnant, was having panic attacks, and was unable to sleep. At the interview, Ms D. presented herself in a very agitated state, feeling terribly persecuted and seeing things on the wall. I discussed with her the possibility of consulting a psychiatrist, and she commented that she had just spent a week as an inpatient because she had been totally unable to sleep. Since returning home, she had started seeing things on the wall as well as being unable to sleep. She would not mind going back to her psychiatrist, but she wanted to see me as I had helped a friend of hers to attach to her baby.

I pursued the thread about attachment and her probable fear of attachment to her baby. She commented that she was working very hard and had very little time to think about it. I asked her about her pregnancy, and she commented on the wonderful circumstances in which she had become pregnant, and how much they were looking forward to the birth. It occurred to me to inquire about previous experiences of any hallucinations, and, when asked, she answered that she had not had any. The narrative continued about her actual illness. The characteristics of her hallucinations were persecutory and were distracting her. In my floating attention, an idea of a traumatic experience was preoccupying me, and I asked about dead siblings. She then suddenly talked about a baby she had had who died when a month old, a cot death. Ms D. then went into a trance, a kind of ecstatic state in which she was remembering and desperate.

The allotted time for the session ended, and I had to delay the next appointment and continue with Mrs D. until she could come out of her trance—remembering something terrifying and traumatic. She recalled in bits and pieces all her illusion in the expectancy, all their joy at birth, all their love for him and her feeling filled by those two little alert eyes every moment, and how much the baby loved her as well.

A month after the birth, the baby was found dead one morning in his cot. They were given no explanation other than "it sometimes happens", and the advice was to get pregnant immediately. So she did, but now she had started panic attacks, and her pregnancy was hell. There was a shocking experience that needed to be mourned and digested. She was, deep down, terrified of the same thing happening, and she could not integrate the experience into her life.

She had four sessions before the baby was born, two of them together with her husband. The psychiatrist was informed, and Ms D.'s panic attacks decreased and then stopped. A care team was formed to help her to talk about rather than deny her fears: the team was comprised of a health visitor, a midwife, a psychiatrist, and a psychotherapist. They had to understand the importance of keeping in mind what had happened, with all its horror and despair, and help to think each step for the future. She was seen fortnightly for a year after the birth, by a colleague whom I supervised.

Discussion.   A vicious circle of denial and lack of help in cases of stillbirth, cot death, or disability can generate breakdowns or pathological attachments. This could be avoided by meetings at the time of the death, to help facilitate proper mourning.

In this case, work had to be done about the fear of pathological consequences in the mind of the mother. Soon after, she could start thinking and integrating the past pain and present anxieties, and she could slowly stop, safely and under control, taking sedatives, which were regulated by the psychiatric team.

CASE 75: MS F. (AGORAPHOBIC AND CHRONICALLY DEPRESSED) AND STACEY, AGE 6 MONTHS

Ms F. was 24 years old, agoraphobic and chronically depressed. Her daughter Stacey was 6 months old and was a failure-to-thrive baby. The mother was well known to the hospital because she had had her baby without ever having attended the outpatient sessions. She had been taken by a friend for the delivery and never attended afterwards.

She was referred by the paediatricians, health visitor, and GP. Briefly, the intervention took place at home, and three interviews made her seek psychiatric help with a counsellor and a psychiatrist. In the interviews, it was noticeable that the baby looked like the babies René Spitz described and showed in his film *Grief, a Peril in Infancy*, about the syndrome of "hospitalism". Stacey had a bald patch on the back of her head because she was never picked up; she had loose limbs and was underdeveloped. However, a grin would appear if she was approached and talked to.

The focus then was to discover and describe the individuality of the baby, and to model for the mother another kind of relationship with her daughter, by talking to Stracey about what her likes and dislikes were and what was frightened of and then describing her reactions to what I was saying and doing with her.

The mother acknowledged my work but went on about her depressing and abused background. The aim was to hear her, but also to hear the mute communications of the baby and to help them relate, for both to have a new and different kind of relationship. In the third session, the mother was more active with and responsive to the baby, communicating with her, even looking animated and daring some new comments. When she was asked about scars on her right arm, Ms F. came out with a story that after she had broken up with a boyfriend at 18, she was walking on the square and met her boyfriend who had a bottle in his hand. He was drinking when he saw her, broke the bottle, and hit her with it, cutting her arms and leaving her bleeding on the grass, half conscious. She was taken to the hospital and stayed in shock for a while.

She started crying with anxiety, and the baby lifted her hand up to her, making her aware of the already different kind of relationship and world she could start living in. According to Ms. F.'s account, her mother was neglectful and abusive, and so were her boyfriends.

Ms F. acknowledged her wish to go for psychotherapy or further work at the hospital, and our direct work stopped. I followed up with a team of health visitor, GP psychiatrist, and paediatricians. I was only part of the regular team for follow-up to keep an eye on the development of the baby–mother relationship and the emotional development of the baby. (See also Louise, Case 72.)

Discussion.   It was important to be allowed in to rescue the neglected baby. Relating to her to facilitate the mother's narrative helped to develop all her potential. Ms F. appeared to have felt important in the relationship and also felt that the focus was not on her being a bad mother but on leaving the baby unattended, unseen, and unheld. It seems as if an undeveloped potential started its action in a very powerful way, moving aside the contents of the mind that were an obstacle in the process of mothering and caring.

CASE 76: MS G. (SCHIZOPHRENIC) AND ROHAN, AGE 8 MONTHS

The case was referred by the health visitor. The mother was too ill to take care of Rohan, and he was cared for off and on by the grandmother, who also had full-time care of Ms G.'s 12-year-old daughter. Ms G. had a new husband, and she wanted to take care of this child, as well as her 5-year-old son living with her. The 5-year-old was left with the husband when the mother went into hospital.

An assessment was requested of Ms G.'s caring capacities. Ms G., however, did not want any assessment and refused to attend the consulting-room. I did a home visit with the paediatricians, who tested the baby and the 5-year-old boy developmentally. Both were greatly delayed, though they were well fed. The apartment was so dirty that it was impossible to sit or step on anything clean. The mother had hallucinations and persecutory anxieties in a dangerous way. An immediate psychiatric assessment was requested, and the mother was certified and again admitted to hospital.

The following assessment took place in the grandmother's house. She kept her house clean, but she was feeling overwhelmed and in a disrupted state by Rohan being passed back and forth. The 5-year-old seemed to have a relaxed and happy relationship with his sister and his grandmother.

However when he was visited at home, he was still looking unhappy. Meetings with the mother's psychiatrist, together with the paediatricians and the rest of the psychiatric hospital team, were held with regard to the future of the two younger children.

A plan was considered to work with the father and the 5-year-old boy to develop awareness of the child's needs in order to search for an appropriately stimulating place, for the baby to be placed with the grandmother permanently, and for the mother to visit there as and when she wanted. The children would visit their home after the mother's visit to the psychiatrist, but only for short periods. The hospital staff were going to speak with her about the plans for the baby and advise her on prophylactic care and on caring for the boys' needs. If possible, somebody would attend the home if she was with her son and the infant. Gradually, and after a lot of thought about the recurrence of her delusions and her fragility when she was at home, the professionals arrived at the conclusion that even when she was not ill at home, she was not well enough to be a good-enough mother, and that permanent care with the grandmother was better for both these children as well. The father had five sessions with an infant–parent psychotherapist, and the child was never left at home solely in the care of the mother. There had been a fantasy that the mother could do basic mothering, whereas she could not.

Discussion.   This case is an example of how it is necessary to organize the family differently to accommodate an extremely disturbed mother. The mother had an idea that she was normal at times and she could mother babies. She did have a period of stability when she was newly married and was caring for her 5-year-old son, but she regressed to total unbalance again with the birth of the second child.

The father and grandmother were faced with a reality that they had guessed at but did not know. Fortunately, both reacted positively to thinking differently about the situation, and they wanted to take personal responsibility for the new set-up. It might be that both had the opportunity of repairing past relationships with their own difficult relatives (Mr G. said he had not talked much with either his mother or his father; the grandmother said she had always found Ms G. difficult).

Follow-ups showed that the time spent in meetings and thinking had been productive, with both children developing well in a safe and secure-enough environment.

CASE 77: MS K. (CHRONICALLY DEPRESSION) AND SARAH, AGE 4 MONTHS

Ms K. was chronically depressed. She was referred by a paediatrician at the hospital. Sarah was failing to thrive, and the mother did not attend her psychiatric appointments. Sarah was found by the health visitor in a dark room, on the floor, with only an empty bottle, and Social Services were thinking about taking the child into care. There was a husband and a 5-year-old too, who was doing well at school.

This case is presented in more detail in chapter four (Sarah, Case 11). The mother insisted that she was a good mother because she had brought up her eight brothers and sisters. Five sessions were scheduled, and she attended them all promptly with the baby. On several occasions, the bottle was propped up next to Sarah in the pushchair but she was never picked up. Even though the mother was verbal about her depression and complaints, the baby was brought in short-sleeve T-shirts on snowy days, and she was deteriorating rapidly. The work needed with her would be longer than was scheduled. The father was collecting the 5-year-old from after-school activities and was very involved with him.

Meetings were held with all involved: the psychiatrist, paediatrician, nurse of the day-care unit, psychiatric nurse, health visitor, and a "special-needs" child-minder. The father was going to be empowered to supervise the home care of the baby, dressing her before they left in the morning, and feeding and cleaning her. The baby was going to be looked after by the child-minder from 9 a.m. to 5 p.m. The mother was to be a day-patient in the unit. At 5 p.m. the mother would join the baby and the child-minder, who over tea was going to describe the new or usual activities and doings of the baby during the day. The husband would then collect them all and take them home. On Saturdays and Sundays, the father was in charge.

The child-minder started weekly telephone consultations with an infant–parent psychotherapist, and the father too had access to telephone or personal consultations. Neither of them could attend personally since their work did not allow it or they lived too far away. Follow-ups showed a thriving family, with a mother struggling to go forward and being well supported.

Discussion.   The father in this case, as in the previous case, had a better potential than the mother to keep the children, though to a different degree. Her agreement to attend the day unit and for the child to be looked after allowed an acknowledgement of the damaging circumstances that were interfering in the emotional development of her children.

CASE 78: MS J., IN MATERNITY, AGITATED (MANIC BREAKDOWN), AND SAVANAH, AGE 8 DAYS

Ms J. came to the attention of the nurses in maternity because of her odd behaviour: walking around all the time with the baby held in her arms, picking fights with everybody, constantly changing and feeding the baby. At the time I was doing research on early signals of emotional disturbances in neonates. I went to see her with the Sister, and I suggested a psychiatrist be called because the baby was not allowed to rest and I felt the mother to be in an agitated state. The psychiatric assessment reported normal happiness and a dutiful attitude towards the baby.

The mother was discharged ten days after delivery, but on the eleventh day the baby was back in hospital in the paediatric ward. The mother had climbed onto the roof of their house, neighbours called an ambulance, and she was taken to an adult psychiatric hospital with a manic breakdown. The father did not know what to do with the baby, so he brought her back to hospital. He was advised to seek a family member who could look after the baby. After three days in hospital, the baby was taken to an aunt, who passed him on to another aunt, and so on every two days. After twenty days he was found dead in his cot.

Discussion.   The difficulty in assessing manic mothers is that it is easily confused with good, preoccupied, normal mothering. Alarm bells ring sometimes with mothers who are depressed, because they do not take care of the baby in the maternity ward. However, it is important to keep an eye out for early signs, and for that purpose a scale has been created for observing the quality of the relationship, the individuality of the mothering, and the individuality of the baby (see Figure 5.2).

A mother's continuous activity with the baby, without attunement, can be devastating just as much for the baby, producing defences in some cases that protect the baby; however, if these are trespassed, the baby could relinquish hope and die.

With two other subsequent similar cases, it was possible to have the babies under observation for a longer time, to ask psychiatrists for better management, and to arrange a bed in an inpatient mother-and-baby unit in the probability that it would be needed. It was necessary to arrange interviews while in hospital and to have a plan of action before the mother left the hospital for carefully devised interviews to be carried out at home.

In one case the psychiatric nurse, with me accompanying, went to the home the first three times to learn how to help attachment and read the individuality of the baby in parallel to the needs of the mother. The psychiatric nurse continued the case, and I supervised. In another case, the child psychiatrist became the key worker, following the same procedure as before, initially with me, for the purpose of learning to read the clues of the babies and the way to verbalize without acting out the countertransference, and to help the mother to understand the baby herself. Follow-up showed good development of a sensitive, thoughtful relationship between mother and baby.

CASE 79: Ms N. (ABUSER) AND SHONA, AGE 3 MONTHS

Social Services asked for an assessment of quality of mothering because the mother had two other children, aged 10 and 12 years, who had been physically and sexually abused. Ms N. had now been under observation for three months in a home for mothers and babies, and a decision was due as to whether or not she should be allowed to keep the baby. The father of the child was not the father of the other two children, and there was some hope about the case.

There were four meetings. The mother would not agree to meet in the usual place: instead, the interviews had to be in her room. It was small, but she preferred that. She was annoyed about Social Services and said that it was the other man who was abusive. When asked about the baby's actual father, she mentioned that he did not live with her but was married and had another family. Her concerns were about finances and whether she was going to have another child as company for this one.

First interview.   Ms N. was not around when I arrived. The receptionist had to look for her and tell her I was there as arranged. Because this scenario repeated itself many times, I felt unwelcomed. We started a conversation about the circumstances of the interview and the advantages of doing it in her room, so that I could see the space and quality of the accommodation.

She complained about everything. The baby uttered a whine, and the mother propped up a bottle; the baby did not want the bottle but lifted her hand, and I lifted mine and said hello. Ms N. looked at me in amazement as if I were crazy. I mentioned how uncomfortable she was feeling in her room, in the interview, and with me there peeping into her privacy. She said she hated people like me who felt they knew what she was thinking and who she was. I mentioned that that was a scary thought, if true, and that she might be too sensitive to being "invaded" and that being under observation did not help. She said she hated every minute of it; she had had a horrible childhood; she wanted to take care of her children. She was now having a horrible motherhood. People poking in her thoughts, in her mind, as if she were crazy. The baby wanted to come out of the prone position. Ms N. continued on and on about how crazy and perverse the social workers were, and that "they" were judging her. I realized she was feeling extremely persecuted by me as well and was not paying attention to the baby. When she changed the baby, there was no maternal playing or talking at all; rough manners predominated, and it was painful for me to observe that her rage about me and the others observing her was so easily displaced onto the baby. No maternal love seemed to be in evidence—on the contrary, a tremendous loneliness filled the room. It seemed as if Ms N. wanted all the rights but not the responsibilities of taking care of Shona.

Second and third interviews.   Work on describing the baby's individuality predominated. Precise attention was paid to the needs of the baby and the mother, so that these could be compared and, thereby, some maternal reverie facilitated in an attempt to develop mothering capacities.

Fourth interview.   The mother pinched the baby to quieten her, and I felt repulsion for the mother. I pointed out that she did not welcome Shona's liveliness, and I asked whether she knew anything about her own characteristics as a baby. She talked about her mother, saying that "that bitch surely didn't remember or even notice me". Then suddenly she started crying and said she really wanted to protect her baby and she wanted the baby adopted, that she couldn't be a good mother, that she had too much hate inside her. Perhaps in the future she could care for Shona, but not now.

I had helped her to see that Shona was lovely and needed a kind of mother she could not be because she was driven mad by being nasty with her and doing things to her. She asked if I could help her.

We then thought of foster care and individual treatment, coupled with visits with her child on a scheduled basis. Social Services accepted this arrangement. Ms N. attended an abusive-parents group as well as an abused-adults group, with some individual sessions, as she herself had been badly abused and neglected in her childhood. She visited the baby regularly and chose not to have another child. Three years later she took her daughter back into her home, with therapists holding regular follow-ups and with the possibility of some arrangement being reached if she had any worries or was too tired.

Discussion.   I felt that there was space for internal change because she had waited so long before having another child, and also that deep down she was grateful she was under observation. The discomfort produced in me was indicative of her own internal discomfort. The way she perceived me and the others was a first awareness of the way she herself had been treated as a baby. It was important to keep this information for an appropriate time and utilize this knowledge softly in a context where she could feel our delicacy in giving it to her, but in a digested form and held by us. I think she felt the psychotherapist "holding her baby" and giving her the benefit of the doubt about her real motivations and wishes for both the "real baby" and the "baby in herself". When she felt held—contained in her nastiness but loved anyway—I think she felt she had a trusting nest in the attention of the therapist, who became her ally as she explored her deeper feelings.

CASE 80: MS S. (LEARNING-DISABLED AND PARTIALLY SIGHTED) AND SUSAN, AGE 2 MONTHS

Ms S., together with her baby, was in a Social Services home in observation because her mother had adopted her previous children as Ms S. was rough with them and because she had a slight disability. Ms S. wanted to keep this baby, and her mother also said she did not want to adopt any more. I did four interviews. In the first one, Ms S. was feeling uneasy with me and was justifying all her activities. When she changed the baby, I realized she had great difficulty in finding the nappy, in getting hold of the legs properly, in putting the dummy in her mouth, and so forth. I questioned her about her eyesight, and she replied that she wore glasses because she was short-sighted.

When she came for the second interview, I saw Ms S. crossing the road precariously with the pram, and she also knocked over some of the plants in the corridor. I requested an eye test for her and found that she was partially sighted. That explained to the staff why appliances in the kitchen were left on, why she would drop things so easily, and why she found it difficult to prepare the bottle. Further tests revealed that her disability was milder than her capacity to think. An interview with Ms S.'s mother showed extreme contempt towards her daughter. The mother was very smart-looking, seemingly middle-class, with a job as a top executive manager. She had three other daughters, described by her as very pretty and smart from the beginning—the opposite, she said, of Ms S., who had always been the ugly and slow one. She did not want Ms S. around; she had already adopted two other children from her, but she did not want to continue adopting, nor to have Ms S. at home because she was so stupid and stubborn.

When the mother was asked about what made her think that from the beginning Ms S. had been stupid, ugly, and annoying, she answered very quickly that she realized that she was the last one to be born. The floating attention and the countertransference were indicating to me something that might have happened in pregnancy or delivery that had primed this woman to be so horribly rejecting of Mrs S. When asked for information about the pregnancy and delivery, concerns about death appeared. In fact, her own mother had died a year before Ms S. was born, and Ms S. had not been "planned". The mourning had been interrupted or perhaps acted out through becoming pregnant.

Discussion. This case shows poignantly how Ms S.'s mother's unresolved grief for own mother did not allow for proper attachment with Ms S. She was seen as stupid, uninvited at a time her mother was still in the sad process of grieving for her mother. The abusive verbal treatment given to her daughter, not just mentally but physically, did not allow Ms S. to grow internally. Ms S. became pregnant again so she would have company, without realizing the amount of work involved in bringing up a baby. So for two years she could only look after the baby while in an institution, and afterwards they moved to Ms S.'s mother's house.

REFERENCES & BIBLIOGRAPHY

Acquarone, S. (1986). Early interventions in cases of disturbed mother–infant relationships. *Infant Mental Health Journal, 8* (4).

Acquarone, S. (1987). Psychotherapeutic interventions in cases of impaired mother-infant relationships. *Journal of Child Psychotherapy,* 13: 45-63.

Acquarone, S. (1990). "Warning Signals of Emotional Disturbance in Neonates." Unpublished paper presented at WAIMNH Congress, Lugano, Switzerland.

Acquarone, S. (1992). What shall I do to stop him crying? *Journal of Child Psychotherapy, 18* (1): 33–56.

Acquarone, S. (1995). Mens sana in corpore sano: Psychotherapy with a cerebral palsy child aged nine months. *Psychoanalytic Psychotherapy, 9* (1): 41–57.

Acquarone, S. (2002). Mother-infant psychotherapy: A classification of eleven psychoanalytic treatment strategies. In: B. Kahr (Ed.), *The Legacy of Winnicott: Essays on Infant and Child Mental Health* (pp. 50-78). London: Karnac.

Acquarone, S. (2003). Feeding disorders. In: J. Raphael-Leff (Ed.), *Parent–Infant Psychodynamics* (pp. 283–293). London: Whurr.

Adamson-Macedo, E. (1984). *Effects of Very Early Tactile Stimulation on Very Low Birth-Weight "Infants"—A Two-Year Follow-up Study.* PhD thesis, University of London, Bedford College, Faculty of Science.

Allen, N. D., et al. (1995). Distribution of parthenogenetic cells in the mouse brain and their influence on brain development and behaviour. *Procedings of the National Academic of Sciences, USA, 92* (11): 10782–10786

Alvarez, A. (1983). Problems in the use of the counter-transference: Getting it across. *Journal of Child Psychotherapy, 9* (1).

Alvarez, A. (1985). Neutrality: Some reflections on the psychoanalytic attitude on the treatment of borderline and psychotic children. *Journal of Child Psychotherapy, 2:* 87–103.

Alvarez, A. (1992). *Live Company.* London & New York: Tavistock/Routledge.

Badcock, C. (2000). *Evolutionary Psychology: A Critical Introduction.* Cambridge: Polity Press.

Baranek, G. T. (2002). Efficacy of sensory and motor interventions for children with autism. *Journal of Autism and Developmental Disorders, 32* (5): 397–422.

Bell, S., & Ainsworth, M. (1972). Infant crying and maternal responses. *Child Development, 43:* 1171–1190.

Bichard, S., Sinason, V., & Usiskin, J. (1996). *Measuring Change in Mentally Retarded Clients in Long-Term Psychoanalytic Psychotherapy.* Kingston, NY: National Association for the Dually Diagnosed.

Bick, E. (1964). Notes on infant observation in psycho-analytic training. *International Journal of Psycho-Analysis, 45:* 558–566.

Bick, E. (1968). The experience of the skin in early object relations. *Psychoanalytic Journal, 49:* 484.

Bion, W. R. (1959). Attacks on linking. In: *Second Thoughts: Selected Papers on Psycho-Analysis.* London: Karnac, 1984.

Bion, W. R. (1962a). *Learning from Experience.* London: Karnac, 1984.

Bion, W. R. (1962b). A theory of thinking. In: *Second Thoughts: Selected Papers on Psycho-Analysis.* London: Karnac, 1984.

Bion W. R. (1967). *Second Thoughts: Selected Papers on Psycho-Analysis.* London: Karnac, 1984.

Blacher, J., & Meyers, C. (1983). A review of attachment formation and disorder of handicapped children. *American Journal of Mental Deficiencies, 87:* 359–371.

Brazelton, T. B., Koslowsky, B., & Main, M. (1974). The origins of reciprocity: The early mother–infant interaction. In: M. Lewis & L. Rosenblum (Eds.), *The Effect of the Infant on Its Caregiver* (pp. 49–77). New York: Wiley.

Brazelton, T. B., Young, G., & Bullowa, M. (1971). Inception and resolution of early pathology. *Journal of American Child Psychiatry, 10:* 124–156.

Britton, R. (1989). The missing link: Parental sexuality in the Oedipus complex. In: *The Oedipus Complex Today* (Chapter 2). London: Karnac.

Burman, E. (1994). *Deconstructing Developmental Psychology*. London: Routledge.

Casement, P. J. (1985). *On Learning from the Patient*. London: Tavistock Publications.

Chatoor, I. (1989). Infantile anorexia nervosa: A developmental disorder or separation and individuation. *Journal of the American Academy of Psychoanalysis, 17* (1): 43–64.

Clar, P. (1933). *The Nature and Treatment of Amentia*. London: Bailliera.

Cooper, P. J., Murray, L., Wilson, A., & Romaniuk, H. (2003). Controlled trial of the short- and long-term effect of psychological treatment of post-partum depression: 1. Impact on maternal mood. *British Journal of Psychiatry, 182*: 412–419.

Cramer, B. (1995). Short-term dynamic psychotherapy for infants and their parents. *Child and Adolescent Psychiatric Clinics of North America, 4* (3): 649–660.

Cramer, B., & Stern, D. (1986). "Mother–Infant Psychotherapy: Objective and Subjective Changes." Paper presented at the Third World Congress, WAIPAD, Stockholm.

Damasio, A. (2000). *The Feeling of What Happens: Body, Emotion and the Making of Consciousness*. London: Vintage.

Darwin, C. B. (1872). *The Expression of Emotions in Man and Animals*. Chicago, IL: University of Chicago Press, 1965.

Daws, D. (1989). *Through the Night*. London: Free Association Books.

Dawson, G., Ashman, S. B., & Carver, L. J. (2000). The role of early experience in shaping behavioural and brain development and its implications for social policy. *Developmental Psychopathology, 12* (4): 695–712.

Deacon,T. (1997). *The Symbolic Species*. London: Penguin

DiLalla, D. L. (1990). Age of symptom onset in young children with Pervasive Developmental Disorders. *Journal of the American Academy of Child and Adolescent Psychiatry, 29*: 863–872.

Ekman, P. (1972). Universal and cultural differences in facial expressions of emotion. In: *Nebraska Symposium on Motivation*. Lincoln, NB: University of Nebraska Press.

Eliot, L. (2001). *Early Intelligence: How the Brain and Mind Develop in the First Years*. London: Penguin

Emde, R. N., Gaensbauer, T. J, & Harmon, R. J. (1976). *Emotional Expression in Infancy: A Behavioural Study*. Psychological Issues, Monograph No. 37. New York: International Universities Press.

Fairbairn, W. R. D. (1952). *An Object Relation Theory of the Personality*. New York: Basic Books.

Ferenczi, S. (1929). The unwelcomed child and the death instinct. In: *Final Contributions to the Problems and Methods of Psychanalysis*. London: Hogarth Press, 1955.

Fonagy, P. (2001). *Attachment Theory and Psychoanalysis*. New York: Other Press.

Fraiberg, S. (1971). Smiling and stranger reaction in blind infants. In: J. Hellmuth (Ed.), *The Exceptional Infant, Vol. 2: Studies in Abnormalities* (pp. 110–127). New York: Brunner/Mazel.

Fraiberg, S. (1977). *Insights from the Blind*. Human Horizon Series. London: Souvenir Press.

Fraiberg, S. (1980). *Clinical Studies in Infant Mental Health: The First Year of Life*. London: Tavistock Publications.

Freedman, D. A. (1968). Blind child. *Psychoanalytic Study of the Child, 19*: 133–169.

Freedman, D. G. (1974). *Human Infancy: An Evolutionary Perspective*. Hillsdale, NJ: Lawrence Erlbaum Associates.

Freud, S. (1912). The dynamics of the transference. *S.E., 12*.

Freud, S. (1914). The history of the psycho-analytic movement. *S.E., 14*.

Freud, W. E. (1967). Assessment of early infancy: Problems and considerations. *Psychoanalytic Study of the Child, 22*: 217–237.

Gewirtz, J. L. (1965). The course of infant smiling in four child-rearing environments in Israel. In: B. M. Fox (Ed.), *Determinants of Infant Behaviour, Vol. 3* (pp. 205–260). London: Methuen.

Gewirtz, J. L. (1969). Level of conceptual analysis in environment–infant interaction research. *Merrill-Palmer Quarterly, 15*: 9.

Greenspan, S. I. (1992). *Infancy and Early Childhood: The Practice of Clinical Assessment and Intervention with Emotional and Developmental Challenges*. Madison, CT: International Universities Press.

Greenspan, S. I., & Wieder, S. (1984). Dimensions and levels of the therapeutic process. *Psychotherapy: Theory, Research, and Practice, 21* (1): 5–23.

Greenspan, S. I., & Wieder, S. (1999). A functional developmental approach to autism spectrum disorders. *Journal of the Association for Persons with Severe Handicaps (JASH), 24*: 147–161

Haig, D. (1999). Genetic conflicts of pregnancy and childhood. In: S. C. Stearns (Ed.), *Evolution in Health and Disease*. Oxford: Oxford University Press

Heimann, P. (1950). On counter-transference. *International Journal of Psycho-Analysis, 31*: 81–84.

Hobson, P. (1993). *Autism and the Development of the Mind*. Hove: Lawrence Earlbaum.

Hopkins, J. (1992). "Parent Infant Psychotherapy." Paper presented at the Forum of the Infant–Parent Clinic, London.

Izard, C. (1978). On the development of emotions and emotion-cognition relationships in infancy. In: M. Lewis & L. Rosenblum (Eds.), *The Development of Affect*. New York: Plenum.

Johnson, F. K., Dowling, J., & Wesner, D. (1980). Notes on infant psychotherapy. *Infant Mental Health Journal, 1*.

Joseph, B. (1975). The patient who is difficult to reach. In: P. L. Giovacchini (Ed.), *Tactics and Techniques in Psychoanalytic Therapy, Vol. 2: Countertransference*. New York: Jason Aronson.

Kennell, J., & Klaus, M. (1984). Helping parents after the birth of a baby with malfunction. In: *Frontiers in Infant Mental Health, Vol. 2: Psychiatry* (Chapter 42). New York: Basic Books.

Keverne, E. B., Martel, F. L., & Nevison, C. M. (1996). Genomic imprinting and the differential roles of parental genomes in brain development. *Developmental Brain Research, 92*: 91–100.

Klaus, M. H., & Kennell, J. H. (1976). *Maternal-Infant Bonding: The Impact of Early Separation or Loss on Family Development*. St. Louis, MO: C. V. Mosby.

Klein, M. (1932). *The Psycho-Analysis of Children*, trans. Alix Strachey. London: Hogarth Press and the Institute of Psycho-Analysis.

Klein, M. (1937). Love, guilt and reparation. In: *The Writings of Melanie Klein, Vol. 1: Love, Guilt and Reparation and Other Works* (pp. 306–343). London: Hogarth Press, 1975.

Klein, M. (1945): The Oedipus complex in the light of early anxieties. *International Journal of Psycho-Analysis, 26*: 11–33. Also in: *The Writings of Melanie Klein, Vol. 1: Love, Guilt and Reparation and Other Works* (pp. 370–419). London: Hogarth Press, 1975.

Kling, P. (1978). Affective response of the analyst to the patient's communications. *International Journal of Psycho-Analysis, 59*: 329–334.

Kobayashi, R., Takenoshita, Y., Kobayashi, H., Kamijo, A., Funaba, K., & Takarabe, M. (2001). Early intervention for infants with autistic spectrum disorder in Japan. *Pediatrics International, 43* (2): 202–208

Kreisler, L., & Cramer. B. (1983). Infant psychopathology: Guidance for examination, clinical groupings, nosological propositions. In: J. Call, E. Galenson, & R. Tyson (Eds.), *Frontiers of Infant Psychiatry* (Chapter 12). New York: Basic Books.

Kumar, S. (1986). Impact of maternal depression on cognitive development of young children. *British Medical Journal, 292* (3 May): 1165–1167.

Lebovici, S. (1984). Comments concerning the concept of fantasmotic interaction. In: *Frontiers in Infant Mental Health, Vol. 2: Psychiatry* (Chapter 15). New York: Basic Books.

Lebovici, S. (1988). Fantasmatic interaction and intergenerational transmission. *Infant Mental Health Journal, 9* (No. 1, Spring).

Lebovici, S., & Stoleru, S. (1983). *La mère, le mourrisson et le psychanalyste, les interactions prècoces*. Paris: Le Centurion.

Lipsitt, L. (1966) Learning process of newborns. *Merrill-Palmer Quarterly, 12*: 45.

Little, M. (1951). Counter-transference and the patient's response to it. *International Journal of Psycho-Analysis, 32*: 32–40.

Littlewood, R., & Kareem, J. (1992). *Intercultural Therapy: Themes, Interpretations and Practice*. Oxford: Blackwell.

Maestro, S., Muratori, F., Cavallaro, M. C., Pei, F., Stern, D., Golse, B., & Palacio-Espasa, F. (2002). Attentional skills during the first 6 months of age in Autism Spectrum Disorder. *Journal of the American Academy of Child and Adolescent Psychiatry, 41*: 1239–1245.

Mahler, M. (1975). *The Psychological Birth of the Human Infant: Symbiosis and Individuation*. London: Hutchinson.

Mannoni, M. (1973). *The Retarded Child and the Mother*. London: Tavistock.

Massie, H., & Campbell, B. K. (1984). Appendix: The Massie–Campbell Scale of Mother–Infant Attachment during Stress. In: H. Massie & J. Rosenthal, *Childhood Psychosis in the First Four Years of Life*. New York: McGraw-Hill.

Massie, H., & Rosenthal, J. (1984). *Childhood Psychosis in the First Four Years of Life*. New York: McGraw-Hill.

McFarlane, A. (1977). *The Psychology of Childbirth*. The Developing Child Series. Cambridge, MA: Harvard University Press.

Mead, M., & Newton, N. (1965a). Childbearing: Its social and psychological aspect. In: *First International Congress of Psychosomatic Medicine & Childbirth*. Paris: Gauthier-Villars.

Mead, M., & Newton, N. (1965b). Conception, pregnancy, labour and the puerpericum in cultural perspective. In: *First International Congress of Psychosomatic Medicine & Childbirth*. Paris: Gauthier-Villars.

Meltzoff, A. N., & Borton, R. W. (1979). Intermodal matching by human neonates. *Nature, 282*: 403–404.

Meltzoff, A. N., & Moore, M. K. (1977). Imitation of facial and manual gestures by human neonates. *Science, 198*: 75–78.

Menzies Lyth, I. (1988). *Containing Anxieties in Institutions: Selected Essays*. London: Free Association Books.

Middlemore, M. (1941). *The Nursing Couple*. Edinburgh: Hamish Hamilton.

Millican, F. K., Lourie, R. S., Layman, E. M., et al. (1962). The prevalence of ingestion and mouthing of nonedible substances by children. *Clinical Proceedings of the Children's Hospital of DC, 18*: 207–214.

Muratori, F., & Maestro, S. (2004). "Certitudes et interrogations sur l'autisme au cours de la premiere année de vie." Paper presented at 13th Association de Sante Mentale Conference on Early Signs of

Infantile Autism and Their Therapeutic Implications, Centre Alfred Binet, Paris (June).

Murray, L., Cooper, P. J., Wilson, A., & Romaniuk, H. (2003). Controlled trial of the short- and long-term effect of psychological treatment of post-partum depression: 2. Impact on the mother–child relationship and child outcome. *British Journal of Psychiatry, 182*: 420–27

Newson, J., & Newson, E. (1975). Intersubjectivity and the transmission of culture: On the social origins of symbolic functioning. *Bulletin of the British Psychological Society, 28*: 437–446.

Ogden, T. H. (1987). The transitional Oedipal relationship in female development. *International Journal of Psycho-Analysis, 68*: 485.

Ogden,T. H. (1992). *The Matrix of the Mind: Object Relations and the Psychoanalytic Dialogue* (pp. 71–76). London: Karnac.

Palacio Espasa, F., & Manzano, J. (1988) Problèmatique psychique et interactions parents-bebè lors des interventions thèrapeutiques. In: B. Cramer (Ed.), *Psychiatrie du bebè, Nouvelles Fontaières*. Paris: Eshel.

Panksepp, J. (1998). The sources of fear and anxiety in the brain. In: *Affective Neuroscience: The Foundations of Animal and Human Emotions*. New York: Oxford University Press.

Perry, B. D., Pollard, R., Brakely, T., Baker, W., & Vigilante, D. (1995). Childhood trauma, the neurobiology of adaptation and "use dependent" development of the brain: How states becomes traits. *Infant Mental Health Journal, 16* (4): 271–291.

Rabain-Jamin, J. (1984). Survey of the infant's "sound envelope" and organisation of parent-infant communication. In: *Frontiers in Infant Mental Health, Vol. 2: Psychiatry* (Chapter 12). New York: Basic Books.

Racker, H. (1951). *Transference and Countertransference*. London: Karnac, 1982.

Raphael-Leff, J. (1991). *Psychological Processes in Motherhood*. London: Chapman & Hall.

Reich, A. (1951). On counter-transference. *International Journal of Psycho-Analysis, 32*: 25–31.

Restak, R. (2001). *The Secret Life of the Brain*. Washington, DC: Joseph Henry Press.

Robinson, B. A., Tolan, W., & Golding-Beecher, O. (1990). Childhood pica: Some aspects of the clinical profile in Manchester, Jamaica. *West Indian Medical Journal, 39*: 20–26.

Rosenthal, M. (1984). *Childhood Psychosis in the First Four Years of Life*. New York: McGraw-Hill.

Sanders, L. W. (1977). Regulation of exchange in the infant caretaker system: A viewpoint on the ontogeny of structures. In: N. Freedman & S. Grant (Eds.), *Communicative Structures and Psychic Structures* (pp. 13–34). New York: Plenum Press.

Sanders, L. W., Stechler, G., Burns, P., & Julia, H. (1970). Early mother–infant interaction and 24-hour patterns of activity and sleep. *Journal of the American Academy of Child Psychiatry*, 9: 103–123.

Sandler, J. (1976). Countertransference and role-responsiveness. *International Review of Psycho-Analysis*, 3: 43–47.

Schore, A. (1994). *Affect Regulation and the Origin of the Self.* Hillsdale, NJ, & Hove: Lawrence Erlbaum Associates.

Schrader, A. (1997). Thornton woman nurtures infected, addicted babies. *The Denver Post Newspaper*, Sunday, 16 February.

Seigal, D. J. (1999). *The Developing Mind: Towards a Neurobiology of Interpersonal Experience.* New York: Guilford Press.

Selwyn, R. (1993). Psychodynamic aspects of failure-to-thrive: A case study. *Journal of Child Psychotherapy*, 19 (2): 84–110.

Sinason, V. (1986). Secondary mental handicap and its relationship to trauma. *Psychoanalytic Psychotherapy*, 2: 131–154.

Sinason, V. (1988). Richard III, Hephaestus and Echo: Sexuality and mental/multiple handicap. *Journal of Child Psychotherapy*, 14 (2): 93–105.

Sinason, V. (1992). *Mental Handicap and the Human Condition.* London: Free Association Books.

Spensley, S. (1985). Mentally ill or mentally handicapped? A longitudinal study of severe learning difficulty. *Psychoanalytic Psychotherapy*, 7 (3): 55–70.

Spitz, R. (1945). Hospitalism: An inquiry into the genesis of psychiatric conditions in early childhood. *Psychoanalytic Studies of the Child*, 1: 53–74; 2: 113–117.

Spitz, R. (1946). Anaclitic depression. *Psychoanalytic Study of the Child*, 2: 313–342.

Spitz, R. (1948). *Emotional Starvation in Infants: Somatic Consequences.* Video.

Spitz, R. (1957). *Dialogues from Infancy: Selected Papers*, ed. R. N. Ernde. New York: International Universities Press.

Spitz, R. (1961). Some early prototypes of ego defences. *Journal of the American Psychoanalytic Association*, 9: 626–651.

Spitz, R. (1965). *The First Year of Life.* New York: International Universities Press.

Stern, D. (1974a). Mother and infant at play: The dyadic interaction involving facial, vocal and gaze behaviour. In: M. Lewis & L. Rosenblum (Eds.), *The Effects of the Infant on Its Caregiver* (pp. 187–213). New York: Wiley.

Stern, D. (1974b). The goal and structure of mother–infant play. *Journal of the American Academy of Child Psychiatry*, 13: 402.

Stern, D. (1985). *The Interpersonal World of the Infant.* New York: Basic Books.

Stern-Buschweiler, N., & Stern, D. (1989). A model for conceptualising the role of the mother's representational world in various mother–infant therapies. *Infant Mental Health, 10*: 3.

St. James-Roberts, I. (1989). "Crying Babies and Difficult Infants: Are We Starting to Get a Hold on Them?" Paper presented at the 9th SRIP Conference, Oxford.

Tomkins, S. (1963). *Affect, Imagery, Consciousness, Vols 1 & 2*. New York: Springer.

Trevarthen, C. (1979). Communication and cooperation in early infancy, a description of primary intersubjectivity. In: M. Bullowa (Ed.), *Before Speech: The Beginnings of Human Communication* (pp. 321–347). London: Cambridge University Press.

Trevarthen, C. (1999): Musicality and the intrinsic motive pulse: Evidence from human psychobiology and infant communication. *Musicae Scientiae*: 157–213. (Special Issue: "Rhythm, Musical Narrative and Origins of Human Communication.")

Trevarthen, C. (2001). Intrinsic motives for companionship in understanding: Their origin, development and significance for infant mental health. *Infant Mental Health Journal, 22* (1–2): 95–131. (Special Issue, ed. Allan Shore: "Contributions from the Decade of the Brain to Infant Mental Health.")

Trevarthen, C., & Aitken, K. J. (1994). Brain development, infant communication and empathy disorder: Intrinsic factors in child mental health. *Developmental Psychopathology, 6*: 597–633.

Trevarthen, C., & Aitken, K. J. (2001). Infant intersubjectivity: Research, theory and clinical applications. *Journal of Child Psychology and Psychiatry, 1*: 3–48.

Trevarthen, C., & Hubley, P. (1978). Secondary intersubjectivity: Confidence, confiding and acts of meaning in the first year. In: A. Lock (Ed.), *Action Gesture and Symbol* (pp. 183–229). London: Academic Press.

Trevarthen, C., Kokkinaki, T., & Fiamenghi, G. A., Jr. (1999). What infants' imitations communicate: With mothers, with fathers, and with peers. In: J. Nadel & G. Butterworth (Eds.), *Imitation in Infancy* (pp. 128–185). Cambridge: Cambridge University Press.

Van Rees, S., & de Leeuw, R. (1987). *Born too Early: The Kangaroo Method with Premature Babies*. Video by Stichting Lichaamstaal, Heythuysen, The Netherlands.

Volkmar, F. R., & Cohen, D. J. (1985). The experience of infantile autism: A first- person account by T.W. *Journal of Autism and Developmental Disorders, 1*: 47–54.

Winnicott, D. W. (1931). A note on normality and anxiety. In: *Collected Papers: Through Paediatrics to Psycho-Analysis*. London: Tavistock Publications, 1958.

Winnicott, D. W. (1947). Hate in the countertransference. In: *Collected Papers: Through Paediatrics to Psycho-Analysis*. London: Tavistock Publications, 1958.

Winnicott, D. W. (1951). Transitional objects and transitional phenomena. In: *Collected Papers: Through Paediatrics to Psycho-Analysis* (pp. 229–242). London: Tavistock Publications, 1958.

Winnicott, D. W. (1952). Anxiety associated with insecurity. In: *Through Paediatrics to Psychoanalysis*. London: Hogarth Press, 1975.

Winnicott, D. W. (1953). Transitional objects and transitional phenomena. In: *Playing and Reality* (pp. 1–25). New York: Basic Books, 1971.

Winnicott, D. W. (1956a). Paediatrics and childhood neurosis. In: *Collected Papers: Through Paediatrics to Psycho-Analysis*. London: Tavistock Publications, 1958.

Winnicott, D. W. (1956b). Primary maternal preoccupation. In: *Collected Papers: Through Paediatrics to Psycho-Analysis*. London: Tavistock Publications, 1958.

Winnicott, D. W. (1957). Mother and child: A primer of first relationships. In: *Collected Papers: Through Paediatrics to Psycho-Analysis*. New York: Basic Books, 1958.

Winnicott, D. W. (1958a). *Collected Papers: Through Paediatrics to Psycho-Analysis*. London: Tavistock Publications; revised edition, *Through Paediatrics to Psycho-Analysis*, London: Hogarth Press, 1975; reprinted London: Karnac, 1987.

Winnicott, D. W. (1958b). Maternal reverie. In: *Through Paediatrics to Psycho-analysis*. London: Hogarth Press.

Winnicott, D. W. (1960). Parent–infant relationship. In: *The Maturational Processes and the Facilitating Environment*. London: Hogarth Press, 1965; reprinted London: Karnac, 1990.

Winnicott, D. W. (1983). Problems in the use of the counter-transference: Getting it across. *Journal of Child Psychotherapy, 9* (1).

Zero to Three (1994). *Diagnostic Classification of Mental Health and Developmental Disorders of Infancy and Early Childhood*. Washington, DC: National Center for Infants, Toddlers, and Families Publications Department.

LIST OF CASES

INDEX